Student Cheating and Plagiarism in the Internet Era

A Wake-Up Call

Ann Lathrop
and
Kathleen Foss

2000
Libraries Unlimited
A Division of Greenwood Publishing Group, Inc.
Englewood, Colorado

Libraries Unlimited
A Division of Greenwood Publishing Group, Inc.
P.O. Box 6633
Englewood, CO 80155-6633
1-800-237-6124
www.lu.com

Library of Congress Cataloging-in-Publication Data

Lathrop, Ann.
    Student cheating and plagiarism in the Internet era : a wake-up call
/ Ann Lathrop and Kathleen Foss.
      p. cm.
    Includes bibliographical references and index.
    ISBN 1-56308-841-X (pbk.)
    1. Cheating (Education) 2. Internet (Computer network) in education.
I. Foss, Kathleen II. Title.

LB3609.L28 2000
371.5'8--dc21   00-030937

BK
$ 31.50

Dedication

This book is dedicated to honest students.

Their integrity and hard work need to be recognized, supported, and protected by parents, teachers, administrators, and all concerned members of society.

Contents

Summary List of Copy-Me Pages viii
Acknowledgments ix
Preface xi
Introduction xiii

Part I: A Wake-Up Call: What's Going On

Chapter 1: Overview of Student Cheating and Plagiarism in the Internet Era 1
    Part I: A Wake-Up Call: What's Going On...1
    Part II: A Call to Action: What We Can Do...3
    Part III: Taking Action: Making It More Difficult to Cheat and Plagiarize 7

Chapter 2: High-Tech Cheating 10
    Cheating with New Technologies 11

Chapter 3: Electronic Plagiarism..17
    What's Available on the Internet?...18
    Plagiarizing 1-2-3 19
    Plagiarizing from Electronic Encyclopedias 20
    Downloadable Term Papers: What's a Prof to Do? by Tom Rocklin....................25

Chapter 4: Why We Are Alarmed 29
    Things Are Bad and Getting Worse 30
    Are Elementary School Students Cheating?..31
    Student and Teacher Attitudes toward Cheating 32
    What the Students Say...33
    Data and Conclusions from Four Surveys...35

Part II: A Call to Action: What We Can Do

Chapter 5: High-Tech Defenses against Cheating and Plagiarism 47
    Information as a First Line of Defense..48
    High-Tech Defenses against Cheating Technologies....................................48
    Blocking, Filtering, and Rating Systems 50
    Can Legislation Deter Plagiarism?..51
    Using Technology to Identify Plagiarism...52
    Web Sites with Resources for Countering Plagiarism 53
    Searching the Internet for the Originals of Plagiarized Papers 54
    Student Plagiarism in an Online World by Julie J. C. H. Ryan 56

Chapter 6: Parents: Vigilant, Informed, Involved 60
    Be Vigilant about Cheating and Plagiarism 61
    Be Informed about Technology in Your Schools...64
    Be Involved in School Activities and Assignments 64
    Be a Model of Ethical Behavior 65
    Be Ethical in Dealing with Student Cheating or Plagiarism 66
    Can "Too Much" Help Be Harmful?..68
    Honoring Tomorrow's Leaders Today by Paul C. Krouse....................................71

Chapter 7: Integrity, Ethics, and Character Education 72
   1997 Yearbook of the National Society for the Study of Education 73
   Character Education at Teacher–Training Institutions...74
   The Power of Story—Literature that Models Ethics and Integrity 75
   Institutes and Centers that Support Ethics, Integrity, and Character Education 76
   Resources to Support Integrity, Ethics, and Character Education 83
   Student Discussions of Integrity and Ethical Behavior..84
   The Six E's of Character Education: Practical Ways to Bring Moral
      Instruction to Life for Your Students by Dr. Kevin Ryan...........................89

Chapter 8: Academic Integrity Policies 92
   Initiating an Action Plan 93
   Gathering Local Statistical Data...96
   Honor Code or Integrity Policy? 96
   School Board, Administrative, and Faculty Leadership..97
   Student Leadership 98
   Acceptable Use Policies 99
   Fair Enforcement and an Ethical School Culture 100
   Publicizing the Academic Integrity Policy...101
   Working with New Students 104
   Academic Integrity Policies and Honor Codes Online..104
   One High School's Academic Honesty Code 108
   Honor Codes: Teaching Integrity and Interdependence by Lewis Cobbs 112

Chapter 9: Defining Cheating and Plagiarism for Students 115
   Learning to Recognize Cheating and Plagiarism 116
   Permissible Collaboration 118
   Ethical Use of Writing Centers and Private Tutors 119
   Copyright Issues 121
   Explaining Collaboration and Plagiarism to Students from Other Cultures 122
   But I Changed Three Words! Plagiarism in the ESL Classroom
      by Lenora C. Thompson and Portia G. Williams.......................................127

Chapter 10: Dealing with Student Dishonesty 129
   Why Shouldn't I Cheat?..130
   Dealing with Suspected Cheating or Plagiarism 131
   Suggestions for Informing Parents 133
   Fair and Effective Penalties..134
   Concern for Privacy Rights 135
   Requiring that an Assignment or Test Be Completed Fairly 136
   Notes on Cheating for the Busy Classroom Teacher by Berk Moss 138

Part III: Taking Action:
Making It More Difficult to Cheat and Plagiarize

Chapter 11: Reducing Cheating on Tests and Assignments 140
   "Smart-People" Tests 141
   Grading for Mastery vs. Grading on a Curve..141
   Teachers Who Care about Cheating..142
   Reducing Cheating on Tests...143
   Discouraging Cheating on Class Assignments, Homework, Lab Reports, Etc. 151

Chapter 12: The Librarian–Teacher Team 152
    The Librarian as Team Teacher..153
    Real-Life Importance of Research 153
    Librarians Are Sources of Information about the Internet 154
    Teachers and Librarians Collaborate on Research Assignments 155
    Librarians Make Research Materials Easily Accessible 157
    Cyber-Plagiarism Faculty Workshop 158

Chapter 13: Identifying and Reducing Plagiarism 161
    "High-Tech" and "Low-Tech" Plagiarism 162
    Unintentional Plagiarism..162
    Indicators of Possible Plagiarism 163
    Dear Teacher, Johnny Copied by Louise A. Jackson, Eileen Tway,
        and Alan Frager...170

Chapter 14: Structuring Writing Assignments to Reduce Plagiarism.......................174
    Evaluating Both the Research *Process* and the *Product* 175
    Student Writing Handbook 176
    Structuring an Effective Assignment for a Report or Research Paper 178
    Teaching Practices that Encourage or Eliminate Student Plagiarism
        by Susan J. Davis 182

Chapter 15: Tools for Writing without Plagiarizing 188
    Lessons 189
    Antiplagiarism Strategies for Research Papers by Robert Harris 193

Chapter 16: Alternatives to Traditional Writing Assignments.................................197
    Lessons 198

Chapter 17: Online Sites for Reports and Research Papers 213

    References Cited...227
    Further Readings 237
    Summary List of Web Addresses 239
    Index 247

Summary List of Copy-Me Pages

Chapter 2
- Copy Me: "High-Tech Devices Used for Cheating" 15

Chapter 3
- Copy Me: "Online Sites for Reports and Research Papers" 22

Chapter 4
- Copy Me: "Cheating and Succeeding: Record Numbers of Top High School Students Take Ethical Shortcuts" 36
- Copy Me: "1998 Report Card on the Ethics of American Youth" 40
- Copy Me: "Research Highlights" 46

Chapter 6
- Copy Me: "Willful Blindness about Cheating" 63
- Copy Me: "Help, But Not Too Much" 69
- Copy Me: "Practical Suggestions to Support Students at Home and School" 70

Chapter 7
- Copy Me: "Does Cheating Harm Your Career?" 87
- Copy Me: "Are These Valid Reasons to Cheat or Plagiarize?" 88

Chapter 8
- Copy Me: "How to Develop a Strong Program for Academic Integrity" 95
- Copy Me: "One Principal's Commitment to Ethics" 102

Chapter 9
- Copy Me: "When Is Collaboration OK?" 124
- Copy Me: "Are Any of These Cheating?" 125
- Copy Me: "Are Any of These Plagiarizing?" 126

Chapter 10
- Copy Me: "A Case of High School Plagiarism" 137

Chapter 12
- Copy Me: "Cyber-Plagiarism Faculty Workshop" 159

Chapter 13
- Copy Me: "An Electronic Scavenger Hunt" 168
- Copy Me: "Plagiarism and the Web" 169

Chapter 14
- Copy Me: "Research Portfolio Cover Sheet" 177

Acknowledgments

We gratefully acknowledge the many educators and friends who have given freely of their time and expertise to help bring this book from idea to reality. Their assistance enabled us to identify ways students try to circumvent the educational process by cheating and plagiarizing, and to suggest practical, classroom-tested strategies in response.

We thank Kevin Bushweller for writing the preface, Paul Krouse for the message to parents in Chapter 6, and Rush Kidder for his thoughtful response in Chapter 10 to the student who asks, "Why Shouldn't I Cheat?" We are grateful to the many other authors who strengthened the book by granting permission to include their articles and lessons.

Darielle Tom provided valuable assistance in explaining technical aspects of high-tech devices and ways they can be used for cheating. Ann Busenkell, Alice Littlejohn, Sharon Martin, Zhita Rea, and Marsha Span brought to our attention the concern and scope of the problem facing classroom teachers and librarians. Catherine Light was our accurate and always-patient typist.

We received much-needed support and encouragement from our families throughout the entire process of researching and writing this book. Our special thanks go to Rick Lathrop and Diane Baker for their timely suggestions and extensive, careful editing.

Readers with a serious interest in preventing cheating and plagiarism in our schools are encouraged to take special note of the articles by Kevin Bushweller and Don McCabe referenced extensively throughout the book. Their research provided invaluable material and both of them were generous in sharing their time and expertise.

While researching this book, we became ardent admirers of the wonders of electronic databases, especially those that provide full text of the articles located. Many listservs and original articles published on the Internet proved to be excellent resources. Electronic directories made it possible to locate elusive authors and email made it simple to contact them as well as to dialogue with colleagues who patiently answered our many questions. In short, this book would not exist as it is today without the Internet and all that it offers. But how does one say "thank you" to the Internet?

With our deepest appreciation for the many ways you helped,

Ann Lathrop   **Kathleen Foss**

Preface

Cheating: A Plague on American Schools

Kevin Bushweller

Senior Editor, *American School Board Journal*

On a breezy fall day at a suburban Atlanta high school, a cadre of honor students was mingling in a courtyard around a concrete picnic table. They were telling me about the practice of falsifying data for high stakes science fair projects. It happened, but it was wrong—they all seemed to agree on that.

Except for one boy. He chuckled and stepped back from the table. "Making up [false] data for the science fair?" he exclaimed. "If you don't, you're abnormal."

Abnormal not to cheat? Initially, his response startled me. I had just started working on a special report on cheating for the *American School Board Journal* and this high school was my first stop. But as I talked to more kids and teachers around the country—and conducted national surveys of teachers and school board members—I came to the troubled conclusion that this boy's attitude was anything but unique. In fact, it might be closer to the norm than most of us would like to think.

Don McCabe, a Rutgers University professor who has conducted an exhaustive amount of research on cheating for decades, told me he was equally troubled. In one focus group he held of students from high achieving high schools in New Jersey, a girl stated: "It's almost a big deal if you don't cheat."

During my visits to schools, the question kids often threw back at me was "what's the big deal?" They believed cheating didn't hurt anybody. Unfortunately, some educators share that view. Yet cheating strikes at the very heart of whether students are learning what they are supposed to. And it raises grave concerns about the ethics of the nation's future workers and business and political leaders.

To be sure, a student who cheats only once in a school year is not likely to be cutting corners on his academic learning. But when the practice is so deeply rooted in teen culture that kids describe cheating as a necessary high school skill—well, then it's likely students are cutting corners whenever the opportunity arises. Marcia Humbert, a social studies teacher in Atlanta who I interviewed at length, believes the problem goes beyond simply cutting corners. Cheating, she told me, has become "a plague on the American school system. It really is an epidemic."

What must be done? To begin with, everyone should understand that students who cheat are not necessarily bad kids. Some are struggling to get through school—others are reacting to competitive pressures from parents and peers. On the other hand, we cannot ignore the erosion of ethics in a teenage culture so accepting of cheating that high school students were unusually candid in admitting to me that they had cheated.

To confront the problem, students who are struggling should be given extra help so they don't feel pressure to cheat. At academically competitive schools, teachers and parents must find a better balance between pushing kids to do their best and pressuring them to do more than they can. Mostly, though, I believe teachers need to be more aware of the ways kids cheat. That helps them stay one step ahead of the cheaters.

When I was doing research for the *American School Board Journal* special project, I was somewhat surprised by how little had been written about cheating. It has been, unfortunately, a much-neglected topic. That's why I was pleasantly surprised when Ann Lathrop called me last spring to tell me she and Kathy Foss were working on a book about student cheating in K–12 schools.

Simply recognizing the depth of a problem is often the first step toward solving it. I hope this book serves as a first step for you.

Introduction

A Word to Our Readers . . .

We have written this book with the belief that each person who reads it can and will help to reverse the steady increase in student cheating and plagiarism.

Again and again, students who are being interviewed say their teachers don't care about cheating. They say their parents don't know whether or not they cheat and many add that their parents wouldn't care about the cheating if they did know.

Teachers and parents, tell your students and your children that *you* care. Help them to understand they are lying when they turn in a test or homework with their name on it if it is not their own work. They are thieves when they steal work done by someone else. *You can teach them that each of us makes a difference when we choose honesty instead of lying and stealing, and integrity instead of cheating and plagiarizing.*

Scope and Content of the Book

The book is organized as a practical guide for educators and parents who want to reduce cheating and plagiarizing. Helpful ideas and strategies to counter both high-tech and more traditional "low-tech" cheating and plagiarism in K–12 schools come from dozens of authors and educators. References to online and print resources can be useful at home and in the classroom. The articles that follow many of the chapters were selected to extend the discussions, perhaps from a different perspective, or to summarize the chapter. As you read, identify those ideas that will work best for you.

We know that plagiarism actually is one form of cheating but we have chosen to treat it here as a separate issue. New "paper mills" on the Internet and other electronic sources make it so easy for students to copy a report or term paper that plagiarism warrants this special attention.

Two serious types of cheating problems are beyond the scope of this book: (1) cheating by students on standardized tests administered nationally, and (2) dishonesty by administrators or teachers who promote or allow cheating on standardized tests, or report false test data to improve the ratings of their schools or districts. Also, although we discuss the Internet as an easily accessible source for plagiarism, we do not address the issues involved in helping students learn to assess the accuracy and authenticity of online information.

The policies, lessons, and other materials come from friends and colleagues, our research online and in print, and our own years of experience as educators and parents. The survey data and articles on special aspects of cheating and plagiarism are reprinted with permission, as noted, from the authors and publishers.

We realize our descriptions of how educators and parents can identify and prevent cheating and plagiarism may be read by students for an entirely different purpose. We regret this, but hope the good we do by alerting educators and parents to new cheating practices will counter any dishonest use of this information by students.

Format

A "Chapter Overview" introduces each chapter—except the first—and lists the chapter subheadings, including any Copy-Me pages. "Pointers" at the end of each chapter—except the first—direct the reader to related information in other chapters.

Copy-Me pages are provided for use as discussion starters with students, faculty, or parents. They are listed in the "Chapter Overviews" and in the "Summary List of Copy-Me Pages." The content of Copy-Me pages must not be edited and the following credit statement must be included whenever the page is reproduced: Reprinted with permission from *Student Cheating and Plagiarism in the Internet Era: A Wake-Up Call* by Ann Lathrop and Kathleen Foss. Englewood, CO: Libraries Unlimited, 2000.

The "Summary List of Web Addresses" includes all web addresses mentioned in the book. The addresses were accurate as of March 2000.

The style manual used is the *MLA Handbook for Writers of Research Papers,* 5th ed. (Modern Language Association of America, 1999), selected because of its frequent use in high schools. In references to online sources without page numbers, the abbreviation "par." is used to indicate the paragraph quoted.

Request for Readers' Stories

The Internet and other new technologies make the entire issue of cheating and plagiarism one that constantly is evolving and changing. We hope that you, our readers, will share your own experiences with us for inclusion in an anticipated second edition.

Ann Lathrop
alathrop@csulb.edu

Kathleen Foss
kfoss@earthlink.com

Chapter 1

Overview of Student Cheating and Plagiarism in the Internet Era

It's a great mistake to understate the significance of cheating in schools. Cheating is habit-forming. It becomes a way to cope with any situation where we want something we haven't earned or shouldn't have. So cheating leads to cheating. Thus, 44 percent of the high schoolers admit to cheating at least twice in the past year. And since cheaters are likely to cheat on a survey, we know that these figures significantly understate the problem.

If parents and schools took cheating seriously–for instance if school funding was tied to the cheating rate–all sorts of effective methods would be developed to create an academic environment with integrity. Our failure to do so makes a mockery of the empty slogans about the importance of honesty and betrays every child who believes our preaching about character and virtue. (Josephson. *Cheating Leads to Cheating*, pars. 4-5. Reprinted with permission of the Josephson Institute of Ethics)

We know students are cheating more often today; their cheating techniques are increasingly sophisticated, and many express guilt or remorse only if they are caught. Why do they cheat? The bottom line seems to be (1) it's easy, especially with new technologies, (2) fewer than 10% are caught, and (3) most of those who are caught get off without serious penalty. The byword appears to have changed from *Don't cheat* to *Don't get caught.*

Articles in the popular press and research papers in scholarly journals agree that cheating and plagiarism are more serious today. Although many students' grades continue to reflect their competence and knowledge, the grades of others can indicate only that they have become accomplished cheaters.

1

High-Tech Cheating (Chapter 2)

A variety of high-tech electronic devices helps students to improve their school performance in many legitimate ways. Unfortunately, the same devices can be used illicitly by dishonest students. They have become the new "cheat sheets" for tests.

Students use palm-sized computers and electronic calculators to store formulas, dates, spelling words, or any other data likely to be needed during a test. They use silent pagers to send test questions to friends outside the classroom and then receive the answers, or to access information stored on the pager before the test.

Lab results and homework assignments are shared electronically by fax and email. Cautious students change enough words to make the resulting paper sound different or change the margins and use another font to give it a different appearance. Other students just change the name, print the paper, and hand it in.

Electronic Plagiarism (Chapter 3)

Thousands of reports and research papers can be downloaded free and thousands more are available for sale from Internet "paper mills." Electronic research services prepare "original" papers for a fee; one even asks for a writing sample from the student in order to produce the appropriate level and style of writing. Most sites gladly accept credit cards.

Students use word processors to edit and reformat the papers, making it more difficult to identify the original online source. Just how easy is it to create a "new" paper from one of the Internet paper mills?

> With three keystrokes, Smith copied a paper about alternative medicine from the site and pasted it into his word processor. After quickly reformatting the paper, he used the word processor's search-and-replace feature to change certain words in the paper. Finally, he used a grammar-checking program that suggested ways to rephrase sentences, making the original source more difficult to identify. (Magney, par. 16)

Electronic encyclopedias online and on CD-ROM are another source for plagiarized reports and term papers. Some students simply copy and hand in an article "as is." Others edit and reformat the material, sometimes combining verbatim paragraphs from two or more encyclopedias to create an "original" paper.

Why We Are Alarmed (Chapter 4)

> Cheating has not only become more socially acceptable, but in many ways, it has also become more sophisticated. In some schools cheating is highly organized. Students discuss methods and ways to cheat and it becomes almost a way of life. Learning how to cheat, it seems, is almost as important as some of the more academic classes. It is not uncommon for students to brag about the ways they do their cheating and to proudly display the means by which they were able to get around a certain teacher. (Fowler 94)

Data from regional and national surveys of middle school, high school, and college cheating document a steady growth in the percentage of students who cheat. There is an even greater increase in the frequency and seriousness of cheating. These data are disturbing in themselves. Equally disturbing is the cynical attitude expressed by many students. During interviews they brag about their cheating, criticize teachers for not catching them, and scoff at the likelihood of any serious penalty.

The excerpts that follow are from three surveys reported more fully and documented in Chapter 4. In the first report, Schab questioned a cross section of high school students over a twenty-year span. His results reveal a sharp drop in students' belief in honesty in the first statement, and a definite rise in cheating and copying behavior in the following two. The figures are the percentage of *yes* responses to each question. The study will be updated in 2000.

	1969	*1979*	*1989*
• Honesty is always the best policy.	82.3	73.3	59.9
• Have you used a cheat sheet on a test?	33.8	59.5	67.8
• Have you let others copy your work?	58.3	92.5	97.5

(Schab 842–43)

The publisher of *Who's Who Among American High School Students* conducts an annual survey of the academically top 5% of American high school students. These results are from 1998:

- 83% said cheating was either "fairly common" or "almost everybody does it"
- 40% had cheated on a quiz or test themselves
- 67% had copied someone's homework
- 34% said their parents never talked about cheating

Only 6% were caught cheating and the most frequent punishment was being told "never do it again" (*Who's Who*).

The Josephson Institute of Ethics surveyed more than 20,000 middle and high school students, from a cross section of schools, in October 1998; 70% admitted to cheating on an exam within the previous 12 months (Josephson. *1998,* par. 3).

One student took a strong public stand in favor of honesty in a letter to the editor of the *Indianapolis Star:*

> As a student at a public high school, I have observed a decline in morality among my peers. Fights, conversations about personal experiences with drugs and alcohol, smoky bathrooms and cheating seem to be as much a part of the average school day as books, tests, homework and lectures. This is a result of bad parental upbringing, which is only reinforced at school when bad behavior is tolerated. (Preston, pars. 3–4)

It is important that we encourage students like this by assuring them we *are* listening and we *will* act.

Part II: A Call to Action: What We Can Do

Increasingly, cheating is seen as the means to a profitable end, an opportunity to secure the highest grades in order to get into the best colleges. Students who do not cheat are not only at a disadvantage, but are dubbed fools for not playing the system, a system that has grown so tolerant of cheating that punishments tend to be lenient. And it is a system that continues to place more and more emphasis on getting the grade by any means possible, tossing the benefit of learning aside. (Stansbury. *For*, par. 12)

The development of moral character begins at home. Good parents set clear ethical standards for their children and model integrity in their own actions. Effective teachers establish a classroom culture that expects and values integrity and moral behavior. Strong administrators enforce school and district Academic Integrity Policies fairly for all students.

Students from these homes and schools receive continuous reinforcement of the message that cheating, plagiarizing, and other forms of dishonesty are not acceptable and will be penalized. Such a message provides support for students like this one, who complains bitterly, "It isn't fair to the rest of us who bust our butts to get good grades. . . . The professors need to wise up and catch more of these jokers" (Schmidt, par. 11).

High-Tech Defenses against Cheating and Plagiarism (Chapter 5)

Possibly the best defense against high-tech cheating is information. Explore the hardware and software in computer stores and read instructional technology journals. Attend technology workshops. Explore online paper mills and learn to download and edit a paper. Ask students to explain how technology tools in their classrooms can be used for cheating. Students may be less likely to cheat when they know their teachers and parents are informed.

Software is available to prevent student use of school computers to access online sites considered by school staff to be inappropriate. It can reduce plagiarism by blocking online paper mills so students cannot download papers at school. Teachers who suspect plagiarism can use an unblocked computer to search the paper mills for distinctive word strings that can identify the original paper.

As one response to the problem, Educational Testing Service (ETS) and The Advertising Council have launched a national media campaign against student cheating. It is designed to reach children aged ten to fourteen with a message that "doing what's right brings a feeling of pride and a sense of accomplishment." According to their home page, "The first advertising messages feature a whistle-blowing referee symbolic of the student's conscience and the tagline, 'Cheating is a personal foul.' " Details of the campaign are online at <http://www.nocheating.org/adcouncil/news/launchrelease.html> or by calling 1-888-88-CHEAT (Educational. *ETS*, par 1).

Parents: Vigilant, Informed, Involved (Chapter 6)

Vigilant parents know their children's teachers and administrators, become informed about the technologies students are using to cheat at home or school, and are involved with the total school program. They make a point of being informed about school assignments, homework, and related activities. They encourage their children to do their best, but don't push them beyond their limits. What children learn each day is valued for the learning itself rather than considered to be only an avenue to good grades.

> I think children are cheating more because there's too much value on winning and having, and not enough emphasis on learning and giving. . . . Mrs. Lewis advises parents to recognize the everyday accomplishments of their children—congratulate them for completing homework assignments, compliment them after a practice session on the clarinet, engage in conversations about what they're learning. Communicate the message that what they do all the time—not just during test time—is important. (Barbara Lewis, author of *What Do You Stand For? A Kid's Guide to Building Character,* in interview reported by Asch, pars. 7, 19–20)

The *Los Angeles Times* reported on a 1999 poll of 600 adults in Orange County, California, who were asked about a variety of cheating behaviors. When asked, "How acceptable is it to have parents help on a project that is supposed to be done by the student alone?" only 37% replied "never" while 62% replied "always" or "sometimes" (Martelle B7). Parents who provide such help are teaching their children that it is acceptable to cheat.

Paul Krouse, founder and publisher of *Who's Who Among American High School Students,* identifies parents as a key to controlling student dishonesty. He challenges parents to take total responsibility for the ethical conduct of their children by setting a good moral example. His article, "Honoring Tomorrow's Leaders Today," is in Chapter 6.

Parents make a positive difference when they join teachers and administrators in the effort to reduce cheating and plagiarism. It is especially important that they support the school when their child has been proved guilty of cheating or plagiarizing. Some parents demand that the incident be ignored despite the evidence or even threaten to sue the school. This sends the student a message that the parents support dishonest behavior. Ethical parents accept an appropriate penalty and help the student use the experience as an opportunity for moral growth.

Integrity, Ethics, and Character Education (Chapter 7)

Many scholars and writers today challenge educators and parents to strengthen character education in schools. Sommers is one who argues strongly for a renewed emphasis on ethics and integrity:

> Because the typical course in applied ethics concentrates on problems and dilemmas, the students may easily lose sight of the fact that some things are clearly right and some are clearly wrong, that some ethical truths are not subject to serious debate. . . . In teaching ethics, one thing should be made central and prominent: Right and wrong do exist. This should be laid down as uncontroversial lest one leaves an altogether false impression that everything is up for grabs. (Sommers 4)

Students should receive the following clear and consistent message from adults they respect at school and at home:

Honesty and integrity are the hallmarks of good character and are expected from everyone. Dishonesty in any form, including cheating and plagiarism, is wrong and will not be tolerated.

Educators and parents who send this message, and who model honesty and integrity in their own behavior, *will* make a difference in students' lives.

Many of the centers and institutes that foster the development of integrity, ethical behavior, and moral character provide online information and resource materials. One example is the CHARACTER COUNTS! Coalition, a project of the Josephson Institute of Ethics with a focus on K–12 education; their "Six Pillars of Character" are Trustworthiness, Respect, Responsibility, Fairness, Caring, and Citizenship. Descriptions of eleven centers and institutes, with addresses of their informational Web sites, are in Chapter 7.

Dr. Kevin Ryan, founder of the Center for the Advancement of Ethics and Character at Boson University, identifies "The Six E's of Character Education": Example, Explanation, Exhortation, Ethos (ethical environment), Experience, and Expectation of excellence. His article is in Chapter 7.

Academic Integrity Policies (Chapter 8)

We cannot let students make cheating and plagiarizing into a game where *whoever cheats the most is the winner.* This is a game with serious negative consequences for the students, for education, and for society. Time and effort must go into creating a "level playing field" at each school so students' grades will reflect what they have accomplished, not how skillful or daring they have become at playing the cheating game.

One positive approach is the development of an Academic Integrity Policy. It is important that all administrators, school board members, faculty, students, and parents—in effect, the entire school community—participate in the development of the policy. It should define cheating and plagiarism explicitly, prohibit any use of technology for illicit purposes, and establish appropriate procedures and penalties for violations. This policy should be adopted by the school board, publicized throughout the district, and implemented fairly and consistently by all teachers and administrators.

Defining Cheating and Plagiarism for Students (Chapter 9)

Students must have a clear understanding of exactly what constitutes cheating or plagiarism. These simple definitions can help:

- If you had any help that you don't want your teacher or parents to know about, you probably cheated.
- If you didn't think of it and write it all on your own, and you didn't cite (or write down) the sources where you found the ideas or the words, it's probably plagiarism.

Three issues must be clarified for students. First, permissible collaboration on homework, lab reports, or written assignments should be defined clearly by each teacher; this should be contrasted with collaboration that will be regarded as cheating. Second, limits should be set on the permissible use of writing centers or private tutors by students who are seeking their help in completing writing assignments. Finally, the applications of copyright laws to written and electronic source materials should be explained clearly.

Some students from other cultures, especially those new to our schools, may have been taught that collaboration is permissible in all of their work and it is selfish not to share. They need additional assistance in understanding plagiarism and cheating issues.

Dealing with Student Dishonesty (Chapter 10)

Appropriate penalties applied consistently can convince students that we are serious about cheating and plagiarism. The Academic Integrity Policy defines illicit actions, outlines procedures for dealing with violations, and specifies penalties. Impartial implementation of the policy by all faculty and administrators makes it possible to deal effectively with student dishonesty.

Students, and sometimes their parents, appear to have become more accepting of cheating behavior. In an effort to focus on the dishonesty of cheating, one teacher got immediate attention by accusing a student of lying:

> The moral stand against cheating seems grounded in quicksand as people increasingly accept it as "the way things are." Not so for lying. There is still plenty of sting in being called a liar. Students who shrug when accused of cheating get positively outraged at being accused of lying.
>
> "I am not a liar!" the 8th grade offender protested angrily.
>
> "When you handed in this homework to your teacher as if you had done the work yourself, wasn't that a lie? Didn't you misrepresent this as being your own work? Cheating *is* lying." By calling it what it is, teachers can begin to make a dent in the widespread acceptance of cheating. (Summergrad 46)

Berk Moss recommends that a student suspected of cheating be confronted in private. The teacher should listen to the student's explanation without agreeing or arguing, review the situation carefully, and document the incident and the discussion with the student in writing. The teacher must then decide whether to involve the parents, a counselor, or an administrator, and decide on an appropriate action to take. His article is in Chapter 10.

Part III: Taking Action: Making It More Difficult to Cheat and Plagiarize

Those who enter the teaching profession tend to do so for idealistic reasons. First and foremost, teachers want to make the world a better place. They want to share knowledge with students who are eager to learn. They want to teach their students to deal with today's pressures in a positive way. These goals are not easy to accomplish. . . . Parents are busy and may not emphasize character education at home. The temptation to cheat is everywhere, and the Internet has made it easier than ever. . . . For teachers, cheating is a painful betrayal of an educational system based on trust. To overlook the problem is easy. To confront the problem takes tremendous courage. (Posnick-Goodwin. Truth 7-8)

Teachers who confront the problem *will* make it more difficult for students to cheat or plagiarize. Administrators who demand honesty in their schools *will* act to reduce student dishonesty. Parents who are informed about assignments and are monitoring their children's work at home *will* reduce opportunities to cheat or plagiarize. Students who know their parents and teachers are collaborating on efforts to promote ethical behavior *will* find it more rewarding to complete their tests and assignments honestly rather than risk detection and punishment.

Reducing Cheating on Tests and Assignments (Chapter 11)

Identifying cheaters and assigning punishments are necessary, but prevention strategies are needed as well. They often are preferable and will be well worth our efforts. Testing procedures are less susceptible to cheating when tests are designed to focus on interpretation and critical thinking, security precautions are in place, and students are closely monitored. When asked, "How difficult would it be for you to obtain test questions or answers at your school?" 57% of the students in the *Who's Who* survey in Chapter 4 responded either *easy* or *not very difficult.* We can reduce cheating when we (1) convince students that all of the teachers are committed to creating an honest and ethical school environment, (2) develop an Academic Integrity Policy that is enforced fairly and consistently, and (3) involve parents in our efforts.

The Librarian–Teacher Team (Chapter 12)

The librarian helps to reduce plagiarism by taking an active role in the research process, collaborating with the teacher in designing and implementing projects to build information literacy. Students may be less inclined to plagiarize when they are able to locate, analyze, and use information effectively. They learn to value the research process as a practical life skill. Librarians offer faculty workshops, student orientation sessions, and individual assistance to teachers and students in developing these skills to locate appropriate research materials online and in print.

Identifying and Reducing Plagiarism (Chapter 13)

Students use a variety of techniques to disguise a plagiarized paper. They can insert deliberate spelling and grammatical errors or use an electronic thesaurus to replace many of the words with synonyms. As they become more sophisticated, students learn to break up distinctive word strings to make it more difficult to locate the original of a paper copied from the Internet.

Experienced teachers may suspect a paper has been plagiarized when it is written well above a student's usual ability level, doesn't quite fit the assignment, has footnotes that are not found in the bibliography, cites a number of college-level references, has no current references, etc. The sudden appearance of a completed paper can be questioned in cases where the teacher has not observed any work being accomplished in class or in the library. Parents can suspect plagiarism when they have not observed any of the research or writing being done at home or they have been put off with excuses when they ask to see a draft of the paper.

Unintentional plagiarism can occur when students do not understand the concept clearly; this happens more often in the primary grades. Students in middle school and high school can plagiarize unintentionally when they have not learned the necessary research and writing skills.

Structuring Writing Assignments to Reduce Plagiarism (Chapter 14)

Grading the writing *process* as well as the *product* can reduce plagiarism. Papers available online or from other sources will not have the outline, note cards, rough drafts, or working bibliography required by a teacher who tracks each step of the research process.

Placing a strong emphasis on careful analysis and creative presentation of research data makes it more difficult to substitute a plagiarized paper from an encyclopedia or online paper mill. According to Magney, "Simply assigning students to write a research paper on a general topic, then collecting the papers a few weeks later is an invitation to plagiarism" (par. 34). In her model research assignment, Susan Davis recommends building background knowledge, providing easy source texts, being flexible regarding paper length, and providing a variety of ways for students to present their results; her article is in Chapter 14.

Tools for Writing without Plagiarizing (Chapter 15)

Students should develop a clear understanding of plagiarism and how unintentional plagiarism can slip into a paper. They need to learn to paraphrase, quote, summarize, footnote, and cite all references in a consistent style. Providing specific instruction for these elements of the research process can remove "I didn't know how to do it" or "I didn't understand" as excuses for plagiarism.

The article by Robert Harris in Chapter 15, "Antiplagiarism Strategies for Research Papers," emphasizes the importance of working with students on each step of the research process. He suggests that students write a summary essay at the end of the project to reflect on what they learned about their topic and about the research process.

Alternatives to Traditional Writing Assignments (Chapter 16)

It is more difficult for students to locate a paper online or from other sources when an assignment is unusual, requires a particular focus or point of view, lists quotations from one or more specific reference sources that must be included, or is individualized in some other way. Suggested ideas are writing a paper based on a survey, interview, or other primary research data collected by the student; comparing and contrasting two points of view on a controversial topic; or writing a letter describing a dinner with a historical person, author, or other famous person from the era being studied. Assignments of this type make plagiarism much less likely to occur.

Online Sites for Reports and Research Papers (Chapter 17)

Fifty online sites have been identified as representative of those available to students who want to avoid writing their own report. Nineteen sites offer some or all of their papers for free; others charge $5 to $20 per page. Some sites offer to write custom papers on any topic for $10 to $40 per page. Many of the sites have a disclaimer that their papers are to be used for research only and must not be turned in as the student's own work.

> *"Where do you find history?"*
> *I imagine asking the students of the future.*
> *"On the Web," they answer.*
> *"How do you get at it?"*
> *"By surfing."*
> *"What method will you use to write your paper?"*
> *"Access, download, hyperlink and printout."*
> (Darnton A17)

Chapter 2

High-Tech Cheating

Inside Connecticut classrooms, attached to the waistbands of pants and the lips of bookbags, electronic pagers are quietly vibrating. Need an answer to that tough math question? Check your pager. The electronic pager has been given a new name in Connecticut high schools—the vibrating crib sheet—and, students say, it is becoming one of the easiest ways to cheat because pagers are so common in America's classrooms. One student who has already taken a test earlier in the day has only to call a telephone pager number and punch in the numerical answers to the test questions. A pager on the quiet vibrating setting then alerts the test-taker [who may be a friend or may be paying for the information] that the answers have arrived, visible on the tiny pager screen. (Stansbury. Technology, pars. 5–7)

Chapter Overview

Students today enjoy the challenge of discovering what they can accomplish with each new "high-tech toy." Unfortunately, many are quick to see the possibilities of using the new technologies to cheat on tests and homework.

This chapter explores illicit applications of new electronic technologies. Small hand-held computers, electronic calculators, pagers, Web sites, and computer networks can be used legitimately to enhance students' work. They also give some students an unfair advantage when used for cheating. Copy Me pages describing three high-tech devices are designed as handouts for faculty or parent meetings.

Chapter subheadings:

- Cheating with New Technologies
- Copy Me: "High-Tech Devices Used for Cheating"

Cheating with New Technologies

Hand-Held Computers and Watches

Small hand-held computers are equipped with personal information management (PIM) software and can be linked to a personal desktop computer or network. An infrared transmitter allows users to send and receive text files or applications. Students can simply pull up the appropriate information on the computer while taking a test or use the infrared transmitter to send questions and answers across the classroom or into the hall.

- Notes and formulas can be stored in a personal electronic organizer such as a PalmPilot for retrieval during a test (Mahoney).

- Students can load textbook chapters onto a small hand-held computer and do quick electronic searches for information to ace a test (Fishlock, par. 10).

- Advanced design digital watches store information downloaded from a student's computer for retrieval during a test (Stephen Davis, par. 10).

- An infrared transmitter allows students to send and receive test questions and answers within the classroom or from a student just outside. The receiving computer must confirm willingness to accept the message so the receiving student cannot claim innocence or lack of knowledge (Mahoney).

Programmable Calculators

A portable, hand-held calculator can handle a broad range of mathematical or scientific applications from algebra to calculus, including interactive geometry, symbolic manipulation, statistics, and 3-D graphing. It also can display text. Students can program a calculator with all the formulas needed for a test, definitions and spelling words, important dates, or other information. Students can send lists, answers, and information to other students in class.

- Baker refers to programmable calculators as "electronic cheat sheets" and warns that they can be programmed with whatever information a student might anticipate needing during a test (131).

- A student who finished his test early asked permission to play games on his pocket calculator. Actually, he entered the test questions into the calculator and emailed the questions that night to students who would take the test the next day (Posnick-Goodwin. *Catching* 10).

- One student programmed his spelling words into a graphing calculator and had it on his desk during the spelling test; the teacher was not suspicious at first because he thought calculators were useful only in science and math classes.

- Students who share calculators during a test can leave answers on the calculator when it is passed to another student (Corbett 60).

- Teachers can erase calculator memories before a test but "some whiz kids program their calculators to look as though the memory has been erased when in fact it hasn't." One teacher smiled, "If they're that clever, then I guess they win" (Bushweller. *Digital,* par. 26).

Pagers

Most pagers have a small screen for the viewer to read numeric or full-text messages. They can be set to vibrate rather than beep to announce an incoming message. Students can preprogram their pagers with all the information needed during the test. They can send test questions to someone outside the testing room, requesting and then receiving answers. Questions and answers can be sent back and forth between students who are taking the same test. Watch pagers can be worn as a watch, worn around the neck on a cord, attached to a belt or other article of clothing, or slipped into a pocket, backpack, or purse.

- "Before an exam, call the pager and leave as much test information in a message as possible. Then set the pager to vibrate rather than beep. When test time arrives, turn on the pager and it instantly becomes an electronic cheat sheet" (Bushweller. *Digital,* par. 28).

- Croucher reports on the coordinated use of pagers by two students in high school. One finished early, stood outside near a window, and transmitted answers via pager to his friend still in the classroom. "Their teamwork might have gone undetected, except that the slower student drew attention to himself by repeatedly glancing into his shirt pocket before ever writing anything down" (87).

Web Sites

Students in a class can now create an "underground" Internet Web site to share homework or other assignments, answer questions for one another, and post copies of old tests with answers. When properly managed according to guidelines set by the teacher, such a site can be a valuable study aid. Its clandestine use by students to avoid doing their own homework and assignments is cheating.

- Cheaters Paradise at <http://www.jaberwocky.com/cheat/index2.html> and similar free Web sites on the Internet tell students how to cheat and offer them opportunities to brag online about their successes.

- Chat rooms exist on the Internet for almost any subject imaginable and many students are willing to trade papers (Bushweller. *Digital,* par. 7). Complete papers posted to the chat room by participants can be copied or long strings from the discussions can be worked into an "original" paper.

- Other sites exist where "students can submit math homework problems to a resident math whiz and online message boards where students with very specific needs can help each other" (Benning, par. 25). These sites can fill a positive need when they provide legitimate assistance to students. They unfairly improve students' grades when work actually has been completed or precorrected by someone else.

- Students use free translation programs on the Internet to do their homework in foreign language classes, writing an essay or story in English and then having the software translate it into the language of their class (Mosholder, par. 1).

Computer Networks

School computer networks serve a variety of positive educational functions. They make it possible for teachers to distribute lesson materials and monitor student performance. Students can legitimately share email, compositions, and other work. Giving tests on a computer might make it more difficult to cheat than with paper and pencil tests. Unfortunately, computer networks that are not monitored carefully can be used to cheat and plagiarize.

- When computers used for testing are on a school-wide network some computer-savvy students might send the exam to students who will be taking it later in the day and want to know what to study (Wentzel, par. 18).

- Students bring reports and term papers to school on disk to load onto the network to share with friends.

- Exams and electronic grade books kept on a teacher's desk computer on the school network can be vulnerable to hackers trying to get an advance copy of a test or to alter grades (Benning, par. 22).

- Hackers have changed grades and transcripts, deleted unfavorable information from a student's electronic file, and planted viruses that can destroy the student records of a school or district (Baker 133).

- Hackers can break into school networks to copy work from other students (Wentzel, par. 6). As an ironic twist, if the hacker hands the work in first, the student whose files were copied may unfairly be accused of cheating.

Distance Learning

Tests are difficult to monitor in some distance learning situations and cheating becomes harder to detect.

- Students at isolated sites, who are not part of an established class group and complete tests without supervision, have ample opportunity to cheat by accessing notes, textbooks, or another person in the room.

- A person taking an online test at an isolated site can use a "stand-in" unless some controls are in place to determine that the test-taker actually is the student enrolled in the course.

Faxes and Email

It becomes the responsibility of parents to monitor the use of home computers and fax machines for illicit use.

- Students use email to share homework, drafts of reports, and answers for take-home exams (Wentzel, par. 6).

- Students use fax machines to share homework or reports with their friends (Bushweller. *Digital,* par. 8). If they don't have access to a fax machine at home, they easily can pay to send the fax at a local copy center or other store (Baker 135).

- Between classes, students email test questions to others who will take the test later in the day (Kleiner and Lord 61).

Laser Printers and Copiers

- Typed papers could be distinguished by appearance from those that had been photocopied, but papers from a laser printer have the same appearance as those from a photocopier. This makes it very difficult to identify a paper downloaded from the Internet to a laser printer or one photocopied from another source (Rocklin, par. 10).

- Very small cheat sheets can be created by using a photocopier to reduce the size of the page or using the smaller fonts on a laser printer; the smaller cheat sheet is easier to conceal even though it might be more difficult to read (Netherton, par. 7).

Headsets

- Many students ask to wear headsets and listen to music on their cassettes or CDs during an exam. The student can have recorded dates, formulas, or other information between songs to play back during a test as if listening to music (Stephen Davis 12).

- Teachers checking a music tape for such information must listen to both sides; students can press the auto-reverse button and switch to the all-music side before handing it to the teacher to be checked (Baker 135).

Other Electronic Devices

- One student reportedly paid $3,000 for a pen that had a tiny transmitter with a cordless earpiece; he used it during an exam to send questions and receive answers from another student outside the classroom (Croucher 113).

- Miniature, wireless video cameras now available can be used to video each page of a test and transmit the image to someone outside the classroom with a receiver (Dunn 30). The outside person can send answers back to the test-taker via a pager, and distribute the test to students who will be taking it at a later time (or even sell it to them).

Pointers ———————————————————————

Electronic plagiarism, another form of high-tech cheating, is introduced in Chapter 3. High-tech defenses against both cheating and plagiarism are described in Chapter 5. Chapter 6 suggests ways parents can help to control cheating and plagiarism. Strategies to reduce cheating on tests and assignments are in Chapter 11.

COPY ME:
High-Tech Devices Used for Cheating

✍ Palm Computer

Example brand and model: 3Com Corporation PalmPilot
URL: <http://palmpilot.3com.com/>

> *What it is:* Shirt-pocket sized, hand-held personal computer/organizer that enables mobile users to manage their personal and business information remotely. The data can then be linked with a personal desktop computer or computer network.

> *What it does:* Computer/organizers are equipped with personal information management (PIM) software including date book, address book, to-do list, expense management software, calculator, note-taking applications, and games. An infrared transmitter allows users to send and receive text files or applications.

> *How it can be used to cheat:* Students can store information, including entire chapters of books, that they are being tested on. They simply pull up the appropriate information while taking the test. The infrared transmitter can be used to send questions and answers across the classroom or into the hall.

> *What teachers should watch for:* Students checking their pockets, purses, or laps for information; these very small computers easily can be hidden in baggy clothing. Students "pointing" at other students to send or receive information via infrared transmitter.

> *How to prevent cheating:* Inform students in advance that palm computers are not allowed in class during testing and will be confiscated.

✍ Programmable Calculator

Example brand and model: Texas Instruments TI-92
URL: <http://www.ti.com/calc/docs/news/cg-418t.htm>

> *What it is:* Portable, hand-held calculator for electronic calculation in science and mathematics.

> *What it does:* Calculators can handle a broad range of mathematics or science applications from algebra to calculus, including interactive geometry, symbolic manipulation, statistics, and 3-D graphing. They also can display text.

Reprinted with permission from Student Cheating and Plagiarism in the Internet Era: A Wake-Up Call *by Ann Lathrop and Kathleen Foss. Englewood, CO: Libraries Unlimited, 2000.*

How it can be used to cheat: Students can program the calculator with all the formulas, definitions and spelling words, important dates, or other information that can be used on a test. With the press of a button, students can compute answers to the test questions quickly and easily or recall information. Students can link these computers to send lists, answers, and information to other students in class.

What teachers should watch for: Students who do exceptionally well on tests but who do not perform as well in class. Students "pointing" their calculators at other calculators to send or receive information via infrared laser.

How to prevent cheating: Have a classroom set of "simple" calculators for student use during tests or for class assignments. Do not allow students to use calculators from home during testing; warn them they will be confiscated. In classes that do not require students to memorize the formulas, make programmable calculators available to every student in the class and teach them to use them.

Pager or Pager Watch

Example brand and model: Motorola Corporation Beepwear
URL: <http://www.beepwear.com/html/index.html>

What it is: Small, wearable message receiver. Voice pagers let users hear the message. Most pagers have a small screen for the viewer to read numeric or full-text messages. They can be set to vibrate rather than beep to announce an incoming message. The new watch pagers can be worn as a watch, worn around the neck on a cord, attached to a belt or other article of clothing, or slipped into a pocket, backpack, or purse.

What it does: Current pagers have the capability to send or receive messages or email.

How it can be used to cheat: Students can preprogram their pagers with all the information they will need during the test and then read the information from the pager during the test. They can send questions to someone outside the testing room, requesting and then receiving answers to the test. It is possible to send questions and answers back and forth between students as they both take the test.

What teachers should watch for: Students who look at their watch or in their pocket frequently during tests.

How to prevent cheating: Inform students in advance when pagers are not allowed in class; they must be turned off and stored in backpacks. Warn them that their pagers will be confiscated if used during testing.

Chapter 3

Electronic Plagiarism

It's four o'clock in the morning, you're just one page into a 15-page term paper that's due at ten o'clock, and the teaching assistant isn't giving extensions. A few years ago, that would have been it: You would have passed in the paper late, if at all, and dealt with the consequences. But this is 1998, and so, in your most desperate hour, you try a desperate ploy. You log on to the World Wide Web . . . enter "term papers" into an online search engine, and find your way to www.a1-termpaper.com. There you scroll down past the big red disclaimer ("All work offered is for research purposes only"), find a paper that fits the assignment, enter your credit card number, and then wait until the file shows up in your college email account. You feel a little ashamed, but, hey, the course was just a distribution requirement, anyway. You put your own name on the title page, print it out, and set the alarm for nine o'clock. (Hickman, par. 2)

Chapter Overview

Students copy papers from a variety of Internet sites: online paper mills, reviews of films and plays, electronic journals, and legitimate research sites created to share scientific and scholarly papers. Electronic encyclopedias on CD-ROM or online are convenient sources for plagiarizing reports and term papers.

The types of papers available online and the simple steps of downloading a paper are explained. Students are warned against plagiarizing online graphics or other materials to create their own Web sites; these are protected by copyright. Ten representative online sites for research papers are described in a Copy-Me page. Tom Rocklin's article offers one professor's individualized view of Internet plagiarism, a brief history of the paper mills, and some suggested coping techniques he has developed.

17

Chapter subheadings:

- What's Available on the Internet?
- Plagiarizing 1-2-3
- Plagiarizing from Electronic Encyclopedias
- Copy Me: "Online Sites for Reports and Research Papers"
- Rocklin: "Downloadable Term Papers: What's a Prof to Do?"

What's Available on the Internet?

"Cyber-plagiarism" is the new term for student copying from the many online Web sites, or paper mills, which offer thousands of reports and term papers on almost any topic. Student use of the Internet is described by one author as "a big study group and an endless archive of cut-and-paste essay components [where] the ability to easily scoop a little flotsam from the vast oceans of the Internet doesn't seem nearly as nefarious as pilfering a passage from a library book" (Fritz, pars. 6–7).

It is impossible to tell just what is available online for any specific topic without actually searching a number of the paper mill sites for a paper. A student can do comparison shopping by searching several free sites for a specific topic. It is more difficult, and certainly more expensive, to compare papers from sites that charge for each paper or custom write a paper at a per page cost.

Some sites offer all or a significant number of their papers for free; most of these appear to receive income from advertisements for video games, magazines marketing to teenagers, sites selling college information or college entrance essays, etc. About a third of the fifty sites listed in Chapter 17 offer some free papers but charge for the majority of them; others charge for all of their papers. Some sites require that students submit a paper in exchange for one received. More than half the sites offer to write custom papers at a per page cost, usually at least $100 or more per paper.

Many paper mill sites display a statement warning users that their papers are to be used for research purposes only and must not be turned in as the student's own work. This appears to be an attempt to circumvent lawsuits brought against several of the sites (so far without success). A typical statement is the one online at School Paper.com:

> Our research papers are to be used only as references for your paper. We refuse to sell a research paper to any student whom we have reason to believe will submit our work, either in whole or part, for academic credit in their own name. If you choose to quote from our work you must cite our paper as one of your sources.

Owners and developers of the paper mill sites often elaborate on the disclaimers when they are interviewed. They appear eager to counter any accusations that they encourage plagiarism.

> "I help people," says Abe Korn, the man behind The Term Paper, School, and Business Help Line . . . [explaining] that his clients say, " 'Abe, help me, I don't know how to write a paper.' I write them one, as an example, and then they go and pass it in. Is that my fault? No. If I help you in physics and work one problem, and you turn that problem in, am I to blame? No. I'm just a tutor." (Hickman, par. 9)

> Mr. Roberts of Cheat.com agrees that his Web site may make it
> seem easier than ever to fake academic research. But he denies en-
> couraging plagiarism. "The site wasn't at all to promote plagia-
> rism, but to sort of put the library online," he says. "I thought if I
> put term papers online then kids wouldn't have to spend time
> looking in all the encyclopedias and books and stuff like that.
> Kind of like Cliff's Notes®." (Clayton, pars. 16–17)

In addition to the paper mills, Internet sites offer other sources for book reports. Some students plagiarize by downloading television reviews that compare a play or film with the original book (Benning, pars. 16–17). Cyber Classics at <http://www.cyberclassics.com> advertises a package with a print copy of the book, a copy of the book on disk, and an electronic summary. Like Cliff's Notes®, the Cyber Classics summaries can be helpful in interpreting a book. Unfortunately, students might copy all or part of the electronic summary as their book report.

A large number of research sites that share scientific and scholarly papers online provide opportunities for plagiarism, especially for students in Advanced Placement classes. These students can download and hand in the original paper or edit it to sound less scholarly. Articles in electronic journals provide material students can rework into research papers or even copy and hand in "as is."

Versity.com at <http://www.versity.com> will provide detailed lecture notes from large classes at several major universities without charge. Their income appears to come from the many advertisements on each page. A disclaimer states: "Versity.com is not affiliated with, sponsored, or licensed by any of the universities or professors teaching courses contained within the site." The site grows by hiring students to provide lecture notes for popular classes at large universities (Horovitz 2B). Students could download lecture notes from an appropriate class and transform them into a report or term paper.

Editing services, originally offered to professional clientele for a fee, accept student papers emailed to them and provide suggestions for correcting grammar, strengthening weak segments, or improving the bibliography. The paper is returned in the format required by the teacher, ready to hand in.

One other form of electronic plagiarism is students' copying of graphics and text material from an existing Web site. Students with an assignment to create an original Web site often "borrow" from a site they find attractive. This can be unintentional plagiarism when students "don't realize that the same rules that cover print, recordings, and videotape also apply to computer software and Internet sites" (Hardy, par. 5). Copyright issues related to using materials from Internet Web sites are discussed in Chapter 9.

Plagiarizing 1-2-3

Downloading a paper requires just a computer, a printer, and access to the Internet. A credit card is needed only when the student does not locate a suitable free paper.

Some students download and print the paper, create a title page, and hand it in. Others, more sophisticated or more cautious, download the paper into a word processor. They "massage" the text, perhaps using a thesaurus to replace words or phrases the teacher might recognize as beyond their usual vocabulary or writing style. Obvious strings of highly distinctive words can be changed or deleted if a student knows the teacher is "Internet savvy" and might search for word strings online.

A student with computer expertise and good vocabulary skills can locate free translation software online, download a paper in that language on the topic needed, run the paper through the translation program, edit the paper for obvious errors in translation, and turn it in. A teacher who is searching the Internet for English word strings from this paper is unlikely to locate any matches and the plagiarism probably will not be identified (Stebelman, pars. 9–10). Taking the translation scheme another step, an English paper can be translated into French and then translated back into English; this makes it even less likely that original English word strings remain to be traced (Magney, par. 17).

Plagiarizing from Electronic Encyclopedias

Copying term papers and reports from encyclopedias is a deeply entrenched approach to "research" on the part of many students. Encyclopedias available online or on CD-ROM now spare students even the labor of actually typing the text. An eighth-grade student explains the process:

> He downloaded text verbatim from Microsoft's *Encarta* encyclopedia and pasted it into a word processing program. Click. Drag. Copy. Paste. Easy as that, he says. . . . "You have to edit all the obvious stuff you wouldn't say," he says, instructing his listeners in the fine art of plagiarism. "Take out the big words. Some teachers know I wouldn't say those long words." Did it work? "Yeah," he says, leaning back in his chair, "I got away with it." (Bushweller. *Digital*, pars. 15–16)

Many students will, in fact, get away with it. But teachers familiar with their students' reading and writing ability will notice a "too good" paper despite attempts to "edit all the obvious stuff."

Some students go beyond using the encyclopedia to create papers only for themselves. McCabe describes one senior as "a budding entrepreneur, running his own little paper mill in order to raise money for the purchase of CDs."

> I got this computer and it came with an encyclopedia. . . . Somebody comes up to me and says, "I need ten pages on Edgar Poe." I can go home, cut and paste, and depending on how smart the person is, I'll add what is appropriate. (McCabe. *Academic,* 683)

Plagiarism can sometimes be quite innocent, especially in elementary schools. Many younger students have not yet learned to make a clear distinction between "research" and simply copying information from reference sources. One elementary school librarian shares her experience:

> When reviewing a 5th grade boy's preliminary work on a National Park report, I commented that the wording he used seemed to be quite advanced, perhaps even verbatim from an encyclopedia. The student responded that he had in fact "cut and pasted" the article, but that it was okay because his mom paid $69 for the CD-ROM encyclopedia, so he "owned" it. After a brief discussion on plagiarism and a quick review of our two-week lesson on citing references,

the student realized that he didn't really own the right to use the words verbatim. Instead of making him feel guilty, I asked if he was willing to share his new source of information because our school did not own any CD-ROM encyclopedias. He asked permission from his parents and brought the CD-ROM to school. We set up a computer station and announced to the class that he was our CD-ROM expert and was responsible for assisting other students in locating information on the CD-ROM. The student felt empowered to be able to help others and his classmates were excited to use the new information. I received a phone call the following week from the child's mother. She initially was suspicious about sending the CD-ROM to school, because her son sometimes was considered to be a bit of a troublemaker and she thought it odd that he was wanting to share. She then expressed her sincere gratitude because she had never seen her son so charged to come to school, so happy to help others, and so eager to spend time browsing an encyclopedia to see what other "treasures" he could find to share. (Tom)

Pointers

Julie Ryan's article following Chapter 5 explains how to search online for the original of a student's plagiarized paper; a similar example is the Copy-Me page in Chapter 13, "An Electronic Scavenger Hunt." Chapter 13 addresses unintentional plagiarism and techniques to recognize plagiarism; it includes Bruce Leland's suggestions to limit student use of online paper sites. Alternative writing assignments are described in Chapter 16. Descriptions of fifty online sites for reports and research papers are in Chapter 17.

COPY ME:
Online Sites for Reports and Research Papers

These ten sites were selected as representative of the online paper mills being used by students as sources for plagiarized reports and term papers. They were available at the URL listed as of March 2000.

1-800 TERMPAPER ACADEMIC AND BUSINESS RESEARCH SOURCE
<www.al-termpaper.com>

> Disclaimer: One line in capital letters says "all work offered is for research purposes only."

> Description: Offers 20,000 on-file papers and custom papers for students and the business community. Has a subject index for broad categories with subindexes for prewritten papers.

> Pricing: Each on-file paper is individually priced. Custom papers are from $19.95 to $35 per page.

ACADEMIC TERM PAPERS
<www.academictermpapers.com>

> Disclaimer: Warns students that these papers "may not be submitted either in whole or in part for academic credit."

> Description: Has over 30,000 research papers. Will custom write a report.

> Pricing: Each on-file paper is $7 per page with a maximum charge of $120. There is no charge for bibliographies, footnotes, or partial pages. Custom papers are $19 and up per page.

BIGNERDS.COM
<www.bignerds.com>

> Disclaimer: None.

> Description: Has over 800 free essays, term papers, and book reports on a wide variety of topics or will have a custom paper written through its partnership with Collegiate Care. Anyone ordering a custom paper is asked to "Please describe the research you need compiled: Include title, topics, length requirement, citation style, and time frame for completion of the report." Also will supply college admission applications and essays. Has links to fifty-plus additional paper sites.

> Pricing: Free on-file papers. Custom papers from Collegiate Care are $16.95 per page with a five-page minimum. Rush requests cost more.

Reprinted with permission from Student Cheating and Plagiarism in the Internet Era: A Wake-Up Call *by Ann Lathrop and Kathleen Foss. Englewood, CO: Libraries Unlimited, 2000.*

CHEATER.COM
<www.cheater.com>

> Disclaimer: "Who we are, who we aren't," states that "we provide a service for students, like anything it can be abused if used improperly. Like any Library, we offer lots of information that can be used for facts only. Plagiarism is illegal and Cheater.com does not support it in any way, shape or form." and "For once and for all, all you should gain from this site is other peoples' ideas. We are not here to promote plagiarism. If you turn in a paper from this site as your own you are hurting yourself. Cheater.com is meant to be used as a resource."

> Description: Term papers can be accessed by keyword using a Boolean search or by browsing general categories. Custom papers are referred to School Sucks. Claims 72,000 members.

> Pricing: Free. Must submit a paper for membership.

CHEATHOUSE—THE EVIL HOUSE OF CHEAT
<www.cheathouse.com>

> Disclaimer: No disclaimer is listed on the main page, but a copyright link is at the bottom of the page.

> Description: Claims over 2,000 essays or 9,500 for their members who have a password. Search strategy offers students who submit papers the opportunity to list the title and summary length of their paper, their grade level, school system, author information, and the original grade with comments on the papers in the database. Offers links and tips on how to cheat on exams.

> Pricing: Free, but must register for password.

PAPER STORE
<www.paperstore.net>

> Disclaimer: They state that "the intended purpose of our example term papers is that they be used as study aids or as models of what a term paper should be like."

> Description: "Since 1994, The Paper Store has helped tens of thousands of college & graduate students overcome their greatest fear: WRITING PAPERS." They offer examples of term papers and custom research. Can preview an excerpt of their 15,000 on-file research papers.

> Pricing: Each on-file paper is $8.95. Custom papers are $14.95 per page.

Reprinted with permission from Student Cheating and Plagiarism in the Internet Era: A Wake-Up Call *by Ann Lathrop and Kathleen Foss. Englewood, CO: Libraries Unlimited, 2000.*

RESEARCH ASSISTANCE
<www.research-assistance.com>

Disclaimer: None.

Description: Offers an indexed database of over 25,000 papers. Advertise that they have been providing library research reports to academic and business communities since 1969. Offers a custom service too.

Pricing: Each on-file paper is $7.50 per page plus shipping and tax up to seventeen pages, with a flat fee of $127 for any single report that is longer than seventeen pages. Custom papers are from $20 to $35 per page.

SCHOOL PAPER.COM
<www.schoolpaper.com>

Disclaimer: "Our research papers are to be used only as references for your paper. We refuse to sell a research paper to any student whom we have reason to believe will submit our work, either in whole or part, for academic credit in their own name. If you choose to quote from our work you must cite our paper as one of your sources."

Description: A database of thousands of prewritten "reference papers" and literary summaries for those "who do not wish to waste the time reading all of the novels, plays, and other pieces of literature for your classes."

Pricing: Each on-file paper is $20 per paper regardless of length. Membership fee required.

SCHOOLBYTES.COM
<www.schoolbytes.com>

Disclaimer: None.

Description: Offers free book plot summaries, short story plot summaries, and free term papers.

Pricing: Free.

SMART ESSAYS
<www.FreeEssay.com/smart/>

Disclaimer: Long and very detailed disclaimer fills one page with all legal possibilities.

Description: Essays can be accessed from a general index on the first page or user can request a customized search. The index will tell how many words are in the essay and the approximate number of pages. Downloading is more complicated than just highlighting and hitting the print button.

Pricing: Free.

Reprinted with permission from Student Cheating and Plagiarism in the Internet Era: A Wake-Up Call *by Ann Lathrop and Kathleen Foss. Englewood, CO: Libraries Unlimited, 2000.*

Downloadable Term Papers:
What's a Prof to Do?

Tom Rocklin

I imagine that people have been presenting others' work as their own at least since—well, at least since there have been people. Because students are people, I don't suppose any of us is surprised that some students sometimes present other peoples' work as their own. And, since we live in a market economy, I don't suppose any of us is surprised that some people have found ways to make money off the phenomenon.

People have been selling term papers at least since I started college almost 25 years ago. The nature of the market has evolved as technologies have come along to facilitate it. When I was a student, most papers were locally produced and sold. Shortly after I graduated from college and started graduate school, posters started appearing on bulletin boards advertising catalogs of term papers. The advent of 800-number marketing techniques and the widespread use of credit cards allowed for national markets in term papers.

Enter the Internet

In its August 2, 1996, issue, *The Chronicle of Higher Education* caused quite a stir when it reported on a Web site that allows students to download term papers for free. Locally, both the *Iowa City Press Citizen* and the *Des Moines Register* ran related stories.

It seems that an enterprising soul has created a web site, www.schoolsucks.com, to which students are invited to submit papers and from which students are invited to download papers. Apparently, the proprietor of the site expects advertising to support it. I imagine that advertisers will not be hard to find.

Before reacting in greater detail to the School Sucks site, I'd like to survey the Web scene as it relates to term papers. It looks to me as though there are at least three kinds of term paper sources on the Web.

1. *Traditional paper mills.*

   These sites are really only a new advertising medium. The services being offered are no different from those that have been offered before. For the record, all of these sites admonish customers that the papers offered for sale are for research purposes only and are not to be turned in for a grade.

2. *Papers "published" by students and instructors.*

   The Web has created an unprecedented opportunity for people to publish, and students and instructors have taken advantage of the opportunity. There are a number of good reasons to go this route. Perhaps the most important is that publishing student papers more broadly gives students a real audience to write for.

   Of course, it also gives (other) students a source of papers from which to plagiarize. But those that live by the sword will die by the sword, won't they? If an instructor suspected such a plagiarism, it would be fairly easy to find the source paper. A search with Alta Vista or a similar search engine, using an unusual phrase from the paper that was turned in as the search phrase, would quickly find the source.

3. *Papers free for the downloading.*

Finally, School Sucks offers papers for free. They are categorized by subject and particular topic. A quick click of the mouse, a brief wait, and the text is on your disk, ready to be read into your word processor. If you want to hand it in, all you need to do is add your name and other identifying information, perhaps do some minor formatting, and print. The whole process would probably take less than half an hour.

What's Changed?

I've implied that downloadable term papers are a natural step in the evolution of a market that has long existed. Indeed, there are strong continuities here. At the same time, things **have** changed. For one thing, the combination of Internet access and word processor power have made it almost trivially simple to disguise the origin of a downloaded term paper. In the "old days" a student often ended up having to retype a purchased paper because professors insisted on original typescripts. Remember, in those days, a typewriter made noticeable impressions on the paper, and copiers didn't. These days, of course, a laser-printed paper is indistinguishable from a photocopied paper.

For another thing, downloading a term paper is quick and easy. I imagine that the idea of turning in a term paper written by someone else gains attractiveness as the due date approaches. Imagine a student the night before a term paper is due, with no term paper to turn in. The easier and quicker it is to obtain a term paper, the greater the temptation. I cannot imagine that there is an easier way or quicker way to get a paper than downloading one from School Sucks or from one of the sites on which students and instructors publish papers.

How Do Downloadable Papers Threaten Education?

By making it easier to plagiarize, downloadable term papers undermine the purpose of assigned papers. Instructors assign written work not to test the students' abilities to obtain papers, but to encourage students to engage in certain kinds of intellectual work. This intellectual work is what facilitates the students' educational development.

Downloading a paper does not help students develop their abilities to analyze or synthesize information, to judge the credibility of sources, to express themselves clearly and convincingly. It is because handing in a plagiarized paper to fulfill an assignment undermines our educational goals that we take such a dim view of the practice.

What Can Faculty Members Do to Minimize the Threat?

Remembering the purpose of assigning term papers is the key to one response to the threats posed by downloadable term papers. Because we are interested in helping students develop certain skills, the best writing assignments have always included opportunities for the instructor to observe and coach the **process** of writing as well as judge the product. For example, many instructors require that students turn in a topic statement, or a description of the theme of the paper they plan, or a thesis statement early on in the semester. The instructor might also want to see an early bibliography, notes, an outline, a first draft and revisions before accepting the final product for grading. There are a number of more creative opportunities for helping students think about their writing as well. For example, one instructor I know has asked students to turn in three possible openings for a paper. These are all functional ways to encourage students to do the hard intellectual work that we believe will facilitate their development as writers and thinkers.

If the instructor collects interim evidence of students' progress on the assignment, it is unlikely that the purpose of the assignment will be undermined by downloadable term papers. It would generally be more difficult for a student to construct plausible interim products that might lead to a downloaded term paper than to write a term paper.

In any case, anecdotal evidence suggests that plagiarism is rarely a part of a long-term plan. Most students who plagiarize decide to hand in another's work as their own in a panic at the last moment. If students have been turning in interim evidence of their work throughout the semester, they are less likely to panic at the last moment.

Writing Assignments Closely Tied to the Course's Goals

Some assignments are relatively easy to fulfill with plagiarism. In particular, it is not too hard to find papers to satisfy "generic" assignments on the Web. For example, an introductory social psychology course might include the assignment:

- Choose any topic we cover in this course and explore it in greater depth.
- Write a paper summarizing what you learn by reading at least five reports of empirical research.
- Relate your summary to one of the theories we have discussed.

There are, by conservative estimate, a zillion such papers floating around out there.

Other assignments may or may not be easy to fulfill with plagiarism, but create conditions ripe for plagiarism. We are often tempted to ask students to write substantial papers that they won't be able to begin until later in the semester, because we will not have discussed essential ideas until then. Remember my hypothesis that the closer the due date, the more tempting plagiarism is.

Other assignments are very difficult to plagiarize, particularly by obtaining papers from off-campus sites. I once gave an assignment in an educational psychology class that called on students to analyze the motivational properties of our class. I asked them to think about our class in terms of some specific concepts we had been discussing and some that were mentioned in their textbook. The assignment was specifically connected to our particular goals in that class. It is hard to imagine that somewhere out on the net there exists an analysis of a class just like ours in terms of the particular concepts I specified. Frankly, my purpose in defining the assignment this way had more to do with supporting my goals for the students' learning than it did preventing plagiarism. The fact that the paper is hard to plagiarize is a byproduct of a carefully focused assignment.

As it turns out, a student once did turn in a plagiarism for this assignment, by turning in as his own a paper written in a previous semester. The plagiarism was obvious, because the course had changed and the paper described requirements that were out of date.

Putting Downloadable Term Papers to Legitimate Educational Use

Another approach to dealing with the phenomenon of downloadable term papers involves co-opting the site. The proprietors of both the traditional term paper mills and of School Sucks note that they are providing papers for educational purposes. In fact, I can imagine a variety of educational purposes to which they could be put.

- A faculty member could identify several relevant papers on the Web and grade and comment on them. These graded papers could then be made available to students as examples.

- Alternatively, the faculty member could assign students to identify a paper of their choice and critique it. This could be the basis of a class discussion about the characteristics of high quality student papers.

No doubt, instructors will find other uses for term papers on the Web. In any of these cases, it seems unlikely that students will hand in as their own papers downloaded from a site that the instructor has obviously inspected.

Some Final Thoughts

In thinking about downloadable term papers, I have been struck by the feeling that the issue of plagiarism may be symptomatic of a deeper issue. A student who hands in a plagiarized paper has not bought into the instructor's goals for a course. The plagiarist and the instructor are in an adversarial relationship. Somehow, the student has come to conclude that the goal is to "beat" the instructor, to fool the teacher.

If we can convince our students that the assignments we have developed are truly for the students' benefit, they will understand that beating the assignment harms them, not the instructor. That's really what my thoughts about developing assignments that focus on process and are closely tied to the focus of the course boils down to. If we ask students to complete assignments of demonstrable value and offer to work with them as they complete these assignments, they are likely to join us in the educational enterprise we envision.

Footnote: The section focusing on the process of writing grows out of a comment made by Steven Richardson, Director of the Center for Teaching Excellence at Iowa State University.

[Reprinted with permission of the author: Paper was written in 1996. Tom Rocklin can be contacted at: thomas-rocklin@uiowa.edu]

Chapter 4

Why We Are Alarmed

Man, school is geared so it almost encourages you to cheat . . . like tests, papers, and grades. You gotta do well or your parents get mad or you flunk, so everybody cheats. . . . It's easier to cheat and since it's grades that get you into college and scholarships and stuff, the grade's more important. I get pretty good grades and there's a thousand ways to cheat. If I was honest, I'd flunk, then where would I be? (Gladden ii)

Chapter Overview

The statement above was made by a student interviewed by Gladden in 1973, now almost thirty years ago. Today an increasing number of our own students echo his sentiments. New technologies have expanded cheating and plagiarizing far beyond traditional cheat sheets or term papers copied from an encyclopedia.

Statistical data from regional and national surveys summarized here indicate a steady increase in cheating behaviors. Student attitudes in a number of interviews show a general acceptance of cheating as "no big deal" and document an almost universal reluctance to "rat" on classmates who cheat. The abstract and questionnaires from Fred Schab's longitudinal study can be useful to educators planning a school or district survey. Research on cheating at the college and university level is summarized in a Copy-Me page.

Chapter subheadings:

- Things Are Bad and Getting Worse
- Are Elementary School Students Cheating?
- Student and Teacher Attitudes toward Cheating

- What the Students Say
- Data and Conclusions from Four Surveys
- Survey 1: *Who's Who Among American High School Students*
- Copy Me: "Cheating and Succeeding: Record Numbers of Top High School Students Take Ethical Shortcuts"
- Survey 2: Josephson Institute of Ethics
- Copy Me: "1998 Report Card on the Ethics of American Youth"
- Survey 3: Southern California Suburban High School
- Survey 4: Schab's Longitudinal Study
- Research Highlights on Cheating in Colleges and Universities
- Copy Me: "Research Highlights"

Things Are Bad and Getting Worse

The following data are highlights from four surveys reported more fully and documented in the second half of this chapter, "Data and Conclusions from Four Surveys." Complete data for the surveys by the publisher of *Who's Who Among American High School Students* and the Josephson Institute of Ethics, including all questions and student responses from both surveys, are available online at the URLs listed. The abstract and questionnaires from Schab's longitudinal study are the final survey in this chapter.

The *Who's Who* survey represents the academically top 5% of American high school students. The three other surveys represent a cross section of students. Only the Josephson survey includes middle school students.

Figures from the four surveys all support the same message: Cheating is widespread in our schools today, especially at the high school level. There is a steady increase in the number of students who cheat and in the seriousness and frequency of their cheating behaviors. This means the results of classroom tests used to determine grades and GPAs for college admission and scholarships are skewed. The cheaters are gaining a grossly unfair advantage, and again, the honest students who compete with them are the losers.

1. The 1998 survey by the publisher of *Who's Who Among American High School Students* polled a representative sample of the academically top 5% of all American high school students.

   - 83% said "almost everybody does it" or "fairly common" when asked "How common is cheating in your school?"
   - 80% of the students cheated
   - 95% of those who cheated avoided getting caught
   - 67% cheated by copying homework
   - 40% cheated on tests
   - 29% used Cliff's Notes® or Monarch Notes to avoid reading a book
   - 13% plagiarized part of an essay
   - 56% cheated to get good grades
   - 53% cheated because it "didn't seem like a big deal"
   - 28% cheated because they were not interested in the subject

2. The 1998 survey by the Josephson Institute of Ethics polled more than 20,000 middle and high school students nationwide.

   - 70% of the high school students cheated on an examination within the past year
   - 54% of the middle school students cheated on an examination within the past year
   - 36% of the high school students "would be willing to cheat on a test if it would help me get into college"

3. A survey of one Southern California high school, conducted for this book by the authors in 1999 for comparison purposes, found similar results.

   - 71% have cheated on a test
   - 91% have observed students cheating on tests or quizzes

4. Schab surveyed students in 1969, 1979, and 1989. His longitudinal data show a steady rise in *yes* responses.

   - "Have you used a cheat sheet on a test?" 34% *yes* in 1969, 68% *yes* in 1989
   - "Have you let others copy your work?" 58% *yes* in 1969, 98% *yes* in 1989
   - "Would you cheat if it were the only way to get a diploma?" 49% *yes* in 1969, 60% *yes* in 1989

Schab reports a decrease in *yes* responses for two items we would prefer to see going the other way:

   - "Honesty is always the best policy." 82% *yes* in 1969, 60% *yes* in 1989
   - "If you found a $20 bill at school would you turn it in?" 81% *yes* in 1969, 32% *yes* in 1989

The Schab study reports one other student response that is disturbing to educators; 88% of the students agreed that "some teachers are dishonest." It is difficult to convince students to be honest when they perceive their teachers as dishonest.

Are Elementary School Students Cheating?

Bushweller reports on an Idaho counselor who investigated student attitudes toward cheating in two second-grade and two fifth-grade classes. Students were assigned spelling words to study for a test on the following day. Candy bars were promised to students in one second-grade and one fifth-grade class if they could spell either all the words or all but one of the words correctly; students in the other two classes were not offered any reward.

> [The counselor] collected the tests and graded them but didn't mark her grades on the papers. The next day she asked the students to grade their own papers, and then she compared the student's grades with the grades she had assigned. Among the second-graders and fifth-graders in classes that were not offered candy bars, only one kid cheated by changing wrong answers to correct

ones. In the other two classes, all but three kids cheated just to get the candy bar. Looking beyond spelling tests and candy bars, [the counselor] concludes: "Students will cheat if the stakes are high." (Bushweller. *Generation* 26–27)

Students in elementary and middle schools were caught cheating in a story-writing contest gone awry. Almost 800 Atlanta children ages eight through fifteen entered the *Journal-Constitution* holiday story contest and three of the ten finalists were disqualified for plagiarizing:

> One of the entrants had used a short story and just changed the names of the characters. Another student used elements from a story and a video to create her entry. The third had also taken a favorite published story–but said her teacher had told the class to "just write a story you already know if you can't think of your own idea." . . . In all three cases, the students did not really understand that they were doing something wrong. (Martz, par. 13)

Student and Teacher Attitudes toward Cheating

A 1991 study by Evans and Craig reported perceptions of cheating held by teachers and students at four middle and senior high schools. Cheating was regarded as a serious problem by 70% of the teachers and 71.3% of the students in high school, and by 61.4% of the students and 50.1% of the teachers in middle school. Other findings include:

- A majority (51% or more) of both teachers and students in all schools agreed that students usually know when cheating occurs in class, rarely complain to fellow students whom they know are cheating, and typically do not report cheating to their teachers.
- Students generally agreed—but teachers did not—that teachers who are unfriendly, boring or dull, and have high expectations for student performance are more likely to encounter classroom cheating. In contrast, a strong majority of both teachers (95%) and students (70%) showed strong agreement that cheating is more likely to occur when teachers are disorganized and take no steps to prevent cheating.
- Strong agreements among both groups (60–90% range) included beliefs that students are more likely to cheat if they have a low academic self-concept, budget study time poorly, avoid effort, fear failure, are pressured by their parents to do well, and have friends who cheat.
- Teachers and students both emphasized the value of uniformly enforcing penalties for cheating. (46–50)

Students tell us they are under increasing pressure from parents, teachers, peers, counselors, and others to perform well in school. Perhaps in our minds much of this pressure is well intentioned; we are encouraging students to reach their potential. In reality, some teachers and administrators pressure students to perform well on standardized tests so the school will appear successful. In other cases, parents want to boast of their student's admission to a prestigious college.

> It is the college-bound students who are scrambling to build impressive college resumes: taking honors classes, playing in afterschool sports, joining clubs and committees. Some have part-time jobs. Colleges, which used to require personal interviews as part of an application, now put greater emphasis on grade point averages and class ranking. (Stansbury. *For,* par. 19)

Two surveys were conducted by Stephen Davis over a six-year period from 1987–1992 in large and small, public and private universities and colleges across the United States. He found similar reasons for cheating at all of the sites:

> The most frequently cited reason for cheating was "I do study, but cheat to enhance my score" (29.75%). "My job cuts down on study time" (14.28%) and "usually don't study" (13.60%) also were high on the list. "I cheat so my GPA looks better to prospective employers" (8.16%) and "I feel pressure from parents to get good grades, so I cheat" (6.80%) also received substantial endorsement. (pars. 7–8)

McCabe conducted focus groups with nineteen students from eight New Jersey high schools; all but one were college-bound seniors. Almost every student admitted to having cheated in some way and all were unconcerned about being caught and punished. They indicated a widespread, almost cynical acceptance of cheating as an accepted fact of school life that is unlikely to change. McCabe concluded "high school students were decidedly more blasé about cheating than the college students." He also reported that not one of the nineteen students "even entertained the possibility of reporting any cheating they might observe among their classmates." According to one of the students interviewed, "It's an unspoken rule for people our age—you just don't tell. I don't know why, either, but it's like you make yourself look worse than the person [who cheated]" (McCabe. *Academic* 684).

This attitude is supported by the longitudinal data in Schab's survey. In response to the question, "Would you report a friend you saw cheating?" only 12% of the students in 1969 responded *yes*; this dropped to 4% *yes* in 1989. Responses to a second question, "Would you report a person not your friend?" were only slightly higher, with 21% responding *yes* in 1969 and 17% *yes* in 1989 (Schab 843).

What the Students Say

Cheating and plagiarizing appear to be so widely accepted by students that the byword has changed from *Don't cheat or plagiarize* to *Don't get caught.* The remarks that follow, made by students in a variety of interview situations over the past few years, appear to substantiate this change:

- Students in an advanced placement civics class were discussing cheating: "Told that a recent survey found that 70 percent of high school students admitted cheating on exams, the 30 seniors responded virtually in unison: 'Too low!' The classroom erupted in laughter" (Love, pars. 2–3).

- "Maybe when our parents were growing up or their parents were growing up, it was a lot tighter and stricter on people cheating. Today it's just not happening. I think grown-ups have gotten a little bit more with it in terms of knowing that you're just going to kind of cheat. It's almost a big deal if you don't cheat" (McCabe. *Academic* 682).

- According to one 18-year-old girl, "I'm trying to change, but [cheating] is such a part of everyday life, you don't think twice about it" (Bell, par. 14).

- "There's a feeling like everybody does it," the student said. "And the rationale is, if you are going to be able to look it up in a book anyway in life, you shouldn't be tested on memorization of math formulas" (Stansbury. *Technology,* par. 30).

- A college freshman talks about her high school English class: "You didn't even think of it as cheating because everybody did it. . . . We'd study Macbeth in English and no one could answer one question during class, then everybody would bust out a 98 on the exam. The teachers didn't seem to have a clue" (Barnett, par. 17).

- "Sometimes it's so easy that it's tempting to cheat. . . . The teachers don't pay attention, so you just lay your book down on the floor or ask someone next to you" (Netherton, par. 34).

- "You never see any gratification for being a good person anymore. . . . Once you get to high school, it's all about who has the grades and who's going to get the most scholarships" (Kleiner and Lord 62).

- "Another student says, with a shrug: 'Cheating is something that just happens— it's like asking directions' " (Bushweller. *Generation* 25).

- A student at an Iowa high school justifies cheating as a necessity: "You simply have to do better than your peers, and you'll sacrifice your morals, as long as you achieve and get a good job with lots of money" (Albrecht, par. 2).

- Comments from a high school junior: "Everyone is overwhelmed with what they're doing . . . there's no time to learn the material or understand it [so] you have to find another way to get through it. Each teacher expects so much from you, especially in the higher levels. They don't care what's going on in other classes. . . . It's all very stressful" (McKay, pars. 23–24).

- Two high school junior boys made disheartening comments: "Everybody in school has cheated at some point" and "If they say they don't cheat, they're lying" (Monsour, pars. 8–9).

- "People cheat because it's really easy to cheat, really easy to get away with. . . . They don't get caught and they are the ones getting 100 on the exams when the noncheaters are getting 80s and 90s. Cheaters do win" (Stansbury. *For,* par. 32).

- "Teachers give quizzes and just leave the room . . . and they expect us not to cheat. C'mon, it's like they're asking you to, I mean we're teenagers" (Bushweller. *Generation* 28).

- "If I don't prepare for a test, I either get the answers from someone else or put them on flashcards and use them," says the 14-year-old. . . . "I feel wrong doing it, but it's not like it's a big, big deal" (Bell, par. 4).

- "Sam, a junior at the University of Alabama, can barely recall the first time he cheated. He thinks it must have started back in middle school, copying the occasional math assignment or printing a key formula on his forearm . . . 'I realize that it's wrong, but I don't feel bad about it, either, partly because I know everyone else is doing it' " (Kleiner and Lord 56).

- "It's a lot of fun to outwit the system . . . whose fault is it? Is it mine because I'm smart enough to do this, or is it the school's because they're too dumb to catch me?" (Bushweller. *Digital,* par. 47).

"Instead of saying 'What a horrible thing cheating is,' the attitude of some students is, 'How horrible it is that this guy got caught' "(Wentzel, par. 15). If our students cheat because of mounting pressures, if they rationalize that it's OK "because everybody else does it" and "because it's so easy," or if they simply don't want to study for tests or put in the time required to complete assignments—then it is time we all work together at school and at home to eliminate this attitude that it's OK to cheat.

Data and Conclusions from Four Surveys

Survey 1—*Who's Who Among American High School Students*

The first edition of *Who's Who Among American High School Students* was published in 1967. The current edition lists the academically top 5% of all American high school students; this is more than 750,000 students from public, private, and parochial high schools. Paul C. Krouse is the publisher and founder; he is the author of an article that follows Chapter 6.

Annual surveys conducted by *Who's Who* poll a representative sampling of the students listed in the current edition. The surveys provide the most comprehensive high school survey data available, reflecting the opinions of these top students on a wide range of topics.

One focus of the 29th Annual Survey of High Achievers (1998) was cheating in school. The following excerpt is reprinted with permission from the 1998 *Who's Who* summary report, followed by selected questions and answers. Permission is granted to reprint these pages for use with parent, faculty, or student groups. The full report, with all questions and data from this and previous annual surveys, is online at <http://www.honoring. com/highschool/annualsurveys/>.

COPY ME:
Cheating and Succeeding: Record Numbers of Top High School Students Take Ethical Shortcuts

Who's Who Among American High School Students

Four out of five teens at the top of their classes say they got there the easy way, according to this year's [1998] poll of students honored in *Who's Who Among American High School Students*. A full 80 percent admit to having cheated during their impressive academic careers, the highest percentage in the 29-year history of the survey. Most students seem blasé about their own ethical slips (53% say it was "no big deal") and virtually all (95%) avoided getting caught. Even so, nearly two times as many students this year than last year (46% versus 25%) point to "declining social and moral values" as the biggest problem facing their generation today. Crime and violence came in a distant second place, cited by 15 percent.

"In all likelihood, when these kids look at the examples now being set by traditional role models—the president, business leaders, Hollywood stars, even the clergy—they have an easier time excusing their own behavior," said Paul Krouse, publisher and founder of *Who's Who Among American High School Students*.

In high school, apparently even the academic elite take a ho-hum attitude toward cheating. Eighty-three percent say cheating is common at their schools, and this is one lapse they don't try to pin on the other guy: a full 80 percent say they have done it themselves. More than one-half (57%) say it would be easy or not very difficult to obtain test questions and answers at their schools.

Perhaps lax enforcement of the rules is partly to blame: 95 percent of the cheaters were never caught. Silence might be another culprit: over one-third of top students (34%) have never heard anything from their parents about cheating. Parents seem unaware that cheating might be an issue their children are grappling with. In fact, in a 1997 survey of parents of *Who's Who* kids, 63 percent stated flatly that their children had never cheated; another 11 percent admitted they had no idea whether their youngsters had bent the rules.

"With such a casual attitude toward cheating on the part of so many parents and school authorities, it's no wonder more than half of the cheaters just shrug it off, saying 'it didn't seem like a big deal'," said Krouse. "If the folks in charge of moral guidance don't make a bigger fuss about ethical behavior, it *won't be* a big deal."

(The 1998 *Who's Who* annual survey was conducted among 3,123 high-achieving 16- to 18-year-old students, all of whom have an "A" or "B" average, and 97 percent of whom plan to attend college after high school graduation.)

Reprinted with permission from Student Cheating and Plagiarism in the Internet Era: A Wake-Up Call *by Ann Lathrop and Kathleen Foss. Englewood, CO: Libraries Unlimited, 2000.*

Sample Questions and Answers from the 1998 *Who's Who* Survey

Question: How common is cheating at your school?

Answers:	*Responses*
Almost everybody does it	21.8%
Fairly common	60.9%
Pretty rare	16.5%
Never happens	0.4%
No answer	0.3%

Question: Which of the following have you done?

Answers:	*Responses*
Cheated on a quiz or test	39.6%
Copied someone else's homework	66.7%
Plagiarized part of an essay	13.2%
Used Cliff's Notes® or Monarch Notes to avoid reading a book	28.9%
None of the above	19.5%

Question: If you have cheated, why did you do so?

Answers:	*Students responding "yes"*
Competition for good grades	55.6%
Didn't seem like a big deal	53.0%
Didn't think I'd get caught	23.6%
Not interested in the subject	27.6%
Parents encouraged me	0.2%
To get into a good college	14.4%

Question: If you have cheated, what happened?

Answers:	*Responses*
I was caught and punished	6.2%
I was caught but not punished	6.4%
I was not caught	95.1%

Question: How have your parents talked with you about cheating?

Answers:	*Responses*
Never talked about it	34.1%
They encourage it	0%
They don't care if I do this or not	1.6%
They tell me I should not do this	46.8%
They forbid me to do this	16.1%
No answer	1.5%

Question: Do your parents know you cheat in school?

Answers:	*Responses*
Yes	10.6%
No	39.4%
Not applicable	48.7%

Reprinted with permission from Student Cheating and Plagiarism in the Internet Era: A Wake-Up Call *by Ann Lathrop and Kathleen Foss. Englewood, CO: Libraries Unlimited, 2000.*

No answer   1.3%

Question: How difficult would it be for you to obtain test questions or answers at your school?

Answers:	*Responses*
Very difficult	14.9%
Somewhat difficult	25.5%
Not very difficult	28.2%
Easy	29.1%
No answer	2.3%

Reprinted with permission from Student Cheating and Plagiarism in the Internet Era: A Wake-Up Call *by Ann Lathrop and Kathleen Foss. Englewood, CO: Libraries Unlimited, 2000.*

Survey 2—Josephson Institute of Ethics

The Josephson Institute of Ethics, founded by Michael Josephson in 1987, seeks to improve "the ethical quality of society by advocating principled reasoning and ethical decision making." The Institute sponsors the national CHARACTER COUNTS! Coalition that works with parents, educators, schools, and youth groups to develop strong ethical values; information about CHARACTER COUNTS! is in Chapter 7 and online at <http://www.charactercounts.org/>. Additional information about the Josephson Institute is in Chapter 7 and online at <http://www.josephsoninstitute.org>.

In 1998, the Josephson Institute of Ethics surveyed more than 20,000 middle school and high school students. The results of the survey are summarized in the following press release. Permission is granted to reprint these pages for use with parent, faculty, or student groups. All questions and data from the survey are online at <http://www.josephsoninstitute.org>.

COPY ME:
1998 Report Card on the Ethics of American Youth

Michael Josephson
Josephson Institute of Ethics
Press Release—October 19, 1998

The numbers are in, and they don't look good. Nearly half of all high schoolers say they steal. Seven in ten admit to cheating on an exam within the previous twelve months.

These are among the results of a survey released during National CHARACTER COUNTS! Week, October 18–24, 1998. Conducted by the Josephson Institute of Ethics, the survey is one of the largest ever to focus on the ethics of young people, with over 20,000 middle and high school respondents.

"This report card shows that the hole in our moral ozone is getting bigger," says Michael Josephson, president of the Institute, which organized similar, though smaller surveys in 1992 and 1996. "In terms of honesty and integrity, things are going from very bad to worse."

More highlights: Forty-seven percent of all respondents admit they stole something from a store in the previous 12-month period (with more than a quarter of high schoolers saying they had committed store theft at least two times). In the Institute's 1996 survey, the reported theft rate was 39 percent.

In 1998, seven of ten high schoolers admit they cheated on an exam at least once in the past 12 months. In 1996, the cheating rate was 64 percent.

Almost all teenagers admit to lying. Ninety-two percent of the high schoolers say they lied at least once in the past year; 78 percent say they lied two or more times. In 1996, 85 percent said they lied at least once and 73 percent said they lied repeatedly. More than one in three high schoolers say they would lie to get a good job.

"If we keep in mind that liars and cheaters might lie on a survey it's clear that the reality is even worse than these numbers indicate," Mr. Josephson says.

Curiously, 91 percent report that they are "satisfied with my own ethics and character." Mr. Josephson finds this "especially troubling." He explains: "Young people know what they're doing is wrong. There is an inconsistency in what they say they believe and how they act."

For instance, alongside admissions of frequent lying and cheating, 78 percent of high schoolers and 87 percent of those in middle school say "it's not worth it to lie or cheat because it hurts your character."

Ninety-seven percent of both groups say "it's important for me to be a person with good character" and 95 percent say "it's important to me that people trust me."

Only 69 percent of the high schoolers—compared to 98 percent in middle school—say they are satisfied with the ethics and character of their generation.

Young people say they know their parents and teachers expect them to be honest and ethical: 83 percent say "my parents always want me to do the ethically right thing no matter what the cost" and only 7 percent say that "my parents would rather I cheat than get bad grades."

The report was based on written surveys administered by randomly selected schools throughout the nation in 1998. The margin of error is +/-3 percent. It includes responses from 20,829 students (10,760 high school and 10,069 middle school students).

Sample Questions and Answers from the
1998 Josephson Survey

(percentage of students responding *strongly agree* or *agree*)

What do you really think?	High School	Middle School
A person has to lie or cheat sometimes in order to succeed.	45.2%	31.4%
I would be willing to cheat on a test if it would help me get into college.	35.8%	23.9%
My teachers consistently set a good ethical example.	64.8%	76.4 %
My parents sometimes lie to save money.	32.3%	21.8%

Have you done these things within the past year?

	High School	Middle School
Cheated during a test in school.	70.2%	54.0%
Refused to cheat even though others were cheating.	73.1%	71.7%

[Reprinted with permission of the Josephson Institute of Ethics. The full report and survey results are online at <http://www.josephsoninstitute.org>.]

Reprinted with permission from Student Cheating and Plagiarism in the Internet Era: A Wake-Up Call *by Ann Lathrop and Kathleen Foss. Englewood, CO: Libraries Unlimited, 2000.*

Survey 3—Southern California Suburban High School

We decided to "test the waters" by conducting our own small local survey for this book. The high school selected serves an upper-middle-class suburban community in Southern California with a high percentage of college-bound students. Teachers from several departments participated, including both regular and Advanced Placement classes; 336 of the 400 surveys (84%) were returned.

Student Survey at a Southern California Suburban High School

(percentage of *yes* responses)

Have you observed students cheating on tests or quizzes?	91%
Do you think they cheated because the teacher wasn't paying attention?	51%
Have you ever cheated on a test?	71%
Was it because you didn't study?	62%
Were you under a lot of pressure to get a good grade?	72%
Did you do it because everyone does it?	13%
Have you ever taken a paper off the Internet and turned it in as your own work?	6%
Have you every bought a paper off the Internet?	1%
Do you feel that you understand what the term plagiarism means?	93%

Our goal was to determine whether results from a local high school would be similar to those reported nationally. On the question asking whether students had cheated on a test, 71% of the students from the local high school and 70.2% of the high school students from the national study by the Josephson Institute responded *yes*. These are hard-working, college-bound students, many of whom we know personally. We had not thought of them as cheaters.

Survey 4—Schab's Longitudinal Study

This is the only high school survey located with longitudinal data reaching back across thirty years. Dr. Schab plans to update the survey in 2000.

Schooling without Learning:
Thirty Years of Cheating in High School

Fred Schab

Abstract

A survey instrument, developed in 1968 and administered to 1,629 high school students in 1969, 1,100 students in 1979, and 1,291 students in 1989, asked them to respond to items regarding the following: (1) the amount of cheating believed going on, (2) who was most guilty, (3) reasons given for cheating, (4) the course in which most cheating occurred, (5) how to punish cheaters and by whom, (6) beliefs regarding dishonesty in society, and (7) confessions of their own dishonest behaviors in school. Between 1969 and 1989, student responses reflected increasingly pessimistic opinions about dishonesty in school and society. Fear of failure remained the most common reason for cheating. Math and science were the courses in which cheating most often occurred. The home was considered the best place and school the worst place to inculcate honesty. Over the three decades covered by this study, dishonesty was viewed as increasingly necessary; more people believed advertising was suspect, and success in business was attributed to fraudulent activities. More students admitted to cheating on tests and homework. More parents were now aiding and abetting students in avoidance of school rules. Polls, studies, and reports recently published by state, federal, and private agencies appear to confirm these findings.

Questionnaires and Results

Table 1

Societal Dishonesty
(percentage of *yes* responses)

		1969	1979	1989
1.	A cheater in school will cheat on the job	71.8%	53.6%	42.7%
2.	Sometimes it is necessary to be dishonest	33.5%	64.1%	66.6%
3.	Breaking a law is a form of dishonesty	81.6%	82.3%	82.4%
4.	Cheating to get into college will result in failure there	65.7%	84.2%	68.7%
5.	Cheating hurts only the cheater	81.5%	77.1%	73.5%
6.	A cheater in school will cheat on his family	45.2%	39.2%	26.3%
7.	Cheating is a sin	67.9%	65.4%	54.5%
8.	Honesty is always the best policy	82.3%	73.3%	59.9%
9.	Adults are more dishonest than children	29.5%	45.4%	41.4%
10.	Crime does not pay	88.7%	56.8%	65.4%
11.	Sooner or later cheating will be discovered	83.1%	80.1%	74.6%
12.	Most advertising is dishonest	45.3%	68.5%	65.1%
13.	Some teachers are dishonest	57.0%	83.3%	87.1%
14.	More cheating is done in classes taught by men	27.6%	27.4%	27.8%
15.	Parents who are dishonest have dishonest children	35.1%	40.5%	37.0%
16.	To succeed in business requires some dishonesty	32.3%	42.2%	44.6%
17.	People who cheat can't be trusted	61.1%	47.1%	41.0%
18.	Are most people in the U.S.A. today honest?	49.1%	26.0%	23.8%

Table 2

Confessions of Dishonesty
(percentage of *yes* responses)

		1969	1979	1989
1.	Would you report a friend you saw cheating?	12.4%	7.9%	4.3%
2.	Would you report a person not your friend?	20.8%	20.8%	16.9%
3.	Have you used a cheat sheet on a test?	33.8%	59.5%	67.8%
4.	If you lost a book would you "find" one to to replace it?	25.1%	36.1%	31.7%
5.	If you found a $1 bill at school would you turn it in?	60.9%	20.7%	9.2%
6.	If you found a $5 bill at school would you turn it in?	71.8%	31.3%	17.0%
7.	If you found a $10 bill at school would you turn it in?	72.8%	37.3%	27.5%

		1969	1979	1989
8.	If you found a $20 bill at school would you turn it in?	80.7%	59.8%	31.7%
9.	Would you cheat if it were the only way to get a diploma?	48.5%	50.6%	59.8%
10.	Have you turned in work another student did?	50.5%	43.2%	51.5%
11.	Have you let others copy your work?	58.3%	92.5%	97.5%
12.	Have you turned in work done by your parents?	19.3%	17.4%	19.3%
13.	Do you consider the above to be cheating?	98.9%	74.0%	75.5%
14.	Have you lied to your parents about school?	54.5%	59.9%	69.9%
15.	Have you signed parents' name to an excuse?	25.5%	41.7%	47.8%
16.	Have you signed their names to a report card?	12.6%	14.0%	18.9%
17.	Have you signed your teacher's name to anything?	5.9%	15.7%	16.7%
18.	Have your parents written a false excuse for you?	22.6%	28.6%	50.8%
19.	Have you played sick to get out of school?	43.7%	50.1%	69.8%
20.	Have you taken books from the library without checking them out?	8.1%	17.7%	18.6%
21.	Have you kept anything valuable found at school?	16.3%	27.0%	28.5%
22.	Have you copied anything, word for word, out of a book?	66.5%	79.9%	76.1%
23.	Have you ever cheated in games?	47.3%	70.5%	68.7%

(Schab 839, 842–43)

[Reprinted with permission from Libra Publishers. Originally published in *Adolescence,* vol. 26 no. 104, Winter 1991, Libra Publishers.]

Research Highlights on Cheating in Colleges and Universities

The following data are derived from a 1963 study by William Bowers and a 1993 follow-up study by McCabe and Bowers that investigated changes in college students' cheating behaviors over a thirty-year period. The original study by William Bowers and the 1993 follow-up study by McCabe and Bowers are listed in Further Readings at the end of this book. The comparison data presented here are reported in the McCabe and Trevino article noted at the end of the data table.

Percentage of College Students Admitting to Selected Cheating Behaviors, 1963 and 1993

	1963	1993
Tests/Examinations		
Copied from another student	26%	52%
Helped another student cheat	23%	37%
Used crib notes	16%	27%
Written Work		
Copied material without footnoting	49%	54%
Plagiarized	30%	26%
Falsified a bibliography	38%	29%
Turned in work done by another	29%	14%
Collaborated on assignments requiring individual work	11%	49%

"This [data] suggests that although the number of students who cheat has increased only modestly, the students who do cheat are engaging in a wider variety of test-cheating behaviors today and are also cheating more often" (McCabe and Trevino 31).

The following "Research Highlights" Copy-Me page summarizes conclusions from five research studies dealing with cheating behavior by college and university students. These conclusions have serious implications for all educators and parents working to reduce cheating in our schools. As we know, many college students learned their cheating behaviors in high school or middle school.

Pointers

Additional data in Chapter 6 document a "disconnect" between the level of cheating self-reported by students and the level of cheating as perceived by teachers and parents. Chapter 8 has summary data from a 1998 survey of teachers and school board members; again, the adults seriously underestimate the level of cheating when compared with that reported by students.

COPY ME:
Research Highlights

Five major research projects conducted by Donald L. McCabe of Rutgers University (founder and first president of The Center for Academic Integrity [CAI]) have had disturbing, provocative, and challenging results, among them the following:

- On most campuses, over 75% of students admit to some cheating. In surveys conducted in 1990, 1992, and 1995 involving almost 7,000 students on 26 small-to-medium-sized campuses, almost 80% of undergraduate student respondents reported one or more incidents of cheating.

- Academic honor codes effectively reduce cheating. In surveys conducted in 1990 and 1995 of over 5,000 students on 14 small-to-medium-sized campuses that have strong academic honor codes, 57% of undergraduate student respondents reported one or more incidents of cheating. Giving students significant voice and responsibility in issues of academic integrity appears to significantly reduce cheating.

- Chronic cheating is also prevalent. On campuses without honor codes, one in five students (one in four on larger campuses) self-reported more than three incidents of explicit cheating on tests and examinations. On campuses with honor codes, only one in sixteen students reported such levels.

- Faculty are reluctant to report students for cheating. Less than half of 800 faculty surveyed on 16 campuses in 1992 have ever reported an incident of cheating in their classroom. Student survey data suggest that cheating is highest in those courses where it is well known that faculty ignore cheating or fail to report it to the authorities.

- Cheating is higher among fraternity and sorority members. 75% of Greeks surveyed in 1993 admit to one or more incidents of test/exam cheating versus 61% of Independents. 42% of Greeks versus 36% of Independents in 1993 reported they were likely to help a friend who asked for help on a test or examination.

- Longitudinal comparisons show significant increases in explicit test/examination cheating and unpermitted collaboration. The number of students self-reporting instances of unpermitted collaboration at nine medium-to-large state universities increased from 11% in 1963 to 49% in 1993. This trend seems to be continuing: between 1990 and 1995, instances of unpermitted collaboration at 31 small-to-medium schools increased from 30% to 38%.

[Reprinted with permission from The Center for Academic Integrity, a consortium of approximately 200 colleges and universities and 500 individual students, faculty, and administrator members from those institutions. The Center was established in 1992 to identify and affirm the values of academic integrity and to promote their achievement in practice. Additional information is available at <http://www.academicintegrity.org>.]

Reprinted with permission from Student Cheating and Plagiarism in the Internet Era: A Wake-Up Call *by Ann Lathrop and Kathleen Foss. Englewood, CO: Libraries Unlimited, 2000.*

Chapter 5

High-Tech Defenses against Cheating and Plagiarism

First of all, never underestimate the abilities of your students. And always assume the worst when it comes to security. Otherwise, the worst will happen. (Bushweller. *Digital*, par. 44)

Chapter Overview

Information sources and electronic defenses can limit students' dishonest use of new technology. Teachers can counter high-tech cheating by learning to use the hardware and software and knowing what to watch for in the classroom. Blocking or filtering programs and new plagiarism-detection software are defenses against electronic plagiarism.

This chapter suggests these and other strategies to counter high-tech cheating. New antiplagiarism software is described and Web sites with information to help reduce plagiarism are identified. Instructions here and in Julie Ryan's article at the end of the chapter suggest ways to search online for the originals of suspect papers.

Chapter subheadings:

- Information as a First Line of Defense
- High-Tech Defenses against Cheating Technologies
- Blocking, Filtering, and Rating Systems
- Can Legislation Deter Plagiarism?
- Using Technology to Identify Plagiarism
- Web Sites with Resources for Countering Plagiarism
- Searching the Internet for the Originals of Plagiarized Papers
- Julie Ryan: "Student Plagiarism in an Online World"

Information as a First Line of Defense

A trip to a large computer store can be an interesting family outing or an in-service day for faculty. New technology "toys" can be demonstrated at a faculty workshop or parents' meeting. Newspaper and journal articles on new technology developments can be posted in faculty rooms and summarized in faculty bulletins and parent newsletters. Then make it clear to your students or child that you understand the possible ways of cheating with technology and will not accept such use in your classroom or home.

Several electronic journals deal with educational issues and instructional technology. One cited frequently in this book is *Electronic School,* the quarterly online supplement to *American School Board Journal,* which can be found at <http://www.electronic-school.com>. Permission is granted to reprint articles for educational purposes. According to the home page, *Electronic School* provides "practical advice on a broad range of topics pertinent to the implementation of technology in elementary and secondary schools throughout North America."

Another source of information online is the "Cheating Is a Personal Foul" Web site sponsored by the Educational Testing Service/Ad Council Campaign to Discourage Academic Cheating. Their online articles provide valuable information and statistical data for parents and educators. Curriculum materials for school use are being developed. Their web site is at <http://www.nocheating.org/adcouncil/research/> (Educational. *Academic Cheating Background;* Educational. *Academic Cheating Fact Sheet*).

High-Tech Defenses against Cheating Technologies

Hand-Held Computers, Pagers, and Electronic Calculators

- Become familiar with these devices and learn to recognize their use in the classroom. Using them yourself and letting students know you use them is perhaps the best defense.

- Turn on your own hand-held computer to catch any infrared signals being transmitted.

- Check student watches.

- Students sharing calculators might leave answers on them as they are exchanged. Some schools avoid this possibility by providing classroom sets of calculators to be distributed for use during a test (Croucher xiv).

- One math teacher countered cheating with calculators by dividing a test into two sections; calculators were allowed only for the section that required no memorization (Bushweller. *Digital,* par. 24).

- Announce that any prohibited devices used during tests will be confiscated and returned only to the parent at a meeting scheduled to discuss the cheating incident. (Be sure this is included in the Academic Integrity Policy discussed in Chapter 8.)

Web Sites

- Whenever possible, identify and monitor any underground Web sites, chat rooms, etc., that students use for cheating. Access to these sites can be gained by checking students' bookmarks to Web sites they use, searching online for the name of the Webmaster (if known), searching for keywords associated with the subject, or watching students who are working at computers in the classroom, lab, or library.
- Visit "homework help" Web sites, then make it very clear to students exactly how much electronic "help" is permissible.

Computer Networks

- Students can take an exam in a large computer lab, entering answers directly into the computer. No paper is needed so tabletops should be clear and cheat sheets will be more difficult to conceal.
- The server can be programmed to present questions randomly so no two students get questions in the same order. For multiple-choice tests, both questions and answers can appear in random order; for example, a specific question will not always have "b" for the correct answer. The computer can generate a score sheet for each examination, or better yet, grade the tests online.
- The computer lab being used for testing can be disconnected from the school network to prevent students from sending the test to others who will take it during a later period (Wentzel, par. 18).
- To avoid hackers on a school network, teachers can create and print exams on a home computer and keep grade book programs at home as well (but beware of hackers if the home computer is connected to the Internet).
- Teacher passwords should be changed frequently; many hackers enjoy trying to identify passwords.

Distance Learning

- An increasing number of instructors are moving away from traditional testing using multiple choice tests on scantron sheets to develop alternative assessment tools (Akins).
- Some instructors encourage students to research topics online and cite their sources as active links. The instructors then confirm their research by checking the sites (Akins).
- As a precaution against plagiarism, have each student "write a 500-word essay at the beginning of the semester that can serve as a kind of fingerprint of writing style . . . to help a professor spot a paper that isn't original work later in the semester" (Carnevale, par. 17).
- The test method used most often is proctored exams. Tests are sent via email to a school, community college or university, public library, fire station, etc. Completed tests are returned via email or surface mail (Akins).

- Instructors can telephone a student to clarify test answers, check for understanding and mastery, or ask where certain information was located when there is suspicion of cheating (Carnevale, par. 11).

Software Solutions

- New Xmn8r Examination Security Software from ExamSoft lets students take tests on their own laptop computers. It uses a VBB (Virtual Blue Book) disk as a security lock to prevent access to any other material on the computer (Chang, pars. 5–6). Information is available at <http://www.examsoft.com>. As more high school teachers allow students to use a computer to complete essay exams there may be greater interest in this type of software at the secondary level.

- For distance learning testing at remote sites, new software guards are being developed to authenticate the student's identity (Akins).

- CU-CME or other video teleconferencing can be used for distance learning testing when software and hardware are available (Akins).

Blocking, Filtering, and Rating Systems

Blocking or filtering software, or rating systems can be used to prevent access to specific Internet sites considered inappropriate for students, including explicitly sexual or violent sites. Some educators regard this as censorship; others claim it provides a necessary protection for students. The term "censorware" is used by one author to describe several software programs on the market (Kongshem, par. 6).

A nontechnical description is that blocking software denies students access to any sites at the blocked server. Filtering prohibits access to selected sites on a server. A rating system blocks sites according to self-assigned ratings and local criteria. Software programs now on the market use varied combinations of these techniques.

Those opposed to blocking recommend educating students to be critical and informed users of online information who can make their own decisions about what is appropriate. Others suggest that the Internet Acceptable Use Policies in place in many districts, combined with careful monitoring by teachers, can provide adequate protection. Hinman reflects on the issue of plagiarism from the Internet as a threat to academic integrity:

> There are two response to this challenge—external and internal. External approaches try to block access to sites, to police student behavior on the Web in various ways. Internal approaches seek to develop the skills and motivation in students so that they will restrain themselves, even when no one is watching, from plagiarizing. (B7)

Schools that decide to use blocking software can find that use of generic terms for blocking makes many legitimate Web sites inaccessible. This is true especially of sites used for medical or scientific research; blocking the term "breast" also blocks information on breast cancer, breast-feeding, etc. Another problem is the politically sensitive issue of who is to identify the sites to be blocked; that is, who is to determine what is acceptable for student use.

> But vocal opponents of censorware . . . see schools abdicating their supervisory role to software companies that are ill equipped to discern which sites are educationally appropriate and—in some cases—are motivated by conservative agendas to block students from liberal points of view. (Kongshem, par. 4)

Blocking can create a false sense of security. Many parents assume the blocking is complete, whereas in reality any system will be only partially successful. A student who finds a site blocked at school might access it from home just out of curiosity.

When district-wide blocking has been implemented it is helpful to keep one school computer, located in a secure area, free of the blocking. If an important research site has been blocked inadvertently, the teacher or librarian can verify that the site is appropriate and provide access to the material for the student. The process for requesting that a site be blocked or unblocked should be known to all staff and students.

Pownell and Bailey review the pros and cons of blocking and recommend, as an alternative, that schools develop a curriculum to teach students to make good judgments about the information they access:

> It is our belief that schools need to prepare kids to live in the world, not just "protect" them from it. The rate of change has increased tremendously. . . . Educating and building responsibility need to be foremost in our minds; censoring should only be used as a last resort with kids and the Internet. (57)

Blocking/filtering is an issue to consider seriously. Educators and parents can decide that it is a useful tool despite its limitations, or they can put their emphasis on helping students learn to establish their own criteria for selecting appropriate sites.

Can Legislation Deter Plagiarism?

Legislation and lawsuits seem to have had little impact on widespread plagiarism from Internet paper mills. Boston University's effort to shut down the paper mills through legal action in the courts has so far been unsuccessful. States that do have laws against selling term papers apparently cannot enforce them.

> Massachusetts, along with California, is among 17 states that have laws against selling term papers, though enforcement ranges from spotty to nonexistent. (Fritz, pars. 23–24)

> Texas does have a law on the books, passed in this year's [1997] legislative session, that makes it illegal to sell or buy term papers for the purpose of academic deceit. The law does not regulate free sites. . . . Attempting to close free sites would infringe on free speech rights. (Strickland, pars. 18–19)

> In 1997, Boston University filed a federal lawsuit against several term paper companies after employing a law student to purchase a research paper on author Toni Morrison that was said to be for a literature course assignment . . . the lawsuit charged wire fraud, mail fraud, and racketeering, and targeted eight companies in

seven states with violating a Massachusetts law that prohibits the sale and marketing of term papers. . . . Earlier this month [December 1998] a federal judge dismissed the case. The university plans to refile its case in state court. (Roach, pars. 12–13)

Using Technology to Identify Plagiarism

New electronic tools are being developed to identify plagiarism. Four of these listed subsequently seek to identify student research papers that have been plagiarized. The fifth tool, MOSS, is designed to detect plagiarism in computer code developed by students. The tools are fairly new and no evaluative data were located. The following brief descriptions are from each web site; more complete information is available online.

Glatt Plagiarism Services
<http://www.plagiarism.com>

The web site offers three products: (1) Glatt Plagiarism Teaching Program, a tutorial "on what constitutes plagiarism and how to avoid it [with] practice exercises on rewriting"; (2) Glatt Plagiarism Screening Program, a "highly sophisticated program . . . the first comprehensive computer software program specifically designed for detecting plagiarism [and] a valid and sensitive measure for successfully discriminating plagiarists from nonplagiarists"; and (3) Glatt Plagiarism Self-Detection Program, a test "designed to help you become more sensitive to your own writing style [and] to help detect inadvertent instances of plagiarism." The software removes every fifth word in a student's paper. The student then fills in the words from memory, assuming the student would be more likely to remember words from an original paper than from one that was plagiarized.

IntegriGuard
<http://www.integriguard.com>

The software program "detects sentences that match those in papers already included in what they hope will become a vast data-base." Teachers subscribe to the service for a monthly fee. Their students load their term papers into the online database to be checked against the papers already in the database to find any possible match.

Intelligent Essay Assessor
<http://www.lsa.colorado.edu/essay>

A press release on the Web site states: "New computer software can grade the content of essay exams just as well as people and could be a major boon in assessing student performance. . . . [It] uses mathematical analysis to measure the quality of knowledge expressed in essays [but] is not designed to grade stylistic considerations like grammar and spelling." According to one author, the program "also alerts users to sentences that sound similar to those it has read before" and so might be useful in detecting plagiarism (Guernsey, par. 12).

MOSS (Measure Of Software Similarity)
<http://www.cs.berkeley.edu/~aiken/moss.html>

This free software is described on the Web site as "an automatic system for determining the similarity of C, C++, Java, Pascal, Ada, ML, Lisp, or Scheme programs. To date, the main application of Moss has been in detecting plagiarism in programming classes. . . . Access to Moss is restricted to instructors and staff of programming courses."

Plagiarism.org
<http://www.plagiarism.org/>

This Web site identifies plagiarized papers by evaluating them statistically against their existing database of papers from universities and from other Web sites across the Internet. An instructor registers a class with the service and students upload their papers to the web site. A report is sent to the instructor on the degree of originality for each paper. There is a per class charge for the service.

Web Sites with Resources for Countering Plagiarism

The following Web sites provide articles, discussion groups, links to other Web sites, etc., for educators or parents seeking additional information. Several offer teaching suggestions, clear examples of plagiarism, and specific techniques for reducing plagiarism in term papers.

About Plagiarism, Pixels, and Platitudes
<http://www.svsu.edu/~dboehm/pixels.htm#NextStep>

There are suggestions to counter plagiarism and help students become better writers; the emphasis is on integrity in the classroom.

Avoiding Plagiarism
<http://www.hamilton.edu/academic/resource/wc/wc.html>

Sharon Williams, director of the Writing Center at Hamilton College, offers basic advice on the correct use of sources and suggests how careful note taking can help to avoid errors in paraphrasing.

Combating Cybercheating: Resources for Teachers
<http://www.epcc.edu.library/>

El Paso Community College Libraries maintain lists of Web sites on Discussions of the Cybercheating Phenomenon, Defining Plagiarism: A Guide for Students, and Combating Cybercheating: Strategies for Teachers.

Plagiarism
<http://webware.princeton.edu/writing/wc4g.htm>

The Writing Center at Princeton University defines and gives varied examples of plagiarism; there are links to information on using quotations, documenting sources, and citing sources.

Plagiarism and Antiplagiarism
<http://newark.rutgers.edu/>

This Web site has a discussion of the problem of plagiarism and possible approaches to reducing it, links to related Web sites, a list of recent publications, and suggestions for using specific search engines to locate the original paper online when a suspicious paper is being investigated.

Plagiarism: Definitions, Examples, and Penalties
<http://www.chem.uky.edu/courses/common/plagiarism.html>

Plagiarism is defined in the University of Kentucky Student Rights and Responsibilities Handbook with the associated procedures and penalties; there are very specific examples of plagiarism that might appear in student work.

Plagiarism: What It Is and How to Recognize and Avoid It
<http://www.indiana.edu/~wts/wts/plagiarism.html>

Writing Tutorial Services, the writing center at Indiana University Bloomington, provides examples of acceptable and unacceptable paraphrases, explains the correct use of quotations, and gives a clear definition of what is considered to be "common knowledge."

Policy on Plagiarism and Outside Help
<http://www.ualberta.ca/~german/plagiar.htm>

Policy from the Division of Germanic Languages, Literatures, and Linguistics at the University of Alberta defines plagiarism and states guidelines for quoting correctly from sources, provides very specific limits on types of "outside help" that are acceptable in completing homework assignments or writing papers, and lists penalties for plagiarism.

Searching the Internet for the Originals of Plagiarized Papers

The same electronic search techniques used by students to locate papers to copy from the Internet also can be used to locate many of the original papers and thus prove they were copied. An online search engine will take unique or unusual "strings" of words from the suspect paper and attempt to locate them online; it often finds them in the original paper. The process is described in the article by Julie Ryan that follows.

Science teachers tracking the source of suspect articles can use a new "find related articles" feature of PubMed, the gateway service to the National Library of Medicine's

Medline. It can locate very similar word strings that might identify plagiarized articles <http://www.ncbi.nlm.nih.gov/pubmed/> (Marshall 474).

Sometimes students trip themselves up unintentionally. For example, one science instructor reported that four students turned in almost identical research papers—each copied from the same Internet site (Benning, par. 12). Another student turned in a paper with the Web address printed in the top corner of each page (Bushweller. *Digital,* par. 11). One "Internet legend" actually has been documented as a true story of a high school English teacher whose student turned in a paper she had written some years before; it had made its way onto one of the paper mill sites when her former professor removed student names from his huge accumulation of college student papers and dumped them into the trash (Ropp, par. 6).

Stories such as these demonstrate the fact that electronic plagiarizing is becoming more popular. It also is becoming more difficult to detect as students learn to use a word processor and online thesaurus to "edit" the plagiarized papers.

Pointers

Copy-Me pages in Chapter 2 describe three high-tech tools and suggest ways to prevent their use for cheating. Chapter 8 describes Academic Integrity Policies and Acceptable Use Policies; these should specifically prohibit high-tech cheating and electronic plagiarism. Chapter 11 recommends strategies to reduce cheating on tests and assignments. Chapter 13 describes "An Electronic Scavenger Hunt."

Student Plagiarism in an Online World

Julie J. C. H. Ryan

In academe, the consequences of plagiarism are clear: Using someone else's words or ideas without attribution is grounds for failed assignments, suspension, or expulsion. For some students, however, breaking the rules seems to be an irresistible challenge. And so the game goes: Students continually look for (and find) ways to cheat, and teachers remain on the alert for purloined paragraphs, pages, and even entire papers.

Before the world was linked by the Internet, hard-to-detect plagiarism required ingenuity and skill. But today, with the click of a mouse, even technologically inept students have access to vast information resources in cyberspace without having to leave the comfort of their dorm rooms.

A few words typed into a Web search engine can lead a student to hundreds, sometimes thousands, of relevant documents, making it easy to "cut and paste" a few paragraphs from here and a few more from there until the student has an entire paper-length collection. Or a student can find a research paper published in one of the hundreds of new journals that have gone online over the past few years, copy the entire text, turn it into a new document, and then offer it up as an original work without having to type anything but a cover page. Even recycling efforts and ghostwriters have gone global, with Web sites offering professionally or student-written term papers for sale, some even with a money-back guarantee against detection.

Facing the New Plagiarism Reality

I ran headlong into these new practices during the fall 1997 semester as my husband and I each taught an introductory information security concepts course for George Washington University. When students turned in their required research papers, we were initially surprised at how well they seemed to have mastered the course material. But when we looked closer, we realized that in many cases we were not looking at original student work.

Consider the following extract from one of the student-submitted papers:

> *Both the government and the healthcare unions agree that electronic health records must be at least as well protected as paper ones; the Data Protection Act makes physicians and others responsible for the security of personal health information that they collect; and a recent Directive obliges the government to prohibit the processing of health data except where the data subject has given his explicit consent, and in certain other circumstances.*

The level of erudition, education, and sophistication evidenced in this extract (and the entire document) made it immediately suspect—the student was, after all, taking an introductory course in information-security concepts. To satisfy his curiosity, my husband asked me to research the paper content for possible plagiarism. I did so using the tool most readily available, the Internet. It didn't take me long to find an exact match.

I used the AltaVista Search engine to conduct a search for specific phrases (or strings) in the paper. To search for an exact match, I used quotation marks around the string. If quotation marks are not used, the results will include Web pages that contain some or all of the words in the string.

I also could have performed a category search using one of the comprehensive listing services that index Web sites by category. Yahoo! is one of the most popular sites of this type. Comprehensive list sites give you two search options. You can choose a category from the site's standing lists, or you can type a few words into the search box and the site's internal search engine will retrieve a list of categories and Web sites that include the words in your search parameters.

I found the following extract in an online journal article by Ross J. Anderson, a distinguished University of Cambridge computer researcher:

> *Both the government and the healthcare unions are agreed that electronic health records must be at least as well protected as paper ones; the Data Protection Act makes GPs and others responsible for the security of personal health information that they collect; and a recent EU Directive obliges the government to prohibit the processing of health data except where the data subject has given his explicit consent, and in certain other circumstances [EU95].*

It took me five minutes on the Internet to determine the probable source of the paper, and another 10 minutes to confirm word-for-word plagiarism. The entire paper, including the title, table of contents, and bibliography, was plagiarized. An open-and-shut case. Once I caught the first plagiarism, I decided to check every paper. I discovered that seven of 42 students plagiarized most or all of their papers, and four others turned in papers with footnotes that could charitably be called substandard.

If the student doesn't understand or can't discuss the ideas presented in the paper, or doesn't know the subject matter of the books referenced, then it's safe to assume the student didn't write the paper.

Plagiarism-Fighting Tools

String Search Sites

- altavista.digital.com
- www.lycos.com
- www.netscape.com
- www.metacrawler.com

Search Help Sites

- www.searchinsider.com
- www.cs.uwyo.edu/~drnelson/cs1100/TGSEARCH.html
- www.zdnet.com/products/searchuser.html
- www.albany.edu/library/internet/search.html

Category Search Sites

- www.yahoo.com
- www.infoseek.com
- www.infospace.com
- www.excite.com

Online Bookstores

- www.amazon.com
- www.barnesandnoble.com
- www.borders.com

People Search Sites

- www.bigfoot.com
- www.bigyellow.com
- www.whowhere.com

The papers that are the subject of this article were out-and-out forgeries, with inadequate, nonexistent, or false footnotes. In many cases the plagiary attempts were so patently obvious they were insulting.

The attempted deception is particularly disturbing because the class was an overview of information security concepts and practices. The curriculum focused on the value and protection of information, and specific readings and lectures addressed copyright law and other relevant topics. These students will go on to computer-related careers where they have to deal with information-security issues on a regular basis, yet they showed no regard for information's basic value.

Also disturbing was students' reactions when caught. Instead of expressing shame or remorse, reactions included denial (even in the face of overwhelming evidence) and defiance. One student even exclaimed: "You can't do this to me—I'm on a scholarship!" A response from another student caught plagiarizing is immortalized in the following email:

> Hi prof.
>
> I just wanted to tell you something. I called all my friends and asked them how they usually do their papers. Most of them told me that they do the same thing. They didn't know it is illegal and they can't do that. Can you believe it? Anyway, I told some of them what I did and what happened to me and they were shocked. They didn't know that what they do is wrong. . . . That's why, I did that without knowing it's wrong. Also, I talked to my advisor in the writing center who reviewed my paper. He told me that he didn't notice that, even though I gave him all the articles I used in my paper. . . . All I want to say is that I wanted to get an A in your class and I wanted to give you a good paper. . . .

Several other students made similar ignorance pleas when confronted, despite the fact that we emphasized acceptable footnoting practices for research papers during both semesters. In spring 1998, the emphasis on proper procedure was naturally even higher than it had been in fall 1997, and the repercussions from the preceding semester were still a subject of gossip within the student population. Thus it was quite startling to yet again see students attempt to pass off other people's works as their own.

Virtual Epidemic or Limited Reality?

Computer technology can make it easy for students to pass off others' work as their own—but has the amount of plagiarism on campuses really increased? It's difficult to determine because no one has made a serious effort to compile statistics on cybercheating. However, anecdotal evidence from educators does suggest that Web-aided plagiarism is becoming the method of choice for the lazy and dishonest writer.

Does your school track Internet-related plagiarism? Is it a problem on your campus? ASEE PRISM invites you to share your data, anecdotes, and thoughts on the subject, as well as any "cybersleuthing" suggestions you might have, in our new PRISM Online forum. Send your comments to: prism@asee.org, or see www.asee.org/prism.

Conclusion

Often lost in the discussion of plagiarism is the interest of the students who don't cheat. They do legitimate research and write their own papers. They work harder (and learn more) than the plagiarists, yet their grades might suffer when their papers are judged and graded against papers that are superior but stolen material. Students have a right to expect fairness in the classroom. When teachers turn a blind eye to plagiarism, it undermines that right and denigrates grades, degrees, and even institutions.

Plagiarism is alive and well on campuses and in cyberspace. But educators should take some solace in the fact that while the Internet is a useful resource for plagiarists, it is also an excellent tool to use against them.

[Julie J. C. H. Ryan is a graduate teaching assistant at George Washington University and an information security consultant. Excerpts reprinted with permission from "Student Plagiarism in an Online World," by Julie J. C. H. Ryan; *ASEE Prism*; December 1998. Online at <http://www.asee.org/prism/december/html/student_plagiarism>.]

Chapter 6

Parents: Vigilant, Informed, Involved

> *First, and most important, parents must strive to model positive ethical values for their children. This holds for big things, such as alcohol abuse, and small things, such as lying to a theater ticket-taker about their child's age.*
>
> *Second, they must hold their children accountable for unethical behavior. Even when a punishment is a hardship on the parent, such as grounding a high school-age child and thus losing a driver in the household, it must be done if the child is to learn that there are consequences for wrongful behavior.*
>
> *Third, work to influence the schools. Insist that teachers and administrators set examples of good ethical values—and when teachers legitimately punish students for misconduct, support the teachers.*
>
> *Fourth, be a positive ethical influence in the workplace [especially for] young people entering the work force [who] have something like a child–parent relationship to the more experienced workers.* (Michael Josephson, founder and president of the Josephson Institute of Ethics, in speech reported by Osinski, pars. 94–98)

Chapter Overview

Parents have the most important role in limiting cheating and plagiarism. They set the moral tone in the home and model ethical behavior for their children. Active involvement in a variety of school activities can open important lines of communication with their children's teachers. It is especially important that parents deal ethically and fairly with any instances of cheating or plagiarism by their children.

This chapter urges parents to be vigilant, informed, and involved. Michael Josephson warns against "Willful Blindness" and the statistics support his opinion that such blindness exists in homes and schools. Two Copy Me pages, "Help, But Not Too Much" and "Practical Suggestions to Support Students at Home and School," can be used as discussion starters for parent meetings. The article by Paul Krouse, publisher and founder of *Who's Who Among American High School Students,* challenges parents to take "total responsibility for the behavior and ethical conduct of their children" and "be keenly aware that what we do is more important than what we say to our children."

Chapter subheadings:

- Be Vigilant about Cheating and Plagiarism
- Copy Me: "Willful Blindness about Cheating"
- Be Informed about Technology in Your Schools
- Be Involved in School Activities and Assignments
- Be a Model of Ethical Behavior
- Be Ethical in Dealing with Student Cheating or Plagiarism
- Can "Too Much" Help Be Harmful?
- Copy Me: "Help, But Not Too Much"
- Copy Me: "Practical Suggestions to Support Students at Home and School"
- Krouse: "Honoring Tomorrow's Leaders Today"

Be Vigilant about Cheating and Plagiarism

Parents are often unaware when their children are cheating in school. The following survey results indicate a disconnect between parents' perception of student cheating and the reality (complete survey data and references are in Chapter 4).

How many students cheat?
- 70% of all high school students cheated on a test (Josephson)
- 54% of all middle school students cheated on a test (Josephson)
- 40% of high school students in academically top 5% cheated on a test (*Who's Who*)

What do parents say about cheating?
- 63% of the parents said their child never cheated (*Who's Who*)
- 47% of the parents tell students they should not cheat (*Who's Who*)
- 34% of the parents "never talked about it" (*Who's Who*)
- 16% of the parents forbid cheating (*Who's Who*)

What do students tell their parents about cheating?

- 70% of all high school students said they lied to their parents about school (Schab)
- 39% said their parents didn't know they cheated (*Who's Who*)
- 11% said their parents knew they cheated (*Who's Who*)

Do parents lie for their students?

- 51% of all students answered *yes* to the question, "Have your parents written a false excuse for you?" (Schab)

When we, as parents, don't know whether our kids are cheating; if we don't think it's "a big deal" if we do discover they are cheating; and if we lie for them when it suits our own convenience, then we encourage and permit them to cheat. Michael Josephson, founder and president of the Josephson Institute of Ethics, warns that parents who are "willfully blind" at home let students cheat when and as they choose.

COPY ME:
Willful Blindness about Cheating

Michael Josephson

Of all the ethical problems I talk about, rampant cheating in school is probably one of the most disturbing, partly because of what it says about the next generation of parents, politicians, and business leaders and partly because of what it says about schools that are unwilling to deal with the issue.

Year after year, newspaper articles and television exposés remind us that most high school students cheat—at least 70% every year! Yet only a few schools are seriously attempting to tackle the issue.

Parents should be up in arms, but they're not. In fact, a major reason given by teachers as to why they don't more strictly enforce cheating rules is parents. The parents who threaten to sue if their Bobby or Janie is caught cheating. And the other parents who just don't want to know. According to one study, 83% of parents think their children do not and would not cheat at school. Then whose kids are cheating? This willful blindness to the prevalence and perniciousness of cheating reflects a form of moral agnosticism—doubts about the importance and practicality of honesty. It's positively shameful that we allow our children to grow up in a moral environment where cheaters prosper and the relatively few who struggle to maintain their integrity are viewed, even by themselves, as suckers.

In fact, any school that wanted to could dramatically change attitudes about cheating and cut cheating rates with simple and nonoppressive methods. If we don't become more engaged in the moral lives of our children, we are the cheaters—and our children are the victims.

For KNX 1070, this is Michael Josephson asking you to do something now to show that CHARACTER COUNTS! [August 16, 1999]

[Reprinted with permission from the Josephson Institute of Ethics. Radio addresses are online at <http://www.josephsoninstitute.org>.]

Reprinted with permission from Student Cheating and Plagiarism in the Internet Era: A Wake-Up Call *by Ann Lathrop and Kathleen Foss. Englewood, CO: Libraries Unlimited, 2000.*

Be Informed about Technology in Your Schools

Cheating and plagiarism are facilitated by technology. The better informed you are about the technology being used at school, the more likely you will notice dishonest activity at home. Become familiar with technologies used in classrooms and labs, the ways students use the hardware and software, and how technology impacts their learning. Learn to use the high-tech "toys" described in Chapter 2 and the software programs your children use at school. It can be helpful to buy the same or compatible software for home use.

Access to the Internet is available at almost all schools and in many classrooms. If you have Internet access at home, visit the sites used by your child; become familiar with online research paper sites, cheating tips sites, and other inappropriate Web sites (Chapters 3 and 17). Some schools allow home access to reference databases provided through the school library; this lets parents help students with school research and meet their own reference needs as well. Monitor your children's computer use at home and ask questions when you do not understand what they are doing.

Be Involved in School Activities and Assignments

Vigilant, informed parents are involved in their child's school life. They recognize that, for students, school is their job. Students learn to complete assigned tasks in the allotted time and to get along with a variety of personalities. After mastering the class content and these valuable life skills, they are equipped for success in almost any endeavor. Parents have a large role to play in this learning process.

Good parenting takes time, lots of it. Much of the advice about helping students succeed in school echoes the "common sense" ideas of earlier generations. The crucial point is whether parents actually make available the time needed to do the things they know are necessary. McEwan emphasizes the importance of parent involvement:

> As I looked at the hundreds of kids who came through the elementary school I served as principal, I could usually pick out those whose parents supported and encouraged them. Generally these kids did well in school, liked themselves, and got along well with teachers and fellow students. Their parents were interested in what their kids were doing. They allocated family resources to encourage hobbies, talents, and interests. They attended meetings, volunteered to be leaders, bought supplies and materials, and generally felt that the activities of childhood were worthwhile and important. (57–58)

Lickona makes an especially strong appeal for schools to involve all of the parents and the community as well in character education:

- Parents are a child's first and most important moral teachers, and the school must do everything it can to support parents in this role.
- Parents must in turn support the school's efforts to develop good character.

- The impact of the school–parent partnership is enhanced when the wider community (e.g., churches, businesses, youth organizations, local government, and the media) promotes the virtues that make up good character. (59)

It is important to encourage and support students in school without creating undue pressure. Work with your children in meaningful ways, congratulate them when they are doing their best, and take care not to pressure them into dishonesty by unrealistic expectations.

Pressures in the form of threats when the student does not meet parental expectations are rarely motivational, especially if students know from past experience that such threats usually are not carried out: "You'll be grounded for a month" or "I'll take your car keys away" or "You can't spend the night with a friend." These parents generally provide little positive assistance or motivation, only threats of punishment in case of failure; some students will regard these threats as a justifiable reason to cheat.

Bribes and rewards can create another form of pressure: "If you make an A . . ." or "If you pass a test . . ." or "If you get the top grade . . ."—then "I'll give you a bicycle" or "You can have your own car" or "You get $10 for every A." Adults can see these as positive pressures, but in too many cases, the parents offering the reward accept no responsibility for helping the student achieve the goals set. They do not work with their child or teach study skills; many do not even provide a quiet work area for homework. Again, the pressure can create unrealistic expectations that might lead to cheating behaviors.

A more positive form of parental motivation is an offer to help. This help is continuous across the school year, not given only the night before a test or the week before finals. Parents who practice this positive motivation do not encourage cheating by setting goals the student cannot meet, but instead stress the importance of honesty, hard work, and integrity in approaching any goal, including schoolwork.

Volunteer in the classroom, library, career center, or computer lab. You will have an opportunity to learn how the faculty is addressing the issues of cheating and plagiarism, and what you can do to support their efforts.

Be a Model of Ethical Behavior

"Do as I say, not as I do" is an old adage that is true for most of us, at least occasionally, in dealing with children. Children are very observant and notice how you behave around others. They are great listeners and pick up all the things you say, the way you say them, and whether or not you mean them.

Do you model ethical behavior? Do they hear you brag about "fixing" a parking ticket or "saving" on income taxes? Do they hear you talk on the phone in a very friendly way to someone they know you dislike, then hear you make cruel remarks about that person to a friend? Do they know you always drive ten to twenty miles above the speed limit? Did they see you return a "new" dress for a refund after you wore it to a party? Have they heard you lie to get out of a difficult situation? Adults who model dishonest behavior give tacit permission to children to behave in ways they know are wrong.

What about cheating? Do you tell your child not to cheat and then write a false excuse for a school absence because the family is going on a trip? Do you sometimes write a paper or do a math assignment for your child to turn in, even when you know it is supposed to be the child's own work? Are you modeling cheating with actions that say "it's OK to cheat" even as you say "don't cheat" with your words?

One student said his parents gave him the "don't do it" lecture, but eventually he told them that he sometimes cheats. "It didn't produce that big of an outcome," said the A-student. "They still got mad at me, but they got over it. My dad showed me one way to cheat, but it was so obvious that I told him you'd get caught doing it that way now." (Netherton, pars. 25–26)

It is our responsibility to model the ethical behavior we expect from our children. Anything less offers them permission to behave with dishonesty. Then, when they are guilty of dishonest behavior at school, it is the parents who ultimately must deal with the problem.

Be Ethical in Dealing with Student Cheating or Plagiarism

Involved parents support teachers and administrators in dealing with ethical issues. Enforcement of the school's Academic Integrity Policy (Chapter 8) depends on parental cooperation and support. If there is no Academic Integrity Policy for the school or district, parents can take a leadership role in organizing a committee to create one.

Parent involvement becomes crucial when there is an allegation of plagiarism or cheating. Effective parents seek the truth in such instances. If the student is proved to have behaved dishonestly, parents support integrity and ethical behavior by accepting an appropriate penalty. The dishonest behavior then becomes an opportunity for moral development. Levine suggests five points to discuss with the child who has cheated:

1. School is for learning. If you gain the skills of finding things out, solving problems, and expressing your ideas and feelings, you will succeed.

2. It's okay not to know. Class and homework are for practice, not perfect. If you don't get it, go to a grown-up or a friend and ask for help.

3. Do the best you—not someone else—can do. If you're trying as hard as you can, your family will be proud of you.

4. Even a poor test score can help you. Of course, you need good grades to get into a good high school or college, but use your mistakes as a guide to where to put more effort, and you'll do better next time.

5. Honesty is right. Cheating is wrong. When you secretly copy from a book or your neighbor's paper, you are lying to the grown-ups who trust you, stealing from another child and cheating yourself out of knowing if you've mastered the lessons. And lying, stealing, and cheating are wrong. Period. End of discussion. (56)

When your child is accused of misconduct, a practical first step is to discuss the allegation to get his or her perspective. Next, set up a meeting with the teacher, and perhaps an administrator or counselor, to discuss the problem at school. Stay open-minded and fair to both the student's and the teacher's point of view. Take some time to evaluate what has happened. The suggestions from Moss in Chapter 10 can be helpful.

Teachers are deeply concerned about the possibility of wrongfully accusing a student of cheating. They understand why parents are prompt to defend a child's honor and reputation. But the statistics at the beginning of this chapter document the often serious "disconnect" between what parents believe to be true and what a student actually has done.

McEwan suggests three questions that parents might ask when their child or young adult has been caught cheating:

- Am I realistic in my expectations or demands of my child? Do I continually emphasize the importance of winning or having top grades?

- Are my expectations far greater than my child could be expected to achieve?

- Is my discipline so harsh and punitive that it engenders extreme fear in my children so that they cheat rather than face the consequences of failure? (47–48)

She then suggests that the parents meet with the teacher to explore any other reasons why the cheating occurred, and concludes:

If, after talking to your child's teacher, you determine that competition and pressure might be the reasons for cheating, lighten up. Major on praise and encouragement, rather than pressure. Avoid making comparisons between your child and siblings or friends with regard to report cards, sports achievement, or other accomplishments. (48)

A more serious problem exists when parents refuse to admit that a child has cheated despite overwhelming evidence. They can threaten to bring a lawyer into the dispute if the accusation is not dropped.

These parents may not even question the evidence. Rather, educators say, parents sometimes cut straight to the excuse, hoping to secure more lenient punishments. And teachers often buckle under the pressure. In a survey of 356 high school teachers by the *American School Board Journal,* roughly seven out of ten teachers said parental pressure discourages educators from penalizing student cheaters. (Bushweller. *Generation* 26)

One experienced teacher has had too many parents of this type: "I have parents who will cry 'foul.' They don't want the child's grade to be affected by the action. They might or might not agree that cheating took place, but they don't want consequences for that activity. The ultimate loser, of course, is the child" (DeBoer). Being forced to cope with the consequences of dishonesty can make students realize their behavior was wrong. Parents who seek to shield children from any negative consequences they might deserve are doing an injustice to the child and to the concept of academic integrity.

At the other extreme are those parents who refuse to become involved in any way. They apparently just don't care, will not respond to requests from the school for a meeting, and take no disciplinary action of any kind. Students are left to defend themselves as best they can, and if found guilty, must cope with the penalty alone.

Parents who work cooperatively with teachers and administrators support children's growth in integrity and provide the encouragement that is so important in their lives.

> Besides punishing misbehavior, adults should be more ready to recognize and reward the good that young people do, some of the students said. For example, Donique said, when she brought home a failing grade on a test recently, her mother "went on and on. Pretty soon, everybody at church knew, all my aunts knew. But when I worked hard and brought my grade up, nothing happened." The lesson she said she learned was: "Why work, when you get more attention from being bad?" (Osinski, pars. 19–21)

Donique and all the other students deserve our respect and appreciation when they accomplish good work and achieve positive goals. Parents need to make sure they receive both in good measure.

Can "Too Much" Help Be Harmful?

When do parents cross the line from providing encouragement and needed assistance to actually doing the work? How often does this happen? One of every five students in the survey reported in Chapter 4 replied *yes* when asked "Have you turned in work done by your parents?" (Schab 843).

There are at least three serious negative consequences to helping "too much." The first is that the child does not learn to do the work assigned and does not learn the associated study skills. Second, you could be overemphasizing perfection and creating an impression that the child cannot be successful alone (Lipsett, par. 6). Finally, and perhaps most damaging, you are modeling dishonest behavior. The director of a children's center warns parents:

> By doing their work for them . . . adults teach children that their best isn't good enough if somebody else can do it better. And overemphasizing positive results—such as pleasing artwork, good grades or first-place science-fair projects—can make students feel pressured to win at all costs. Sometimes that inspires positive behaviors, such as vigorous studying and consistent school attendance. It can also lead to taking shortcuts to success— copying, cribbing, plagiarizing, and various other forms of cheating. (Asch, pars. 4–6)

Additional information such as articles of interest to parents, practical suggestions, and links to related Web sites can be located online at the Homework Helper Web site at <http://family.go.com/Features/family_1997_07/dony/dony77lesupervise/>.

The two Copy-Me pages that follow have suggestions for helping students in ways that provide encouragement without taking responsibility for the assignment. The suggestions come from our own experience as educators and parents, from conversations with colleagues and friends, and from suggestions in numerous parenting articles read over the years. The pages are designed as discussion starters and are not intended to be comprehensive.

Pointers

Chapter 7 addresses character education and ethical behavior, and suggests the use of moral tales to develop integrity. Chapter 8 urges parents to be involved in developing and supporting an Academic Integrity Policy for their school and district. The importance of parent support for school policies and personnel when dealing with suspected student dishonesty is stressed in Chapter 10.

COPY ME:
Help, But Not Too Much

What is the message? The message is *do not* complete an assignment yourself, or even help with the actual work. What takes a child all evening to do, even without the moaning and complaining, most parents could do quickly. But remember that children learn the skills of studying, writing, researching, and managing a project by doing the work themselves. You can help in many of the ways listed, but be certain the actual work is done by the child.

- Make interest in your children's schoolwork a daily item.

- Check homework every evening; if there is none, find out why not.

- Ask the teacher for clarification when an assignment seems confusing; additional instructions can often be sent home to assist in completing the work.

- Check backpacks each day for "forgotten" assignments, school messages, or any indication of plagiarized papers.

- When there is a big school project, help to divide the process into manageable pieces and devise a time line.

- Discuss how to build a model of a mission or make a salt map of your state or design a new flag for an imaginary country; go shopping with your child for the supplies needed; help to create a good workspace where the project is safe from siblings; check on daily progress and be encouraging; but don't do the work yourself and don't strive for perfection. It's a student project and the finished product should look like student work.

- Brainstorm ideas for a report or research paper; take your child to libraries or bookstores for information; help to search for information on the Internet; go over model papers in writing handbooks together; but don't take over the research and writing.

- When asked for help with a written assignment, ask leading questions to get the student to suggest how to improve a statement or paragraph; but don't rewrite it yourself.

- Circle misspelled words or awkward phrases, but make the student correct them.

- Read and discuss reports and term papers when they are finished. Ask where they located their sources, why they drew their conclusions, what they learned about the research process, and what they learned about their topic.

- Take children to the public library regularly for pleasure reading and for research.

Reprinted with permission from Student Cheating and Plagiarism in the Internet Era: A Wake-Up Call *by Ann Lathrop and Kathleen Foss. Englewood, CO: Libraries Unlimited, 2000.*

COPY ME:
Practical Suggestions to Support Students at Home and School

Provide space and support materials for homework.

- Provide a study area with good light, proper seating, and minimum distractions.

- Limit telephone and television during time set aside for homework.

- Develop a home reference library, both print and electronic, and provide access to the Internet as appropriate.

- Bookmark good reference sites or virtual library sites on your computer.

- Post a schedule of hours for the surrounding public and college or university libraries on the refrigerator or in another handy place.

Make reasonable rules for use of home computers.

- Set up family rules that balance the student's need for privacy vs. a parent's responsibility to stay informed.

- Check files and bookmarks on home computers. Notice and discuss any bookmarks to cheat sites and term paper sites.

- Ask about email that includes homework or other assignments, and discuss the difference between collaboration and copying.

- Watch for cheat sheets in the trash and for term papers faxed or emailed to your home.

- Check credit card statements for charges to suspicious-sounding companies that might offer research or term papers.

- Read completed reports and term papers and ask about any that might appear to be someone else's work.

Become well acquainted with your child's teachers.

- Meet with teachers more than once a year and keep communication open.

- Many schools have Web sites that allow teachers to post assignments and additional classroom news. Read these often if available at your school.

- Teachers often welcome email messages from parents.

- Most teachers will be glad to schedule a meeting at a convenient time.

Notify the teacher as soon as possible if your child has a health condition or other problem that can affect schoolwork.

- When you call the office about an important family situation or health condition, realize that messages sometimes get misplaced, especially during the first weeks of school or other very busy times, or if the teacher is absent; always follow up on significant calls.

- If your child has a special condition, for example, dyslexia, ADHD, poor hearing, etc., discuss this with the teacher(s) as early in the term as possible. Once teachers know about special conditions they can make any appropriate changes in assignments, seating, etc.

Reprinted with permission from Student Cheating and Plagiarism in the Internet Era: A Wake-Up Call *by Ann Lathrop and Kathleen Foss. Englewood, CO: Libraries Unlimited, 2000.*

Honoring Tomorrow's Leaders Today

Paul C. Krouse

Beginning in 1970 we have annually polled the students listed in *Who's Who Among American High School Students* about their attitudes and opinions covering a broad range of issues and behaviors. Because these students represent what others have called the "best and the brightest," their views frequently put them on the cutting edge of new trends and idea patterns among teenagers.

In 1983 we first asked the *Who's Who* teens about the issue of cheating. We were most surprised to learn that more than 70% of the students acknowledged that they had cheated in some form or another. By 1998 more than 8 out of 10 students acknowledged that they had cheated. Ironically, approximately three-quarters of these students condemned their own behavior as they cite the decline of moral and social values as the number one problem facing our nation.

In my many conversations with the press regarding the cheating issue they frequently ask if I'm surprised that these top students engage in such unethical behavior. My response has typically been that these young people are not living in a vacuum. Hardly a day goes by when we (they) don't read or hear about famous athletes, business leaders, entertainers, clergymen and even the President of the United States engaging in some form of deception, unethical, immoral or even illegal behavior. Consequently, we shouldn't be shocked when the actions of these role models trickles down and influences our young people.

In 1997, however, the issue of why teens and in particular teen leaders, like those listed in *Who's Who,* cheat was further demystified when we conducted a survey of the parents of *Who's Who* students. Virtually an equal number of students and parents, roughly two-thirds of both groups, when asked why students cheat responded, "it didn't seem like a big deal." Obviously when young people receive that kind of message from their parents it is no wonder that they display such a comfort level with unethical behavior.

Clearly, in my opinion, parents need to take more responsibility, in fact total responsibility for the behavior and ethical conduct of their children. We must stop telling our children that it doesn't matter how you achieve as long as you achieve. When Vince Lombardi, the late, great coach of the Green Bay Packers football team said, "Winning isn't everything, it's the only thing," he was talking about a sport, and a business involving grown, adult men. Lombardi wasn't talking to Little Leaguers, their parents, or applicants to selective colleges and universities.

As parents, we need to communicate extensively and frequently with our children. We must serve as role models to the very best of our abilities and be keenly aware that what we do is more important than what we say to our children. We can't preach about honesty and integrity and then boast about cheating Uncle Sam on our income taxes or flaunt other indiscretions in their faces that can only serve to demean our behavior in their eyes.

It's also a good idea for parents to appreciate the importance of working with school administrators and faculty members in combined efforts to improve the school, the community, and the performance of our children. In our litigious society it is too often the teachers who are "put on trial" when they cite some of their students for cheating. Too many parents are ready to threaten litigation when their children are caught, which explains why so few students who cheat are caught and/or disciplined. The teachers and administrators just have too much to lose in that environment. Ultimately we all lose when we allow our children, the future leaders of our country, to take charge of our schools, businesses, and government with their moral compasses dangerously off course.

[Commentary by Paul C. Krouse, Publisher and Founder of *Who's Who Among American High School Students*. Printed with permission of the author.]

Chapter 7

Integrity, Ethics, and Character Education

It is obvious that our schools must have clear behavior codes and high expectations for their students. Civility, honesty, and considerate behavior must be recognized, encouraged, and rewarded. That means that moral education must have as its explicit aim the moral betterment of the student. If that be indoctrination, so be it. How can we hope to equip students to face the challenge of moral responsibility in their lives if we studiously avoid telling them what is right and what is wrong? (Sommers 7)

Chapter Overview

Classroom discussions of each citizen's role in upholding the principles of honesty and fair play begin in kindergarten and continue through high school. Students should receive a clear and consistent message at school and at home:

> *Honesty and integrity are the hallmarks of good character and are expected from everyone. Dishonesty in any form, including cheating and plagiarism, is wrong and will not be tolerated.*

Students need to hear these strong statements from the adults they respect. It is even more important that they see evidence of honesty and integrity in the daily actions of these same adults.

This chapter provides resources to support the efforts of parents and teachers who are helping students to develop an ethical character. The 1997 Yearbook of the National Society for the Study of Education is an excellent review of character education today; the essays by William Schubert and Thomas Lickona are summarized here. Character education in teacher training programs is explored briefly. The use of literature for moral development is suggested with two anthologies as examples. Centers and institutes that provide online information and resources on integrity and ethics are identified, followed by other supporting resources. Two Copy-Me pages are designed to spark classroom discussions. Dr. Kevin Ryan's article on character education closes the chapter.

Chapter subheadings:

- 1997 Yearbook of the National Society for the Study of Education
- Character Education at Teacher–Training Institutions
- The Power of Story—Literature That Models Ethics and Integrity
- Institutes and Centers that Support Ethics, Integrity, and Character Education
- Resources to Support Integrity, Ethics, and Character Education
- Student Discussions of Integrity and Ethical Character
- Copy Me: "Does Cheating Harm Your Career?"
- Copy Me: "Are These Valid Reasons to Cheat or Plagiarize?"
- K. Ryan: "The Six E's of Character Education"

1997 Yearbook of the National Society for the Study of Education

Educators and parents seeking more information on character education in schools today will find a helpful overview in *The Construction of Children's Character,* the 1997 Yearbook of the National Society for the Study of Education (Molnar). Fourteen essays present a variety of viewpoints from well-known educators. Two essays are summarized here.

Schubert identifies and discusses four current approaches to character education:

> The social behaviorist suggests that character worth emulation is right before our eyes, embodied in the activities of successful persons. We need to identify the ideals implicit in what successful persons know and do, and we need to design and organize learning activities to reach these purposes.

> The intellectual traditionalist argues that character is best formed by immersion in the great works because they put students in touch with fundamental questions and mysteries in a way that no other source can provide.

> The experientialist says that each person should follow his or her deepest concerns and interests, which will lead to becoming a curious problem solver and dedicated moral agent who trusts his or her own judgment based on experience.

> The critical reconstructionist sees character best formed in the
> struggle for equity and justice, as the consequence of imaginative,
> democratic, political action, not merely of adherence to precept or
> participation in "interesting" activities. (28)

Schubert does not imply these are the only effective approaches nor does he advocate selecting one approach to the exclusion of others. "My central hope is that as educators reflect on each of these perspectives they will discover more possibilities about how curriculum can provide social and intellectual experiences for students to use in constructing a moral purpose to guide their lives" (28).

Lickona challenges teachers to integrate moral values into all aspects of the curriculum by asking themselves: "What are the moral questions and lessons already present in the subject I teach? How can I make those questions and lessons salient for my students?" (53). He develops a number of possible scenarios:

> A science teacher can design a lesson on the need for precise and
> truthful reporting of data (and how scientific fraud threatens the
> scientific enterprise); a social studies teacher can examine ques-
> tions of social justice, actual moral dilemmas faced by historical
> figures, and current opportunities for civic action to better one's
> community or country; a literature teacher can have students ana-
> lyze the moral decisions and moral strengths and weaknesses of
> characters in novels, plays, and short stories; a mathematics
> teacher can ask students to research and plot morally significant
> societal trends (e.g., violent crime, teen pregnancy, homelessness,
> children living in poverty). All teachers can engage students in the
> study of men and women who have achieved moral or intellectual
> distinction in their fields. (53)

The Construction of Children's Character would be especially helpful in districts preparing a new character education curriculum. Individual chapters provide good background reading for group discussions.

Character Education at Teacher–Training Institutions

Just how well prepared are teachers to address the issues of ethics and integrity in their classrooms? Have they mastered techniques to discourage cheating and plagiarism? According to Carney, "If teachers give slight attention to cheating it may be because little attention is given to the issue during teacher training . . . cheating is not a part of the curriculum of most college education departments" (pars. 36–37).

A recent study by the Character Education Partnership and the Center for the Advancement of Ethics and Character confirms Carney's statement. *Teachers as Educators of Character: Are the Nation's Schools of Education Coming Up Short?* reports: "Only 13.1 percent of the individuals who head schools of education are satisfied with their current character education efforts, and only 24.4 percent say that character education is highly emphasized in their programs' courses" (Jones, Ryan, and Bohlin 2). Other findings include:

- There is little consensus about what character education is and how it should be taught.
- "Community" is a dominant framework and a powerful metaphor in character education efforts.
- The learning process, rather than curricular content, [is cited] as the primary vehicle for character education.
- Colleges and universities that mention character education in their mission statements (63.2 percent of the sample) are much more likely to teach it.
- Schools of education with religious ties are more strongly committed to character education than their secular counterparts.
- Educators generally, but cautiously, favor making character education a requirement for state certification. (Jones, Ryan, and Bohlin 4)

The complete report is available from the Character Education Partnership at <http://www.character.org>.

The International Center for Character Education (ICCE) is sponsoring "A Professional Code of Ethics for Teacher Educators: A Proposal to Stimulate Discussion and Debate." The goal is: "Teacher education is one of the few professions without a professional code of ethics. The author proposes a code specifically designed for teacher–educators. The proposal is intended to stimulate discussion with the eventual goal of adoption by teacher–educators throughout the nation." The contact person is David Freitas at <http://www.teachvalues.org/icce/CodeTE9.htm>.

The Power of Story—Literature that Models Ethics and Integrity

Parents, teachers, and librarians use stories effectively to help children and young adults see and internalize ethical values. Librarians can recommend picture books, easy readers, and novels for leisure reading. These stories lead to thoughtful classroom or family discussions about honesty, moral decision making, and related ethical issues.

Many excellent guides to children's literature are available. The two listed here were selected for their strong focus on ethics and moral values.

Books That Build Character: A Guide to Teaching Your Child Moral Values Through Stories by William Kilpatrick, et al. lists books to help develop virtue and conscience in children from preschool through adolescence. Robert Coles addresses the value of stories in his foreword to the book:

Put differently, our characters are tested constantly by the people, the occasions that all the time come our way. Each day offers us any number of opportunities for affirmation or, alas, calamity. With our children (and with ourselves), we can, then, do no better than to accept the challenge storytelling presents: an openness to life's complexities, ironies, paradoxes, inconsistencies with a willingness as well to examine the most important moral questions with energy and subtlety and seriousness. Stories offer us a chance to affirm our nature, as the creatures of words, of consciousness—and to do so with pleasure and purpose, both: the enjoyment of carefully crafted narration, the chance to reflect, to respond by thinking of one's own life, its nature, its assumptions, its aims. We are lucky indeed to have such stories as a great heritage, a moral reservoir of sorts, from which we can constantly draw. (Kilpatrick 15)

Exploring Ethics through Children's Literature—Book 1 by Elizabeth Saenger, identifies a wide range of books that can be springboards for discussions of moral and ethical issues:

In general, I would say that ethics class literature needs to center on ethical problems, to be full of ambivalences rather than answers, and to be moral in its point of view.... It's not necessary to resolve every question or issue. Some ethical problems will be just left "hanging" for the children to ponder. Possible starting questions include:

- What exactly was wrong about what that character did?
- How do you suppose the other person felt? Why?
- What else could she have said that would not have hurt his feelings?
- Do you think he would have done the same thing if...? Why?
- If the results had been different, would she still have been wrong to do it? Why? (16–17)

Two of the institutes in the next section use literature in character education:

- The Markkula Center for Applied Ethics sponsors the LEAD (Leadership through Ethical Action and Development) project. Student volunteers from Santa Clara University help high school students learn to use children's literature to teach lessons about moral behavior. The high school students then take the stories and lessons to children in local elementary schools (Scheinin, pars. 11–14).

- The Heartwood Institute uses children's stories from around the world as the basis for their ethics curriculum and early childhood curriculum.

Institutes and Centers that Support Ethics, Integrity, and Character Education

These centers and institutes were founded to foster the development of integrity, ethical behavior, and moral character. Many of the Web sites provide information and resource materials for students, parents, and educators. The brief descriptions are taken from the Web sites unless otherwise noted.

The Center for Academic Integrity
<http://www.academicintegrity.org>
Dr. Sally Cole, Executive Director
919-660-3045
Box 90434, Duke University
Durham, NC 27708

"The Center for Academic Integrity is a consortium of approximately 200 colleges and universities and 500 individual students, faculty, and administrator members from those institutions. It was established in 1992 to identify and affirm the values of academic integrity and to promote their achievement in practice.

The Center provides a forum to identify, affirm, and promote the values of academic integrity among students. This mission is achieved primarily through the involvement of students, faculty, and administrators from the member institutions who share with peers and colleagues the Center's collective experience, expertise, and creative energy. There is no single path to academic integrity and the Center respects and values campus differences in traditions, values, and student and faculty characteristics. The membership of the Center is committed to gathering and sharing information about academic integrity via:

- An annual conference; periodic mailings; an electronic listserv; a web site with both public and member-only access; and presentations at the conferences of other associations as well as on the campuses of member institutions;

- Encouraging and supporting research on factors that impact academic integrity;

- Identifying and describing fundamental principles of academic integrity and the sustaining practices that support those principles on a variety of college and university campuses;

- Helping faculty members in different disciplines develop pedagogies that encourage adherence to these fundamental principles; and

- Showcasing successful approaches to academic integrity from schools around the country—policies, enforcement procedures, sanctions, research, curricular materials, and education/prevention programs."

The Center for the 4th and 5th Rs
<http://www.cortland.edu/www/c4n5rs/>
Dr. Thomas Lickona, Director
607-753-2455
SUNY Cortland
Box 2000
Cortland, NY 13045

"The Center for the 4th and 5th Rs (Respect and Responsibility) serves as a regional, state, and national resource in character education. A growing national movement, character education is essential to the task of building a moral society and developing schools that are civil and caring communities. The Center disseminates complimentary articles on character education, sponsors an annual summer institute in character education, publishes a Fourth and Fifth Rs newsletter, offers a browsing library of character education materials, and is building a network of 'Fourth and Fifth Rs Schools' committed to teaching respect, responsibility and other core ethical values as the basis of good character. Character education holds that there are universally important ethical values such as respect, responsibility, trustworthiness, fairness, caring, courage, self-control, and diligence. Character means living by these core values—understanding them, caring about them, and acting upon them."

Center for the Advancement of Ethics and Character, Boston University
<http://www.education.bu.edu/CharacterEd/>
Dr. Karen Bohlin, Director
617-353-3262, ext. 4794
605 Commonwealth Avenue
Boston, MA 02215

"Our mission since 1989 is based on the following simple beliefs:

- that character education is an essential and inescapable mission of schools and thus must be done consciously and well;
- that the human community has a reservoir of moral wisdom, much of which exists in our great stories, works of art, literature, and philosophy and that this treasure must be a regular part of schooling;
- that the teacher is central to the entire enterprise and must be selected, educated, and encouraged with this mission in mind;
- that the most important task facing America's schools today is engaging children in our moral wisdom and aiding them in the formation of the enduring habits that comprise good character.

Goals

- To foster the preparation of teachers who can provide students with an intellectual framework for the discussion, understanding, and practice of the core virtues of our society.
- To develop, in collaboration with the College of Arts and Sciences, a common core curriculum that combines intensive instruction in a wide variety of classic texts with the professional training of teachers.
- To serve as a resource for administrators, teachers, and parents as they seek to fulfill their responsibilities as moral educators.
- To foster research initiatives in, and publications on, all aspects of moral and character education, not only by Boston University's faculty and students but also by the national and the international community.
- To stimulate a national dialogue on issues of moral education, thus helping educators to become more competent in the study of ethics and character in the nation's schools.
- To help develop a model for those throughout the country who wish to establish similar centers or undertake similar work."

A "Character Education Manifesto," created by the Center in 1996, has been signed by President Clinton and a number of state governors and educators. It is online at <http://education.bu.edu/CharacterEd/manifesto.html>.

The article following this chapter, "The Six E's of Character Education," was written by Dr. Kevin Ryan, founder and Director Emeritus of the Center.

CHARACTER COUNTS!

<http://www.charactercounts.org/>
Julie Dwyer, Director
310-306-1868
4640 Admiralty Way, Suite 1001
Marina del Rey, CA 90292-6610

"The purpose of the CHARACTER COUNTS! Coalition is to fortify the lives of America's young people with consensus ethical values called the "Six Pillars of Character." These values, which transcend divisions of race, creed, politics, gender, and wealth, are trustworthiness, respect, responsibility, fairness, caring, and citizenship.

The Coalition works to overcome the false but surprisingly powerful notion that no single value is intrinsically superior to another; that ethical values vary by race, class, gender and politics; that greed and fairness, cheating and honesty carry the same moral weight, simply depending on one's perspective and immediate needs.

The Coalition strives to build consensus that there are values that clearly define us at our best, however diverse our views and backgrounds. It follows that such values are worthy of promotion where they are evident and of repair where they have faltered. The Coalition both builds awareness of these consensus values and teaches them to the young in support of the paramount role of parents." CHARACTER COUNTS! is a project of the Josephson Institute of Ethics.

Character Education Partnership

<http://www.character.org/>
Esther F. Schaeffer, Executive Director
800-988-8081
918 16th Street NW, Suite 501
Washington, DC 20006

"To strengthen civic virtue and moral character in the youth of the United States is to strengthen the very fabric of our nation and to sustain the American experiment in liberty.

We recognize and affirm the primary role of the family in shaping the moral character of children, the vital task of schools in teaching and inspiring civic virtue, and the shared responsibility of each individual and community to model moral character and civic virtue.

The Character Education Partnership (CEP) is a nonpartisan coalition of organizations and individuals dedicated to developing moral character and civic virtue in our nation's youth as one means of creating a more compassionate and responsible society.

CEP is not affiliated with any party or creed. We are a nonpartisan, nonsectarian organization dedicated to the idea that character and education are natural partners in helping children become ethical, responsible adults.

Our members hold that core ethical values such as respect, responsibility, and honesty can both be a matter of consensus and a model for our youth. We are committed to the practical implementation of character education throughout the learning process.

While CEP's primary focus is on young people, it understands that the problems affecting our youth reflect the broader social and economic problems of our country as a whole and that it is the responsibility of all adults to model good character and to help strengthen civic and moral foundations."

The Heartwood Institute
<http://www.enviroweb.org/heartwood/about.html>
Eleanore N. Childs and Marthy Harty, Co-Directors
412-688-8570 or 1-800-HEART-10
425 North Craig Street, Suite 302
Pittsburgh, PA 15213

"Heartwood is a literature-based curriculum that is firmly grounded in the age-old tradition of enriching children's understanding of positive values through the reading aloud of quality literature. In this respect, it is like no other curriculum that exists today.

Heartwood is organized around a group of beautifully written and illustrated stories from many cultures throughout the world. The stories reinforce the notion that all societies share basic moral concepts and rely on attributes such as Courage, Loyalty, Justice, Respect, Hope, Honesty, and Love for their survival.

The Heartwood Ethics Curriculum provides opportunities for teachers, parents and caregivers to discuss ethical concepts with children and build a lifelong vocabulary. It provides a framework around each story that encourages children to share their own life experiences as they relate to the story, and to incorporate the story's message of caring into their daily lives.

Beginning with early childhood, the Heartwood Curriculum offers a comprehensive program for encouraging good citizenship that encompasses all stages of a child's development. It provides teachers with the concepts, tools and support they need to guide students on an exciting journey toward an understanding of ethical behavior."

The Institute for Global Ethics
<http://www.globalethics.org/>
Dr. Rushworth Kidder, President
800-729-2615
Box 563
Camden, ME 04843

"The Institute for Global Ethics is an independent, nonprofit, nonsectarian, and nonpartisan organization dedicated to elevating public awareness and promoting the discussion of ethics in a global context. As an international, membership-based think tank, we focus on ethical activities in education, the corporate sector, and public policy. The Institute's mission is to:

- Discover and articulate the global common ground of ethical values
- Analyze ethical trends and shifts in values as they occur worldwide
- Gather and disseminate information on global ethics
- Elevate public awareness and discussion of global ethical issues

The Institute actively works with schools, community members, state departments of education, and educational organizations. The Institute also has developed curricular materials for use in middle and high schools.

Why do we need to teach children about ethics?

- Because the future promises an ever-increasing number of complex pressures and problems.

- Because the power of technology in the 21st century must be tempered by ethical fitness.
- Because trends in student violence, pregnancies, drug use, vandalism, and cheating need to be reversed.

All of us—parents, schools, and communities—need to provide an ethical foundation to ensure our children's future.

What do we want to teach our children about ethics?

That sound ethics is essential. We must provide our children with a language for talking about ethics and the skills to solve the tough decisions they face now and will face in the future. Our children need to:

- Understand the difference between right and wrong.
- Learn how to tackle difficult right-versus-right ethical dilemmas.
- Understand the growing importance of ethics in a technologically driven world.

Character Education Community Program

We know that a number of communities and school districts have a strong interest in incorporating ethics education into their school curriculums. These districts are beginning to recognize that promoting ethical behavior is one critical key to creating a positive learning environment in the classroom. They also realize that students need to learn ethics-based critical thinking skills if they are to be successful, as adults, in the workforce.

School districts usually agree that a community-based effort is the way to begin. The Institute's program involves a two-phase character-education model that is very specifically community based, on the one hand, but that also equips teachers with the classroom materials and training needed to carry the program forward."

International Center for Character Education (ICCE)
<http://www.teachvalues.org/icce/>
Mary Williams and Edward DeRoche, Co-Directors
(619) 260-5980
University of San Diego Division of Continuing Education-22
5998 Alcala Park
San Diego, CA 92110-2492

"The ICCE is concerned with the four pillars of democracy: home, school, church, and community. The Center's purpose is to enable school personnel, parents, teacher educators, faith community members, youth providers, and concerned individuals to come together to study, discuss, learn, practice, reflect, and write on issues, programs, problems and promises regarding the character education of children and youth. Some center activities include Character Education certificates, program assessment, consulting, publications, courses, workshops, partnerships, academies and conferences."

The ICCE is sponsoring "A Professional Code of Ethics for Teacher Educators: A Proposal to Stimulate Discussion and Debate." The contact person is David J. Freitas, National-Louis University <http://www.teachvalues.org/icce/CodeTE9.htm>. According to Freitas, "Teacher education is one of the few professions without a professional code of ethics. The author proposes a code specifically designed for teacher educators. The proposal is intended to stimulate discussion with the eventual goal of adoption by teacher educators throughout the nation."

Josephson Institute of Ethics

<http://www.josephsoninstitute.org/>
Michael S. Josephson, President
310-306-1868
Josephson Institute of Ethics
4640 Admiralty Way, Suite 1001
Marina del Rey, CA 90292-6610

"The Joseph & Edna Josephson Institute of Ethics is a public-benefit, nonpartisan, nonprofit membership organization founded by Michael Josephson in honor of his parents to improve the ethical quality of society by advocating principled reasoning and ethical decision making. Since 1987, the Institute has conducted programs for more than 100,000 leaders—in government and the armed forces, in business and journalism, in law and law enforcement, and in education and the nonprofit community. The nationwide CHARACTER COUNTS! youth-education initiative is a project of the Institute. To help individuals change, the Institute seeks to:

- Stimulate moral ambition
- Heighten the ability to perceive the ethical dimension of choices
- Teach how to formulate optimal ethical responses
- Show how to implement these responses intelligently

The Institute holds that ethical obligations are based on common ethical values applicable and knowable to all, regardless of gender, race, age, wealth, class, politics, or religion. These values, called the Six Pillars of Character, are: trustworthiness, respect, responsibility, fairness, caring, and citizenship."

(Short daily radio addresses by Michael Josephson dealing with many different aspects of ethics and society today are available at the Web site.)

Markkula Center for Applied Ethics

<http://www.scu.edu/SCU/Centers/Ethics/>
Dennis Moberg, Acting Executive Director
408-554-5319
Santa Clara University
500 El Camino Real
Santa Clara, CA 95053-0633

"The Markkula Center for Applied Ethics . . . operates as a unique community of faculty, students, staff and community members with the common goal of equipping people, both from the on- and off-campus communities, with strategies to heighten ethical awareness and improve ethical decision making. It focuses on providing ethics resources at a critical time in the development of groups, organizations, institutions, or society. The Center:

- focuses on ethical theory, but also offers practical methods for the application of ethical principles in the real world.
- is interdisciplinary in nature. This means that the Center approaches issues from a variety of vantage points, creating an atmosphere of critical thinking and creative problem solving. The topic of fair use in technology, for example, might be examined from philosophical, legal, scientific and social science perspectives.

- enjoys partnership and input from key faculty from all five SCU schools, as well as a group of community professionals who share our goals and commitment. Through this interaction, the Center brings a diversity of expertise to each issue studied.
- suggests what to think about, not what to think."

The LEAD (Leadership through Ethical Action and Development) program trains Santa Clara University undergraduates to teach ethics in school and recreational settings, facilitate ethical discussions, lead group activities in ethics workshops, and mentor students in local schools. LEAD students then use these skills to be effective peer mentors and to deliver literature-based character education lessons for elementary, middle, and high schools through the language arts program. SPICE (Student Performers Involved in Character Education) makes particular use of virtue- and problem-centered skits promoting dialogue between students and performers. Skits developed by the SPICE program are available on the Web site [LEAD and SPICE information provided by the Center].

The Values Institute: The Place for the Thoughtful Discussion of Moral Issues
<http://www.ethics.acusd.edu/values/>
Dr. Lawrence M. Hinman, Director
619-260-4787
University of San Diego
5998 Alcala Park
San Diego, CA 92110-2492

"The principal aim of The Values Institute is to provide a place where people can come together for the thoughtful discussion of troubling moral issues. We seek to provide such a place for members of our own immediate university community (students, faculty, administration, and alumni), for members of our own local San Diego community, and for the larger national and international communities of students and scholars. We seek to do this through courses, lectures, seminars, workshops, and conferences, both on-campus and on the World Wide Web. *Ethics Updates* is designed primarily to be used by ethics instructors and their students. It is intended to provide updates on current literature, both popular and professional, that relates to ethics. *Ethics Across the Curriculum* [is] the basic source for information about activities related to *Ethics Across the Curriculum* at the University of San Diego and *Ethics Across the Curriculum* programs around the nation."

Resources to Support Integrity, Ethics, and Character Education

Center for Applied and Professional Ethics (CAPE)
<http://cape.cmsu.edu/>
Dr. Kenneth Cust, Director
660-543-4268
Central Missouri State University
Warrensburg, MO 64093

"Welcome to the Academic Integrity Project. Central Missouri State University is an institutional member of The Center for Academic Integrity and Kenneth Cust, the Founding Director of CAPE, is on the Board of Directors of The Center for Academic

Integrity. Consequently, and in order to promote academic integrity, CAPE undertook the Academic Integrity Project to create and maintain a searchable database of annotated links to Web sites concerned with and/or promoting academic integrity in one form or another. Thus the Academic Integrity Project, which is part of CAPE's Ethics Portal, includes the following searchable databases: Academic Integrity (3450 annotated links), Honor Codes (3980 annotated links), Codes of Ethics (3400 annotated links)."

The Character Education Pages
<http://cuip.uchicago.edu/~cac/chared>
Dr. Craig A. Cunningham, Editor
312-794-6260
Department of Educational Leadership and Development
Northeastern Illinois University
5500 North St. Louis Avenue
Chicago, IL 60625

"This page will serve as a clearinghouse for a variety of materials [with] links and lists of resources for educators and parents, related to the practice and theory of character education. Links: Internet Resources on Character Education, Some Good Character Education Ideas, Character Education: A General Introduction, A Certain and Reasoned Art: The Rise and Fall of Character Education in America."

The Multimedia Integrity Teaching Tool (MITT)
<http://www.bsu.edu/csh/mitt/>
Dr. Patricia C. Keith-Spiegel
765-285-8197
Department of Psychological Science
Ball State University
Muncie, IN 47306

MITT is a "computerized integrity seminar on CD-ROM. Students are given information about academic dishonesty and sensitized to the importance of integrity in the academy, society, and to themselves. The program offers students alternative responses to consider the next time an urge or opportunity to cheat arises. Each of the 38 lessons is highly interactive [with] colorful graphics, sound effects, music, video clips, and animation [to] sustain attention . . . the program automatically generates a confidential evaluation of the learner's mastery of content." The CD-ROM was developed for individual or class use by college students, with a high school version to be released in 2000 (Keith-Spiegel).

Student Discussions of Integrity and Ethical Behavior

As noted in Chapter 4, many students today view cheating simply as one way to enhance their grades. Preventive measures and penalties are not enough to counter such widely accepted beliefs. A renewed emphasis on integrity and ethical behavior at home and at school is necessary if students are to be persuaded to change their perception of cheating as "no big deal."

Now, much of the research being done on why students cheat has concluded that cheating *is* a problem of moral development—that many students have poorly developed value systems, making it difficult for them to consider issues beyond their desire for a certain grade when deciding whether or not to cheat.

Even though the mission statements of most institutions still include the development of students' ethical standards as an educational goal, many colleges and universities have taken a neutral position concerning traditional values in recent years, including taking a *laissez-faire* attitude toward students' moral development. (Kibler B1)

Classroom discussions about moral character can be developed around a variety of curriculum topics. Creative teachers will find ways to introduce the values of integrity into class work throughout the school year.

Questions that encourage students to express their feelings and opinions about honest and dishonest behaviors can lead to interesting discussions: "In what situation would you definitely *not* cheat?" or "When do you refuse to give test answers to a friend?" Some students might be willing to respond to the question, "Why *don't* you cheat when you know that most of your peers are cheating?" Two topics designed to challenge students to look seriously at their own behavior are suggested in the following pages. These topics are supported by two Copy-Me pages with discussion starters.

Topic 1: Does Cheating Harm Your Career?

Surveys and interviews that document extensive cheating by students raise concerns about the long-term effects on society of such widespread dishonesty. This topic can lead students to discuss how dishonesty in school could lead to dishonesty in college and eventually impact a person's career.

Students can develop their own scenarios. In small groups they might be willing to explore ways their own dishonesty could damage their ability to achieve career goals. Consider the following hypothetical situations:

- The architect who designed your home cheated his way through the mathematics class that provided the basis for determining building tolerances.

- The medical researcher who just announced a new drug fabricated test results in college and plagiarized research reports.

- The young lawyer who wrote your will bought a copy of the bar exam to study.

To what extent have these young professionals transferred their cheating from schools into their careers? Just how worried should we be?

What all the evidence suggests—the use of ever more sophisticated technology and the instances of mass cheating—is a fundamental change of the human condition: The very perception of cheating as sin has begun to drop into the same moral gray zone as infidelity, tax evasion, recreational drug use and a host of other activities that once grimly stood at the gates of hell. Indeed, we live in a world in which our values are in flux, contorting, as it were, to adapt to the fragmented and hyper-speed atmosphere of modern life. (Dunn 31)

Do we want to live in a society where dishonesty is the normal behavior to be expected of each person? Is it important that we trust those with whom we are doing business? How do we know which people are honest and trustworthy?

Topic 2: Are These Valid Reasons to Cheat or Plagiarize?

This list is designed to spark a class discussion about which reasons, if any, would justify cheating or plagiarizing. Honest students can express their reasons for not cheating even when they face the same pressures other students use to excuse their cheating. The discussion can provide an opportunity to honor the ethical students and to reinforce their integrity and honesty.

The students who do cheat, and then justify their cheating to themselves, might begin to re-examine their personal values. Whether these discussions take place with an entire class, in small groups, or individually between a parent and child, thoughtful questioning can guide students toward critical self-evaluation.

Questions to ask students could include "Would any of these be a good reason to cheat or are they all just excuses?" or "Would any of these make it OK to cheat once in a while?" or "Can you think of other reasons that might make it OK to cheat?" A list of reasons why some students do not cheat, or why cheating can be self-defeating, might be generated by the discussion.

These same reasons can be used in discussions about cheating at faculty or parent meetings. Suggested questions to ask teachers include "Are any of these valid reasons? If so, what actions can or should we take to change the situations that might encourage cheating?" For parents: "Do you hear any of these excuses at home? Are any of them valid? Do they indicate school policies we should re-examine?"

These reasons for cheating come primarily from discussions with students, colleagues, and friends, and ideas from the following authors: Alschular and Blimling; Anderman, Griesinger, and Westerfield; Stephen Davis; Maramark and Maline; and Schab.

Pointers

Chapter 8 addresses the development and implementation of an Academic Integrity Policy. Chapter 9 defines cheating and plagiarism and has Copy-Me pages to support discussions of cheating, plagiarism, and permissible collaboration. Penalties for student dishonesty are suggested in Chapter 10.

COPY ME:
Does Cheating Harm Your Career?

Many of today's young professionals cheated in high school and college. Will they transfer their successful cheating techniques into their new careers? How might this threaten society?

- The architect who designed your home cheated his way through the mathematics class that provided the basis for determining building tolerances. *Is your home safe?*

- The medical researcher who just announced a new drug fabricated her test results in college and plagiarized her research reports. *Did she perhaps "adjust" the data in the recent drug tests? Is the new drug safe?*

- Your lawyer paid for a copy of the bar exam to study. *Will the contract she wrote for you stand up in court?*

- The accountant who does your taxes hired someone to write his term papers and paid a "stand-in" to take several major tests. *Does he know enough to complete your tax forms correctly?*

1. What are some examples from other professions?

2. Can this type of cheating in professional preparation put all of us in danger?

3. Do we want to live in a society where dishonesty is the normal behavior to be expected of each person who provides a service to us?

4. Is it important that we trust those with whom we are doing business?

5. How do we know which people are honest and trustworthy?

6. How might cheating cause a problem in the career you have chosen?

Reprinted with permission from Student Cheating and Plagiarism in the Internet Era: A Wake-Up Call *by Ann Lathrop and Kathleen Foss. Englewood, CO: Libraries Unlimited, 2000.*

COPY ME:
Are These Valid Reasons to Cheat or Plagiarize?

Individual Issues

- Lack of ethical training or personal philosophy, moral values
- Lack of time management skills; inability to meet deadlines
- Desire for better grades, scholarships, college admission, etc.
- Test anxiety
- Fear of failure

Family/Peer Pressure

- Unrealistic demands from parents
- Sibling rivalry
- Desire or pressure to help friends and peers

School-Related Issues

- There is no school policy that defines and penalizes cheating, or the policy is unclear
- Teachers expect too much, especially when an older sibling was a strong student
- Class or assignment is boring, isn't relevant, isn't important to the student's life
- Large class sizes alienate students who feel they are "only a number"
- Advanced Placement students, at the top of their middle school classes with very little effort, must compete with students who are just as good or even better
- The teachers don't seem to care about cheating

"Poor Me" (I have no choice)

- Working to pay for a car or to save for college cuts into study time
- Athletes must maintain their GPA to be eligible to play
- Scholarship competition forces me to participate in lots of activities

"Why Not Cheat?"

- Little risk of being caught or of serious punishment if caught
- Perceived disadvantage of not cheating
- Computers make it so easy!

Excuses

- I didn't realize that what I did was dishonest
- We were collaborating—is this cheating?

Reprinted with permission from Student Cheating and Plagiarism in the Internet Era: A Wake-Up Call *by Ann Lathrop and Kathleen Foss. Englewood, CO: Libraries Unlimited, 2000.*

The Six E's of Character Education: Practical Ways to Bring Moral Instruction to Life for Your Students

Dr. Kevin Ryan

Politicians call for it. State education departments write memos about it. Parents and schools now agree on the need for it.

"It" is character education, and lately more and more educators are looking for ways to present and model the definition of it: to help each child know the good, love the good and do the good.

Like many human endeavors, it's easier to talk about character education than to actually do it. Because many secular teacher education programs dismiss the entire field of moral, ethical and character education, a great hole exists in teacher preparation. But there's hope.

Over the years I have developed six E's of character education: example, explanation, exhortation, ethos (ethical environment), experience and expectations of excellence. The six concepts will help educators promote morality within each student and in the class and school environments.

EXAMPLE:

Example is probably the most obvious way to model character education. While I'm not suggesting that teachers be saints, they should take their moral lives seriously by modeling upright behavior. Students imitate their trusted teachers.

Another method of moral modeling is to teach the moral truths embedded in literature and history. Students need to know about George Washington and Benedict Arnold; Hester Prynne of *The Scarlet Letter* and Shakespeare's Richard III; Jonas Salk (who developed the polio vaccine) and Adolf Hitler. A child's education must include such examples of good and evil individuals.

One middle school social studies teacher emphasizes biographies in his curriculum. "When my students studied Harriet Tubman, I had them perform skits with Tubman as the central character," says the New Hampshire teacher, referring to the great abolitionist. "The skits taught them about courage and self-sacrifice. We then placed a poster of Tubman in the classroom so the students would remember her."

EXPLANATION:

We need to practice moral education by means of explanation—not simply stuffing students' heads with rules and regulations, but engaging them in great moral conversations about the human race. The very existence of this dialogue helps make us human.

A private school teacher, tired and discouraged by the hostility of her sophomore students, explained the meaning of friendship to them. "Many had never heard that values like compassion and trustworthiness are needed to be a true friend," says the Boston educator. She also had her students read essays on friendship by Cicero and C. S. Lewis. "My students began to understand what it means to be a friend," she says.

Forty years ago, as an undergraduate at the University of Toronto, I sat dazed listening to Marshall McLuhan, then an obscure literature teacher, rambling about the medium being the message. I see now that his point is relevant to schooling and the moral education of children. Our continual explanation of the rules is one of the most important messages of school.

EXHORTATION:

A child discouraged by academic, athletic or artistic failure often needs something stronger than sweet reason to ward off self-pity. So do students who passively attend school, flirt with racist ideas and get denied entrance into a college of their choice. Sincere exhortation is needed.

When a fifth-grade class in upstate New York learned of its low scores on a statewide test, the teacher exhorted her students with pep talks. "I also led them in discussions about the qualities of a good student," she says. "My class felt that a good student achieved good grades. But I helped them understand that a good student is also someone who makes class contributions, does homework and assists other students."

Use exhortation sparingly and never stray far from explanation. But appeal to the best interests of the young and urge them to move in the proper direction when the need arises.

ETHOS (or Ethical Environment):

A classroom is a small society with patterns and rituals, power relationships and standards for both academic performance and student behavior. Moral climate influences classroom environment.

Does the teacher respect the students? Do students respect one another? Are the classroom rules fair and fairly exercised? Does the teacher play favorites? Are ethical questions and issues about "what ought to be" part of the classroom dialogue?

Disgusted by the bad language used by their students, members of a New Hampshire senior high faculty joined forces to stamp out rudeness and obscenity use. At an in-service just before the school year started, they discussed ways to promote a more positive climate in their classrooms and around campus.

"When the students arrived on the first school day," recalls their principal, "I announced that we were all going to work towards using a new kind of language, one free from obscenities and rudeness. We got the students involved in changing their crude environments into better ones."

There is little doubt that the ethical climate within a classroom promotes a steady and strong influence in the formation of character and the student's sense of what's right and wrong.

EXPERIENCE:

Today's young people have smaller and less stable families than kids two generations ago. A modern house or apartment offers fewer tasks for children other than the laundry and dishes, the trash and a few other light chores. Without the discipline of work-related chores, students have difficulty building sturdy self-concepts.

Today's young people also exist in the self-focused, pleasure-dominated world of MTV, promiscuity, drugs, or simply "hanging out." Only rare and fortunate teenagers have experiences that help them break out of self interest mode and learn to contribute to others.

Many schools respond by providing students both in- and out-of-school opportunities to serve. Within such schools, students help other students; older children often help younger ones learn academic or physical skills. Students also help teachers, librarians or other staff members with routine clerical tasks.

Out-of-school programs represent a larger departure from the ordinary. They enable students to provide services to individuals in need, such as a blind shut-in or a mother with a mildly retarded child. Other students volunteer in understaffed agencies, such as retirement homes or day care centers.

School staff members serve as troubleshooters between students and the individuals or agencies in need of assistance. Such service programs teach valuable humanitarian skills.

Through these activities, abstract concepts like justice and community become real as students see the faces of the lives they touch. Students begin to appreciate the need to couple moral thinking with moral action.

EXPECTATIONS OF EXCELLENCE:

Children need standards and the skills to achieve them. They need to see themselves as students engaged in a continuing pursuit of excellence.

When the faculty of the Dexter School in Brookline, MA, discussed ways to boost high standards, it created the motto, "Our best today, better tomorrow." That brought home the concept in a focused way to the students of this private boys' school. The teachers there encourage their students and help them to set reasonable standards and work toward their goals.

These standards of excellence in school work and behavior will encourage students to develop qualities like perseverance and determination, and those virtues will affect every aspect of the children's lives as they mature.

SUMMARY:

Academic studies change rapidly; what we discuss in class today becomes passé tomorrow. But the values, moral influences and noteworthy characteristics we model and discuss will outlast academic facts and figures. We can leave our students a legacy that will remain constant throughout life: to know the good, love the good, and do the good.

[Reprinted with permission of the author and the Center for the Advancement of Ethics and Character, Boston University.]

Chapter 8

Academic Integrity Policies

> *Thus, I believe we should have clear direction at the institutional level. Policies regarding academic dishonesty should be written, approved, and understood by the entire community. They should be included in the student handbook that is distributed to all students. Penalties should also be clearly stated and uniformly applied.* (Partello 178)

Chapter Overview

Developing and implementing an Academic Integrity Policy is an important step in a district's attempt to control cheating and plagiarism. It is vitally important that such a policy reflect the participation and support of students, parents, faculty, administrators, and school board members. It is equally important that the policy be enforced consistently and fairly.

This chapter gives direct support to districts or schools in developing an Academic Integrity Policy. Leadership, publicity, fair enforcement, and an ethical school culture are discussed. There are references to online integrity policies and honor policies, and one example of a high school academic honesty code. In the article following this chapter, Lewis Cobbs makes a strong statement in support of honor codes.

Chapter subheadings:

- Initiating an Action Plan
- Copy Me: "How to Develop a Strong Program for Academic Integrity" and "Ten Principles of Academic Integrity for Faculty"
- Gathering Local Statistical Data
- Honor Code or Integrity Policy?
- School Board, Administrative, and Faculty Leadership
- Student Leadership
- Acceptable Use Policies

- Fair Enforcement and an Ethical School Culture
- Copy Me: "One Principal's Commitment to Ethics"
- Publicizing the Academic Integrity Policy
- Working with New Students
- Academic Integrity Policies and Honor Codes Online
- One High School's Academic Honesty Code
- Cobbs: "Honor Codes: Teaching Integrity and Interdependence"

Initiating an Action Plan

Why is it important that a school develop an academic integrity policy? Will it have any real impact on student behavior? Research on cheating at the college and university level indicates such a policy can, in fact, make a significant difference.

> Why do college and university students cheat so much? In responding to surveys, the students themselves most often blamed the pressure to succeed—the need to meet the expectations of their families, graduate schools, and prospective employers. Several students even justified cheating by noting the need to maintain a minimum grade-point average to retain their financial-aid awards. The research of Trevino, Butterfield, and McCabe [see article by McCabe, Trevino, and Butterfield in References Cited], however, suggests an additional explanation: that a major factor determining whether a student will cheat or not is the academic culture of the specific institution that he or she attends . . . at the fewer than 100 institutions where traditional academic honor codes are in place—where students pledge not to cheat and where they play a major role in the judicial process—significantly fewer incidents of cheating occur. (McCabe and Drinan B7)

We can expect implementation of an Academic Integrity Policy, or honor code, to lead to a similar reduction in cheating by students in K–12 schools.

A successful Academic Integrity Policy is developed collaboratively by school board members, district and site administrators, teachers, parents, and students. The following is a list of topics for discussions at faculty and school board meetings, preschool workshops, in-service days, parent meetings, student class meetings, or other opportunities for consensus building and decision making:

- Review of what motivates students to commit academic dishonesty
- Definitions of academic dishonesty
- Risks of ignoring incidents of academic dishonesty
- Cheating techniques
- Deterrence tips, suggestions for test preparation, test administration and guidelines for developing marking techniques for grading

- Detection tips
- Institutional policies, procedures, and support systems
- Confrontation guidelines
- Disciplinary referral guidelines
- New technology issues that affect academic integrity
- Legal information
- Current data both from an institutional perspective (number of academic dishonesty cases the institution reports over a period of time) and a national perspective (national survey results). (Rudolph and Timm 63)

Two documents from The Center for Academic Integrity are formatted here as a Copy-Me page to facilitate discussion. These documents can apply to elementary and secondary schools as well as to higher education. The Center defines academic integrity as "a commitment, even in the face of adversity, to five fundamental values: honesty, trust, fairness, respect, and responsibility. From these values flow the principles of behavior that enable academic communities to translate ideals into action" (The Center for Academic Integrity. *Fundamental* 4). Information about the Center and its leadership role is in Chapter 7.

COPY ME:
How to Develop a Strong Program for Academic Integrity

The call to promote academic integrity places responsibility upon everyone in the educational community to balance high standards with compassion and concern. From its study of the processes and practices of successful academic integrity programs, The Center for Academic Integrity has developed seven recommendations that are appropriate to every institution of higher education. An academic institution should:

- Have clear academic integrity statements, policies, and procedures that are consistently implemented.
- Inform and educate the entire community regarding academic integrity policies and procedures.
- Promulgate and rigorously practice these policies and procedures from the top down, and provide support to those who faithfully follow and uphold them.
- Have a clear, accessible, and equitable system to adjudicate suspected violations of policy.
- Develop programs to promote academic integrity among all segments of the campus community. These programs should go beyond repudiation of academic dishonesty and include discussions about the importance of academic integrity and its connection to broader ethical issues and concerns.
- Be alert to trends in higher education and technology affecting academic integrity on its campus.
- Assess regularly the effectiveness of its policies and procedures and take steps to improve and rejuvenate them.

(The Center for Academic Integrity. *Fundamental* 10)

Ten Principles of Academic Integrity for Faculty

- Affirm the importance of academic integrity.
- Foster a love of learning.
- Treat students as ends in themselves . . . deserving [of] individual attention and consideration.
- Foster an environment of trust in the classroom.
- Encourage student responsibility for academic integrity.
- Clarify expectations for students.
- Develop fair and relevant forms of assessment.
- Reduce opportunities to engage in academic dishonesty.
- Challenge academic dishonesty when it occurs.
- Help define and support campus-wide academic integrity standards.

(The Center for Academic Integrity. *Ten* 12)

Reprinted with permission. The Center for Academic Integrity is a consortium of approximately 200 colleges and universities and 500 individual students, faculty, and administrator members from those institutions. It was established in 1992 to identify and affirm the values of academic integrity and to promote their achievement in practice. <http://www.academicintegrity.org>

Reprinted with permission from Student Cheating and Plagiarism in the Internet Era: A Wake-Up Call *by Ann Lathrop and Kathleen Foss. Englewood, CO: Libraries Unlimited, 2000.*

Gathering Local Statistical Data

One of the first challenges is to make the extent and seriousness of student cheating and plagiarism evident to all. This can be done by providing current articles to read, statistical data to analyze, informed speakers to present facts and lead discussion groups, a publicity campaign that involves the entire community, etc. A survey of the entire school community can document the local situation with data that support the call for action.

The questionnaire below might be useful as a model for one part of the planning process; items for administrators, parents, and students should be added. The statements and results are from a survey of 356 high school teachers and 217 school board members conducted by Bushweller for *The American School Board Journal* in 1998. Some questions were asked of both groups; others of only one (n/a = not asked).

Survey of School Board Members and Teachers

	Agree with statement:	
	Teachers	*Board Members*
Student cheating is a problem in my school.	90%	n/a
Student cheating is a problem in my district.	n/a	37%
New technologies such as the Internet have made it easier for students to cheat.	n/a	50%
Increasing number of students are plagiarizing information off the Internet.	89%	n/a
Student cheating is more prevalent now than five years ago.	52%	24%
Parental pressure discourages teachers from penalizing cheaters.	67%	37%

(Bushweller. *Generation* 27, 28, 30)

Based on cheating data in the surveys reported in Chapters 4 and 6, school board members responding to these questions appear to have an overly optimistic view of cheating and plagiarism in schools today. Teachers see the problems as much more serious.

It is important that all of the groups involved be invited to suggest questions for the local survey. The four surveys in Chapter 4 can provide additional items for consideration.

Honor Code or Integrity Policy?

Instead of "Honor Code," the term "Academic Integrity Policy" is used throughout this book to indicate a policy developed by the entire school community and adopted officially by the school board. Such a policy will include, as a minimum:

- a strong statement in support of integrity and ethical behavior;
- a list of actions that are permissible and those that are not, with clear definitions of each;

- a procedure for adjudicating policy violations; and
- specific penalties to be assigned in each instance.

Other elements that might be considered come from Melendez' definition of an honor code as reported by McCabe, Trevino, and Butterfield:

> ... a policy that includes one or more of the following elements: a written pledge in which students affirm that their work will be or has been done honestly; the majority of the judiciary that hears alleged violations of academic dishonesty is comprised of students, or the chair of this group is a student; unproctored examinations; and a clause that places some degree of obligation on students to report incidents of cheating they learn about or observe. (213)

It is this last element, requiring students to report on their peers, that appears to be unacceptable to the majority of students in our schools today. Bushweller investigated students' attitudes toward honor codes as part of his 1998 research into high school cheating and found almost unanimous agreement among the students that they would not turn in another student for cheating. "It's one of those things you just don't do" (Bushweller. *Generation* 29).

One California high school teacher agrees that students strictly enforce their own code of silence. "When I cover Watergate in U.S. history classes, students vilify John Dean because he's the one who told. They think it's worse than anything else. When you talk about the moral issues and the consequences of being guilty through silence, they don't understand it" (Posnick-Goodwin. *Catching* 11).

Teachers and administrators can be reluctant to accept another element, that of allowing students to participate in hearings for students accused of violating the policy and in assigning penalties. Regardless of the outcome, students' opinions on this issue should be considered. The issues of unproctored examinations and student honesty pledges also need to be discussed by students, faculty, administrators, and school board members.

The policy should include specific mention of new technologies that are being used for cheating and plagiarism. Permissible uses of the Internet are addressed in the Acceptable Use Policy and should be included in the Academic Integrity Policy as well.

Full and open discussions of each proposed element of the Academic Integrity Policy should invite active participation from all groups. This is an essential requirement if the resulting policy is to be supported throughout the school community.

School Board, Administrative, and Faculty Leadership

The strong commitment of all school board members to ethics and integrity is a primary requirement for positive change. They can energize administrators, faculty, parents, and students to work on developing and implementing an effective Academic Integrity Policy.

It is important that the Academic Integrity Policy and any related policies be adopted by official action of the school board. This informs the entire school community that the district is determined to make honesty an integral part of its curriculum and value system.

Strong leadership on the part of district and school administrators is crucial to the successful implementation of an Academic Integrity Policy. Administrators and faculty must be perceived by the students as united on the policy. Some teachers can be reluctant to report cheating, or even to admit it happens in their classrooms, because they believe a good teacher would not have students who cheat. Other teachers can hesitate to accuse students of cheating or plagiarism for fear of administrative inaction or reprisals from students or parents.

When administrators and teachers ignore official procedures and respond to cheating incidents informally, frequently with little or no penalty, they undermine school-wide programs to reduce cheating in three ways:

- Students will be convinced that "the teachers don't care" and behave accordingly;
- Students with multiple offenses, but only one in each class, can go unpunished because each offense appears to be their only one; none is reported to a central monitor who would note a pattern of repeat offenses; and
- Inaccurately low statistics on cheating will create a false sense of "all is OK."

Administrators can speak to these concerns in faculty meetings or in discussions with individual teachers. The important result is a willingness of the entire faculty to adhere uniformly to the Academic Integrity Policy. They must convince students by their actions that there is "zero tolerance" for cheating and plagiarism.

> At most Connecticut high schools, carrying a Swiss army knife in a backpack is grounds for expulsion. Smoking a cigarette can carry the same punishment as possession of heroin. Sexual harassment, absenteeism and tardiness are all covered in student handbooks. Yet students are cheating every day to get better grades, and very little is done about it . . . "zero tolerance" weapons policies were designed to send an absolutely clear message that violence would not be tolerated in school. A tolerance for cheating shows young people that it is an appropriate way to get what you want . . . (Stansbury. *Popular,* pars. 5–8, 14)

Once the policy has been adopted by the school board and implemented throughout the district, it should be reviewed periodically. A committee of students, faculty, administrators, school board members, and parents can assess how well the policy is meeting the desired goals and make any appropriate changes. The Center for Academic Integrity (Chapter 7) is developing assessment tools with "guidelines that will allow an institution to assess the effectiveness of the efforts of each of its major constituents . . . to promote academic integrity" (McCabe and Drinan B7). When available, these guidelines can be helpful to schools and districts in strengthening their Academic Integrity Policy.

Student Leadership

It is essential that all students, and especially those in student government, participate actively in the development of the Academic Integrity Policy. The proposed policy should be debated in student government sessions and through letters in the student newspaper. Making sure students' opinions are reflected in the final document can build the student support necessary for successful implementation.

> Finally, changing the campus culture requires that students be involved from the outset. Interestingly, inspiration and initiatives for reform often come from good students who are fed up with competing at a disadvantage. Students should participate in formulating academic integrity codes, educating their peers, helping proctor exams, and serving as members of judicial boards on cases of alleged academic dishonesty. They must be partners with faculty if a new norm of academic integrity is to move from intention to reality. (Alschuler and Blimling 125)

Following adoption of the policy, students should have a meaningful role in confronting their peers who cheat or plagiarize. Student courts or combined student–faculty courts can adjudicate a variety of student offenses.

> It also is essential that students be involved in developing and carrying out systems to promote academic integrity. Failure to involve students creates an "us vs. them" atmosphere, which tends to promote cheating. Students can serve on honor or disciplinary boards and on review committees that assess how well an institution's process for assuring academic integrity is working. (Kibler B2)

The student newspaper can publicize the new Academic Integrity Policy and report periodically on instances of student dishonesty. No names would be used and no attention drawn to specific cases. Simply listing the types of cases and the penalties once each quarter or semester reminds students, faculty, and parents that cheating is taken seriously.

Student involvement in implementation of the policy, and their acceptance of it as reasonable and appropriate for their campus, can make a significant difference in student attitudes toward cheating.

> Although honor codes appeared to be a major influence in reducing cheating among students, McCabe and Trevino concluded that a more significant influence was the student culture that developed on campus concerning the question of cheating—whether it was considered socially acceptable, whether students felt they had primary responsibility for controlling cheating or whether the faculty and/or administration did, what their peers thought about the issue, and how their peers behaved . . . perhaps the most significant element of any strategy designed to create a positive peer culture on a campus is the ability to create a shared understanding and acceptance of the institution's policies on academic integrity among both faculty and students. (McCabe and Pavela 98)

Acceptable Use Policies

Closely related to the Academic Integrity Policy, or perhaps one component of it, is the Acceptable Use Policy. Many schools today require that students and parents sign such an agreement listing acceptable student uses of school computers and of any Internet access provided by the school.

The Acceptable Use Policy can be expanded to cover permissible uses of school computer labs, reference databases on CD-ROM, etc. Any use of school technology for cheating and plagiarism can be prohibited explicitly. Term paper sites can be included in the list of inappropriate Internet sites declared "off limits" for students. The policy should deal with Internet access in three situations:

- at school, in classrooms, labs, library;
- at home, using a school password to access electronic databases and other reference tools; and
- at home, using an individual or family password.

Admittedly, the school cannot control this third use, but including it in the policy alerts parents to the potential problem. Because many students regard everything on the Internet as being fair to copy, it is important that the policy explicitly forbid home as well as school use of the Internet for plagiarism.

Fair Enforcement and an Ethical School Culture

"The campus culture must be one that values integrity and encourages all campus constituencies to accept mutual responsibility for issues of academic integrity on campus" (McCabe. *Faculty* 656). Anything less than this commitment to mutual responsibility can make an Academic Integrity Policy powerless and ineffectual. Yet some educators can be reluctant to implement the new policy fairly and fully.

Teachers' effectiveness in dealing with cheating can be compromised by the fact that educators usually were good students themselves and probably didn't cheat in school. They know that some cheating probably occurs in their school but generally are unaware of how widespread it is, the frequency of cheating by individual students, or the variety of cheating techniques used in their classes. Unfortunately, some teachers choose to ignore cheating and thereby confirm their students' opinions that teachers don't care about cheating.

> Those who refrain from discussing the importance of academic integrity, or look the other way when students engage in academic dishonesty, alienate honest students and foster a climate of moral cynicism on campus. (McCabe and Pavela 101)

Administrators can be concerned that acknowledging the level of cheating will show the institution and its administration in an unfavorable light. They can hesitate to insist that teachers report all cheating incidents because they do not want to deal with irate parents or lawyers. Any lack of full enforcement by administrators undermines the Academic Integrity Policy and can result in even more cheating.

Favoritism and influence can result in selective enforcement of the rules against cheating and plagiarism, depending upon which students have been caught. In other cases, teachers or administrators can agree to adjust a grade for one student but not for another who appears to have an equally good reason to request a change. Such unfairness can be perceived by students as a form of dishonesty by the adults.

Any of these factors make it difficult to establish and maintain an ethical school culture. Administrators and faculty have a responsibility to make it clear that any unfair or dishonest action by an administrator, teacher, or student is unacceptable. Students and parents must be convinced that enforcement will be equitable for all.

> Preserving academic integrity is a collective responsibility involving students, faculty, and the administration. . . . Those institutions that have nurtured an environment characterized by a genuine care for students should have a minimum of cheating incidents. In addition, a well-developed plan will minimize the prospect of litigation and maximize fairness to all concerned. (Raffetto 27)

Writers and scholars recommend that schools infuse the curriculum with a strong emphasis on character education. Often one or two strong administrators or teachers take the lead in making this happen. Stephen Falcone described what one administrator is accomplishing in his doctoral dissertation, "A Comparative Case Study of the Ethical Functioning of a Public and Catholic High School." The Copy-Me page that follows is a recent summary, based on his dissertation, of the impact one principal had on his school. It can be used in faculty discussions of ways to work toward a more ethical school culture.

Publicizing the Academic Integrity Policy

All students and parents in the district should receive a copy of the Academic Integrity Policy each year. One way to accomplish this is to publish it in the student handbook mailed to all parents each fall. In schools where teachers are required to write an annual Classroom Management Plan, the policy can be included in the portion of the plan that parents are asked to sign.

Students in high school and middle school, and perhaps in elementary school, can be required to sign an integrity statement that is based on the policy and appropriate to their grade level. A parent also signs the policy and returns it. This makes students and parents fully aware of procedures and penalties.

The Academic Integrity Policy can be publicized at each school and throughout the entire community. Suggested publicity ideas include:

- Discuss the official policy against cheating and plagiarism during the first week of classes.
- Ask students to write in their own words about what the policy means.
- Organize debates on the ethics of cheating or plagiarism with a focus on moving students beyond the "it's OK if you don't get caught" concept of cheating.
- Discuss the policy at parent meetings, Back-to-School Nights, and at meetings of community service clubs.
- Post the policy in classrooms near a clock or bell schedule, in computer labs and near other computers throughout the school, in the library, in the counseling office, in the cafeteria and gym, and other areas of the school as appropriate.
- Discuss the policy in the student newspaper and in parent newsletters.
- Post a copy of the policy on district and school Web pages.
- Publicize the policy in local newspapers and on television and radio stations.
- Include the statement defining plagiarism in the student writing handbook.

COPY ME:
One Principal's Commitment to Ethics
Stephen V. Falcone

Mr. Public High School is a principal fully committed to establishing an ethical culture at his high school. His philosophy includes creating a caring community, establishing a system of justice based on democratic principles, and serving all 600 of his students—those enfranchised and those "on the outs."

Mr. Public consistently delivers a message that promotes interdisciplinary instruction, teacher/student advisory groups, personalized learning, and democratic governance. He has established a communitarian mission within an often complex and divisive democratic process. It can appear that this public school does not have a normative orientation—but it does—one grounded in the principles of democracy.

Random Advisory Councils

Ten to twelve students are selected randomly by Mr. Public to meet with him for an informal discussion of school issues every two weeks. No agenda is provided and students are limited only in that they cannot talk about a specific person if that person is not present; teachers can not be critiqued. This is an effective way to gather student opinion, meet with students he might not otherwise have the chance to see, and personalize the school experience for all involved.

Faculty Random Advisory Councils

A similar program for faculty, also randomly selected, is hosted by Mr. Public every two weeks. Teachers meet across disciplines to break departmental isolation common in high schools.

Ethics Class (elective)

Students in a recent Ethics class pursued the creation of an honor code for the school. Their concern was in response to a perceived increase in cheating at the school and to a recent accreditation report that had raised the issue. Class dialog led to this effort; it was supported by Mr. Public and the faculty.

Humanities Class (senior requirement)

Humanities is a team-taught interdisciplinary course focusing on the nature of truth, goodness, and beauty. Mr. Public is one of the lead instructors. Students actively participate in class discussions, maintain journals, and write papers. It is one of the few "untracked" courses, so students of varying abilities work together. The course gives all seniors a common intellectual experience, one that addresses universal issues.

Mastery Project (required)

All students complete an in-depth research "mastery project" in cooperation with a faculty mentor. This year-long project must reflect one of the themes developed in the four-year literature program but can focus on any related discipline, e.g., science, history, etc. Each student completes an original research project and presents it in the medium of his or her choice. The finished products of their mastery projects are displayed at an annual community open house.

Reprinted with permission from Student Cheating and Plagiarism in the Internet Era: A Wake-Up Call *by Ann Lathrop and Kathleen Foss. Englewood, CO: Libraries Unlimited, 2000.*

Activities to Inhibit Cheating Behavior

Mr. Public facilitates these personal connections and student investment in projects and coursework as a way to positively influence the school culture. Developing a culture that promotes cooperation, collaboration, and openness can limit students' proclivity toward academic or personal dishonesty.

To the degree that teachers in and across departments share students' writing, coordinate testing times, and compare assignments, incidents of cheating decrease. Also, the degree to which students' work is more public, as at the community open house, can make students more cautious and less apt to pass off another's work as their own.

[Printed with permission of the author. Based on: Falcone, S.V. (1999). "A Comparative Case Study of the Ethical Functioning of a Public and Catholic High School." Unpublished doctoral dissertation, University of Connecticut.]

Reprinted with permission from Student Cheating and Plagiarism in the Internet Era: A Wake-Up Call *by Ann Lathrop and Kathleen Foss. Englewood, CO: Libraries Unlimited, 2000.*

Working with New Students

New students entering at the beginning of a term or transferring from another school need an orientation. Students and parents should receive a copy of the Academic Integrity Policy and the accompanying agreement form to be signed. In addition, new student orientation could include the following:

- A meeting with a counselor for the student and parents to discuss the Academic Integrity Policy and answer any questions;
- A meeting with the librarian for an assessment of the student's information literacy and research skills, to reinforce ethical issues during the research process, and to assist in helping students evaluate appropriate materials;
- Occasional after school or Saturday sessions for students who received poor preparation at lower grade levels in other districts and lack the skills to research and write reports and term papers;
- A "student buddy" to introduce the student to the school and explain the seriousness with which the school treats cheating and plagiarism; and
- Monthly "new student" orientation meetings that include a discussion of the Academic Integrity Policy.

Academic Integrity Policies and Honor Codes Online

These school policies are available online. The excerpts from each policy printed here come from the online text and were selected to highlight different areas of emphasis. Some policies are relatively brief and general; others cover several pages with specific and increasingly serious penalties for first, second, or third violations. Plagiarism and cheating are defined briefly in some policies and in great detail in others.

It is interesting to notice variations in the titles: eight have *honor, ethics,* or *integrity* in the title; six use *cheating, dishonesty,* or *misconduct;* and two combine one term from each group. One policy uses simply the word *"Discipline."* The policies vary from encouragement of honest behavior to a focus on defining dishonest behavior and penalties.

Middle Schools

Blocker Middle School (TX): Honor Code and Academic Dishonesty

<http://www.texascity.isd.tenet.edu/academic.html>

"Honor Code: Blocker Middle School expects and encourages all students to contribute to an atmosphere of academic integrity. The code states that all students will be honest in all of their academic activities and will not tolerate dishonesty.

Academic dishonesty includes cheating or copying the work of another student, plagiarism, and unauthorized communication between students during an examination. The determination that a student has engaged in academic dishonesty shall be based on the judgment of the classroom teacher or other supervising professional employee, taking into consideration written materials, observation, or information from students. Students found to have engaged in academic dishonesty shall be subject to disciplinary penalties as well as academic penalties."

H. E. Huntington Middle School (CA): Cheating Policy
<http://www.san-marino.k12.ca.us/~heh/binderreminder/cheatpolic.html>
"The goal of our discipline program is to promote responsible decision making, respect for other people and property, and pride in appropriate behavior. A key to successful discipline is communication and teamwork between the home and school. Student behavior must always demonstrate respect, promote safety, and be appropriate for school.

We seek to provide positive reinforcement to encourage appropriate student actions. We have programs such as the Outstanding Citizens breakfast in order to recognize and support those students who do make good choices. In spite of our efforts, sometimes rules are broken. When this happens, it is our desire to include parent support in mutually guiding the student so that the inappropriate behavior is not repeated. The goal is integrity."

St. Patricks School (NY): Discipline
<http://www.stpatrick-school.org/Discipline/discipline.html>
"The primary right and duty of education rests on the parents. When you send your child to school, you are delegating some of your teaching authority to the school. Parents must, while their child is in school, support the authority of the school and be alert to see that this authority is not abused. . . . The ultimate goal of learning is self-discipline, a sense of responsibility, and self-direction. Helping the student grow in these areas should be the constant aim of both parents and teachers."

Webb School of Knoxville (TN): Middle School Honor Code
<http://www.webbschool.org/info/enrollment/Honor.html>
"Middle School students are expected to live by this code: 'I will not lie, cheat or steal.' Students who see the Code being violated should report it to a teacher or administrator. Teachers are required to report infractions to the administration. . . . Students are expected to write the words 'I pledge' on all papers, tests, and quizzes, signifying that unauthorized aid was neither given nor received on the assignment."

Students, parents and faculty members sign the reaffirmation pledge annually.

High Schools

Citizens' High School (FL): CHS Honor System
<http://www.citizenschool.com/40.html#honor>
"A high sense of personal honor and integrity is imperative in the completion of Citizens' courses. . . . Although students may receive help from others in preparing for exams, all exams must be done without cheating or plagiarizing. Students might discuss any of the lesson material with others, but the actual responses on work submitted to the school must be the student's own."

El Toro High School (CA): Ethics and Cheating Policy
<http://www.svusd.k12.ca.us/schools/eths/ethcspol.htm>
"All tests, quizzes, reports, assignments, and any school related test (SAT, PSAT, etc.) are subject to this policy. . . . Students who violate the Ethics and Cheating Policy while taking major national examinations, such as SAT, PSAT, etc., will be removed from any and all elected leadership positions for the remainder of the school year."

Langley High School (VA): Honor Code
<http://www.fcps.k12.va.us/LangleyHS/saxon/honor.html>
"The honor code of Langley High School addresses cheating, plagiarizing, lying, and stealing. Parents will:

- Have knowledge of the Langley High School Honor Code and its consequences.
- Provide a positive example for adhering to the Honor Code.
- Support faculty and administration in enforcing the Honor Code."

Providence High School (CA): Academic Dishonesty
<http://www.providencehigh.org/hb/hb.htm>
"Honesty is primarily the responsibility of each student. Providence High School considers cheating to be a voluntary act for which there might be reasons, but for which there is no acceptable excuse."

Webb School of Knoxville (TN): Upper School Honor Code and Procedures
<http://www.webbschool.org/info/enrollment/Honor.html>
"Lying, cheating (including plagiarism) and stealing are Honor Code violations. Every faculty member must, and parents and students should, when aware of an Honor Code infraction, report it to the Honor Committee or to a faculty member. Cases are investigated and heard by a committee of Upper School students, working with three faculty advisors.

After acceptance and before official enrollment, all Webb students and their parents must sign brief statements affirming their understanding of and adherence to the Honor System and Honor Code. Students, parents and faculty members sign the reaffirmation pledge annually."

West Springfield High School (VA): Honor Code
<http://www.wshs.fcps.k12.va.us/info/hcode.htm>
"The honor code obligates students to neither give nor receive aid on any examination, test, quiz, or other specified assignments. The honor code is explained by teachers in their policies and procedures statements distributed in writing at the beginning of school."

Universities and Colleges

Queen's University (Kingston, Ontario, Canada): Policy on Academic Dishonesty
<http://www.queensu.ca/secretariat/senate/policies/acaddish.html>
"Academic dishonesty includes plagiarism as well as any deliberate attempt to gain advantage. . . . Plagiarism should be distinguished from cooperation and collaboration. Often, students can be permitted or expected to work on assignments collectively, and to present the results either collectively or separately. This is not a problem so long as it is clearly understood whose work is being presented, for example, by way of formal acknowledgment or by footnoting."

State University of West Georgia: Cheating and Plagiarism
<http://www.westga.edu/~vpaa/handbook/207.html>
"Just as complete honesty should be the Professor's standard in his or her presentation of material, this same standard should be demanded from students when they respond for purpose of evaluation through tests, reports, projects, and term papers. Every professor has the responsibility to inculcate in students the ideal of academic honesty and to take all practical precautions against its violation."

University of Arizona: Code of Academic Integrity
<http://w3.arizona.edu/~uhap/appendg.html>

"Students engaging in academic dishonesty diminish their education and bring discredit to the academic community. . . . Failure of faculty to prevent cheating does not excuse students from compliance with the Code."

University of Kansas: Academic Misconduct
<http://www.cc.ukans.edu/cwis/units/safacts/codes.html#AcademicMisconduct>

"Academic misconduct by a student shall include, but not be limited to, disruption of classes; threatening an instructor or fellow student in an academic setting; giving or receiving of unauthorized aid on examinations or in the preparation of notebooks, themes, reports or other assignments; knowingly misrepresenting the source of any academic work; unauthorized changing of grades; unauthorized use of University approvals or forging of signatures; falsification of research results; plagiarizing of another's work; violation of regulations or ethical codes for the treatment of human and animal subjects; or otherwise acting dishonestly in research."

University of Maryland, College Park: Code of Academic Integrity
<http://www.inform.umd.edu/JPO/AcInteg/code_acinteg2a.html>

"Apathy or acquiescence in the presence of academic dishonesty is not a neutral act. Histories of institutions demonstrate that a laissez-faire response will reinforce, perpetuate, and enlarge the scope of such misconduct. Institutional reputations for academic dishonesty are regrettable aspects of modern education. These reputations become self-fulfilling and grow, unless vigorously challenged by students and faculty alike. All members of the University community, students, faculty, and staff share the responsibility and authority to challenge and make known acts of apparent academic dishonesty."

University of Virginia: The Honor System
<http://www.virginia.edu/%7eregist/ugradrec/chapter5/uchap5-3.2.html>

"University of Virginia students have entered into an agreement, embodied in the Honor System, that they shall not tolerate lying, cheating, or stealing from their fellow students. . . . Students are thus presumed to be honorable unless their actions prove otherwise. Students who violate this spirit of mutual trust have committed an offense against the community. Hence, their continued residence at the University would undermine the basis of this community that holds that personal fulfillment is best achieved in an atmosphere where only honest means are used to achieve any ends."

University of Washington (WA) College of Engineering: Academic Misconduct
<http://www.ee.washington.edu/undergrad/handbook/misconduct.html>

"Academic misconduct or violation of Engineering Ethics is unacceptable in the practice of engineering. . . . The College expects you to behave in a mature manner and to be responsible for your own actions. The College does not accept excuses for misconduct and will prosecute all allegations of misconduct according to the procedures outlined."

One High School's Academic Honesty Code

The policy on pages 109–111 was developed by the faculty with support from the administration and approved by the Faculty Forum at Los Alamitos High School (Los Alamitos, CA) in December 1997. It would be strengthened substantially by school board action making it an official district policy.

Pointers

Student attitudes toward reporting cheating by their peers are reported in Chapter 4. The important role of parents in the development and implementation of an Academic Integrity Policy is discussed in Chapter 6. Chapters 9 and 10 focus on two essential elements of the Academic Integrity Policy, defining cheating and plagiarism for students and dealing with student dishonesty.

Academic Honesty Code—Los Alamitos High School

Los Alamitos High School requires all students to demonstrate honesty and to abide by ethical standards in preparing and presenting materials, as well as in testing situations. Grades should reflect the student's own work in the fairest possible way. Academic dishonesty, cheating, or plagiarism involves an attempt by the student to show possession of a level of knowledge or skill that he or she does not possess. It involves any attempt of a student to substitute the product of another, in whole or in part, as his or her own work. It also includes theft, possession, or unauthorized use of any answer key or model answers.

Violation of the Los Alamitos High School Academic Honesty Code will be subject to disciplinary action up to and including: suspension, dismissal from student offices and all athletics and extracurricular activities, involuntary transfer, and expulsion. This policy covers all school-related tests, quizzes, reports, class assignments, and projects, both in and out of class.

CHEATING

Cheating includes but is not necessarily limited to:

Copying/Sharing Assignments

- Copying or giving an assignment to a student to be copied, unless specifically permitted or required by the teacher

Plagiarism

- Plagiarism* or submission of any work that is not the student's own
- Submission or use of falsified data or records

Cheating on Exams or on Major Projects

- Use of unauthorized material including textbooks, notes, calculators, or computer programs during an examination or on a major project
- Supplying or communicating in any way unauthorized material including textbooks, notes, calculators, or computer programs during an examination or on a major project

Forgery/Stealing

- Unauthorized access to an exam or answers to exam
- Use of an alternate, stand-in or proxy during an examination
- Alteration of computer and/or gradebook records or forgery of signatures for the purpose of academic advantage
- Sabotaging or destroying the work of others

*Plagiarism: "Plagiarism" is the "act of appropriating the literary composition of another, or parts or passages of his writings, or the ideas or language of the same, and passing them off as the product of one's own mind." It involves "the use of any outside source without proper acknowledgment." In the academic setting, an "outside source" includes "any work, published or unpublished, by a person other than the student." *(continued)*

Note: The following could be given to students or posted in classrooms to clarify the cheating policy.

You Are Cheating If You:

- Copy, fax, duplicate, or transmit using any technology, assignments that will each be turned in as "original" work.
- Exchange assignments by printout, disk transfer, modem, or other electronic or recorded means, then submit it as "original" work.
- Write formulas, codes, key words on your person or objects for use in a test.
- Use hidden reference sheets during a test.
- Use programmed material in watches, calculators, or computer programs when prohibited.
- Exchange answers with others (either give or receive answers).
- Submit someone else's assignment as your own, in whole or part.
- Submit material (written or designed by someone else) without giving the author/artist name and/or source (e.g., plagiarizing or submitting work done by family, friends, or tutors).
- Take credit for group work when little contribution was made.
- Do not follow additional specific guidelines on cheating as established by a department, class or teacher.
- Steal tests, answers, or materials, or have unauthorized possession of such materials.
- Sabotage or destroy the work of others.

METHODS OF HANDLING CHEATING

1. There must be clear objective evidence of cheating for this policy to be used. There must be NO REASONABLE DOUBT.
2. In cases of observance of cheating, clearly document student behavior on referral form. If there is reasonable suspicion of cheating but no physical evidence, teachers can opt to re-test the student(s) under different conditions.
3. When you obtain evidence of possible violation of the policy, it must be stapled to the referral and sent to the counselor as soon as possible. If there is any doubt concerning the potential offense, contact an administrator immediately for assistance in investigation of the matter.
4. If the evidence is on the body, you are to detain the student and send to the office for a counselor or administrator to escort the student to the office for second verification of the cheating. Turn in the referral with all facts stated.

(continued)

FOR STAFF USE ONLY

*Guidelines**

The range of consequences allows for flexibility given the severity of the offense. Some or all of the options can be exercised.

Type/Level of Offense	Range of Consequences	
	Less Severe	**More Severe****
Copying/Sharing Assignment	• '0' on Assignment	• '0' on assignment • Parent Notification
Plagiarism or Cheating On Exams or Major Projects	• '0' on assignment or loss of One Grade Pt. • Parent Notification • Teacher Issued Suspension or Referral to Admin. for Saturday School	• '0' on assignment or loss of One Grade Pt. • Parent Notification • Referral to Admin. (Suspension) • Dismissal from Student Office, Athletics, and Extracurricular Activities
Stealing/Forgery	**Referral to Administration** • Suspension • "U" in Citizenship • Dismissal from Student Office, Athletics, and Extracurricular Activities	• Involuntary Transfer • Expulsion

* The options listed above are intended as guidelines for the purpose of consistency in enforcement of consequences. If a violation appears to warrant consequences beyond the range listed, confer with an administrator.

** Repeat offenses need to be referred to administration.

Honor Codes: Teaching Integrity and Interdependence

Lewis Cobbs

When they work properly, honor systems function as much more than mere means of identifying and punishing cheaters. . . .

Halfway through his senior year, Greg is not sure he wants to complete his precollegiate education at the competitive independent school he entered as a kindergartner. With the backing of several of his classmates, Greg recently reported four of his peers for cheating. The results of the test in question appeared to corroborate the allegation. When confronted, however, the accused students denied the charge; judged guilty and suspended by a disciplinary committee of students and teachers, they threatened the school with legal action. And when the headmaster still refused to alter the decision, the offenders and their parents offered to "plea bargain" the case. What mattered most to them, it seemed, was not the original question of academic honesty or even the larger issues of character, but rather the possible repercussions of any action on college-admission decisions.

The case stirred controversy among the school's students. A disturbingly common ethic among adolescents dictated the response of many. According to this outlook—which might be called the "Milli Vanilli syndrome"—the ends of personal gain or fame justify means perceived as questionable only because risky; the offenders in the cheating episode deserved to be punished not so much because they did something wrong as because they were caught. And although a sizable contingent supported Greg, an equally large number felt that, by violating the immemorial code among young people against "ratting," he had committed a more grievous offense than the cheaters.

Greg's own distress resulted less from the isolation and bullying he has had to endure than from disillusionment with his peers' values and frustration with the school's inability to respond quickly and decisively to such situations. Ironically, in a year when the school had suspended its long-dormant honor system for review, these events underlined the usefulness of just such a guideline as a vital element in moral education.

In deference to the cultural diversity of their student bodies and the moral relativism of the times, most public schools and many nonparochial private schools forgo explicit efforts to teach values. If they address ethical issues at all, they are more likely to do so in a format that, without advocating any values as "right," exposes students to different sets of beliefs, or teaches ways of analyzing moral questions and defending alternative resolutions.

To the ears of many, the term "honor" itself sounds archaic, and the designation "honor code" connotes an elitist, vaguely militaristic outlook that is long outmoded and better left dead and buried, like the hero of a lost cause. But the principles of academic honesty defy cultural boundaries and historical eras. Beyond providing a means of enforcing academic accountability, honor systems can foster in students respect for ideas, for classmates and teachers, and for themselves; they can teach integrity.

The proposition of honor codes is clear and elegant: That ideas belong to those who create and articulate them; that to submit work that is not one's own is to insult the efforts of one's peers; that to claim the thoughts or words of another as one's own is to steal from the originator and to deceive those to whom the material is presented; that to cheat or lie or steal—ideas or property—is to degrade oneself.

And just as important, honor systems clarify and reinforce the practice of community: Students learn that responsibility for maintaining values shared by a group must lie with each of its members, and that violations undercut trust not just in the offender but among all those connected with the school. When they work properly, the systems function as much more than mere means of identifying and punishing cheaters; they become methods of education in human interdependence.

Indeed, because schools cannot assume any sort of shared ethic among their entering students, honor codes must take education, in all senses of the word, as their first charge. For many young people, participation in an honor system will initially be based on compulsion rather than choice: Whether or not they have selected the school they attend, it imposes its standards on them. Explanation of attitudes that can be new to many must be unambiguous and convincing, enforcement consistent.

And from the start, students must teach students. Even in schools with active honor systems, the commonplace adversarial attitude of young people toward teachers prevails when students' voices are subordinated to adults'—and teenagers perceive the system as simply one more weapon for repressing their individuality. To see why they should accept an honor code, students must be directly involved in its operation.

The steps by which honor systems are instituted and run should mirror these principles of education and student involvement. Primary responsibility for teaching the values of academic honesty and reviewing violations typically rests with a committee consisting of students elected by their peers and teachers appointed by the school head. Students constitute a majority and the committee is chaired by a student. The faculty membership guides and counsels; it shares the accumulated experience of the school and of individual adults but does not dictate decisions.

Teaching should occur regularly in large-group (grade level or entire student body) and small-group (homeroom or advisee cluster) meetings. Student members of the honor committee lead all sessions with the presence and support of teachers. Although the frequency of such meetings will vary depending on the needs of the school, they should take place, if at no other times, during the opening days of the term and during examination weeks or other periods of heavy testing.

In addition, honor committees can publicly announce and explain briefly any actions they have taken. The purpose of this step is to educate students about the nature and gravity of acts that might be considered honor offenses, not further to punish or humiliate guilty parties. To protect the latter, their names can and should be withheld, and the announcements made on a regularly scheduled (monthly or quarterly), rather than an ad hoc basis.

At appropriate times during the year—for instance, as a class begins work on a research paper—teachers review particular points of the code as they apply to the task at hand. On each written assignment, students pledge that they have neither given nor received assistance.

Beyond their strictures against cheating, lying, and stealing, honor codes can require students to report offenses they witness. Such a provision, at which even some of the most zealous of a system's student supporters might balk, is virtually impossible to enforce. There is no sadder testimony to the narcissistic relativism of the times than the common rationalization among students that "it's up to them to catch us; why should we turn each other in if teachers don't see what's going on?" And even the best intentioned of young people will often hesitate to report a violation when one consequence will be ostracism. Moral courage is just as rare among adolescents as it is among adults—and its absence more easily forgiven.

But even as schools concede that many students who respect the honor system will nonetheless falter on this point, they should also recognize its symbolic importance: No other component of the code can suggest so clearly that academic honor is a set of values fostered within and among individuals, rather than a disciplinary regimen imposed from without. If an honor system is to be the foundation for a self-regulating community of trust, the willingness of students to participate in its sometimes painful responsibilities is crucial.

Even the most effective honor system will not eliminate cheating or lying, nor will it obviate the need for vigilance by faculty members. This approach's emphasis on education, after all, rests on the premise that lapses are likely and that growth is nourished by experience and instruction. But with the moral guidance imparted by honor systems, young people can gain an understanding vital to their flowering as adults: That the good of others—as individuals or as group—is also their own good.

[Reprinted with permission of the author and publisher from *Education Week,* Volume 10 Number 28 April 3, 1991.]

Chapter 9

Defining Cheating and Plagiarism for Students

> *Students lack a basic reference point for ethical academic be-*
> *havior. Too often learning and the evaluation of that learn-*
> *ing—namely grading—are considered one rather than two distinct*
> *processes. For some students, getting the grade becomes the goal,*
> *and they might see any behavior as appropriate which results in*
> *good grades. Thus, lacking clear guidance from faculty and con-*
> *fused about the goal of education, students do not know what consti-*
> *tutes academic dishonesty.* (Peterson 169)

Chapter Overview

Simple definitions of cheating and plagiarism are important to help students develop a very clear understanding of what is and is not permissible. Copyright issues and the permissible use of writing centers or private tutors can impact student understanding of cheating and plagiarism. Student discussion is sparked by two Copy-Me pages, "Are Any of These Cheating?" and "Are Any of These Plagiarizing?" The issue of collaboration is explored with a Copy-Me page, "When Is Collaboration OK?" Students who are learning English as a new language might have difficulty understanding the concept of plagiarism; this is addressed in the article by Lenora Thompson and Portia Williams.

Chapter subheadings:

- Learning to Recognize Cheating and Plagiarism
- Permissible Collaboration
- Ethical Use of Writing Centers and Private Tutors
- Copyright Issues
- Explaining Collaboration and Plagiarism to Students from Other Cultures

115

- Copy Me: "When Is Collaboration OK?"
- Copy Me: "Are Any of These Cheating?"
- Copy Me: "Are Any of These Plagiarizing?"
- Thompson and Williams: "But I Changed Three Words! Plagiarism in the ESL Classroom"

Learning to Recognize Cheating and Plagiarism

> **Cheat:** the act or action of cheating or fraudulently deceiving; to practice fraud or trickery; to violate rules dishonestly. (*Webster's Third New International Dictionary of the English Language, Unabridged*, p. 381)

Try using this simple working definition: "If you had any help that you don't want your teacher or parents to know about, you probably cheated." Cheating can be explained to students as copying someone else's work on a test or assignment, sneaking a look at a cheat sheet for answers during a test, or claiming someone else's lab data, research, or other work as their own.

> **Plagiarize:** to steal and pass off as one's own (the ideas or words of another); use (a created production) without crediting the source; to commit literary theft; present as new and original an idea or product derived from an existing source. (*Webster's Third New International Dictionary of the English Language, Unabridged*, p. 1728)

A simple working definition for plagiarism might be, "If you didn't think of it and write it all on your own, and you didn't cite (or write down) the sources where you found the ideas or the words, it's probably plagiarism." Students are plagiarizing if they use someone else's words or ideas and present them as their own.

Clear definitions of cheating and plagiarism, and the associated penalties, should be included in the Academic Integrity Policy adopted by the school board (Chapter 8). The policy should make specific reference to cheating with high-tech devices and to plagiarizing from the Internet.

It is important that teachers explain the section on cheating and plagiarism in the Academic Integrity Policy to students in language appropriate to their grade level. Older students can read and discuss the entire policy. As part of these discussions, each teacher will make a clear distinction between cheating and permissible collaboration. Definitions and examples of plagiarism should be included in the student writing handbook.

Many students and parents are accustomed to signing an annual Acceptable Use Policy required for online access to the Internet (Chapter 8). This policy should prohibit any use of the Internet for electronic plagiarism and include an honesty pledge signed by students that they will neither cheat nor plagiarize. Parents can sign a pledge agreeing to support the school and district in efforts to prevent cheating and plagiarizing.

It is important to bring the issues of plagiarism and copying into the open. Students can discuss their past experiences as a prelude to setting and accepting new standards of honesty:

> Students are much less defensive and more open to training when as a class we discuss our common experiences with copying and not acknowledging sources. After such a discussion ranges over

why other teachers might not have discouraged plagiarism but why it is important to avoid it, my students ask questions about specific passages in their papers. They more willingly wrestle with the problems of determining what is not common knowledge and are relieved to learn the list of items that are always documented. They become concerned with paraphrasing properly instead of merely reshuffling phrases. (Dant 83)

In talking with his high school English class about plagiarism, Sterling and the students devised some tests for plagiarism:

One was to ask of any particular passage, "Who is making the point?" If you are making it and establishing the context of discussion, and if your source materials support and illustrate in a subordinate way, you're on track. A simple question: "Who wrote more words, you or the source?" If a quoted source makes the point and you don't incorporate or elaborate on it, you yourself haven't done anything but a copying exercise. I tell students I'm not teaching handwriting. . . . What began as a simple definition of terms and clarification of values expanded to two days of in-class discussion, followed by many hours of evaluation of written responses, of individual conferences, and of re-evaluation of revised papers. But it was time well spent. (pars. 6, 15)

Part of helping students learn to recognize and avoid plagiarism is teaching the specific skills required. These include (1) quoting with correct citations, (2) paraphrasing with integrity and documenting the source, and (3) extracting meaning and summarizing passages in their own words, again with credit to the source.

One question that arises is whether it is permissible to turn in the same, or almost the same, paper for two different classes. Most teachers consider this to be cheating or plagiarizing. It is an issue that should be addressed in the student writing handbook and in each class that requires reports or term papers. Whenever possible, all teachers at a school will agree to a uniform policy.

Serafin suggests two situations in which reworking an earlier paper might be an interesting assignment: "using a different statistical approach in analyzing the data collected from previous research," or "using conclusions from previous papers to lead to research topics for new papers" (Serafin. *About* 3). This would be acceptable only if the student presents an honest proposal to rework an earlier paper and the teacher agrees.

The "Are Any of These Cheating?" and "Are Any of These Plagiarizing?" Copy-Me pages later in this chapter can be discussed by teachers with their students or parents with their children. They could be discussion starters in faculty or parent meetings. Questions might include: "Is this wrong to do?" "Have you done this in the past year?" "Have you seen a friend or classmate doing this?" or "Did you tell your teacher when you saw it?" The Copy-Me pages are based largely on personal experience and conversations with colleagues. Articles by Aiken; Graber; Maramark and Maline; Raffetto; Serafin (*Academic*); and Singhal and Johnson provided additional ideas.

Permissible Collaboration

Student collaboration raises several difficult issues for faculty. Among the most difficult is the inherent conflict between the university's need to recognize collaborative work as a model that serves students well in their careers and lives, and the need to teach students to do their own, independent work. The conflict is heightened by the current generation of faculty having inherited an academic tradition of assigning individual grades that reflect individual accomplishment. (McCabe and Cole 4)

This conflict exists in K–12 education as well. Teachers need to help students learn to collaborate; it is a highly valued life skill. Teachers also need independent student work that allows them to assign an individual grade. Permissible collaboration should be clarified for students who are learning to collaborate and are expected to do so with honesty. The suggestions that follow are based on our own experience, suggestions from colleagues, and ideas from the article by McCabe and Cole.

Students must learn to differentiate what they do collaboratively from what they take credit for independently so teachers can assign a fair grade to each student.

- Design collaborative assignments so each student has a specific, identifiable task; students might be reluctant to tell a teacher when only one or two did all the work for a group.

- Students can turn in their research note cards, done in their own handwriting, to indicate the part of the project they completed.

- All students collaborating on a project can present their results as a panel discussion with each one describing the specific work individually accomplished.

- A collaborative group can write their own report of "who did what" in the project.

Teachers should make it quite clear what is "permitted" collaboration and what is "unpermitted," especially for homework assignments and lab reports.

- Specific guidelines should be in writing, should be discussed in class, and should be provided to the parents through the student handbook, class syllabus, or in some other written form.

- Be very certain that all students clearly understand the guidelines for collaboration in terms of the distinction between individual and group work.

Teachers within a school might set different standards for permissible collaboration, confusing students when permitted collaboration in one class is penalized as cheating by another teacher.

- Each teacher should state standards clearly at the beginning of the term.

- Clarification in written policies and class discussions is essential.

- Teachers who teach different sections of the same course can work together to develop models that clarify "permitted" and "unpermitted" collaboration for that course.

A high school teacher explains the issue of collaboration for his students by telling them: "What you need to be is very forthright: If you did [the work] with someone else, put both names on it. . . . If your name goes on it, then clearly you're the one that assumes responsibility for it." A principal in the same school asks teachers to clarify their policies for student collaboration: "The key is that students do their own work when they're turning something in, speak in their own voice, use their own language and their own knowledge" (Anderson, pars. 20–24).

In her research study on student collaboration, Peterson concluded that students frequently had difficulty understanding the difference between actually copying another student's work and working together on a project at the end of which the students hand in the same or very similar papers. She quotes a student who expressed some confusion about the ethics of the situation:

> Yes, if both participated in discovering/producing the answers, there should be no problem in both people claiming the work. Unless it was specifically stated that all work was to be [done] independently. This reasoning applies only to classes of this nature though, that is, classes in which material is learned. In classes where creative thought is involved, that is, English papers, creative writing, art, etc., then it would be wrong because two people cannot truly come up with [one] idea. (173)

A Copy-Me page later in this chapter addresses the question of "When Is Collaboration OK?" It can be used in classroom discussions to help students understand the types of collaboration that are permissible. Teachers might find it helpful in formulating a written school policy on collaboration or for clarifying parents' understanding of permissible collaboration.

Ethical Use of Writing Centers and Private Tutors

When is tutoring in a writing center or lab legitimately helping students to improve their writing and when does the amount of assistance become unfair? A closely related issue is how much help, and of what kind, it is fair for students to receive from individual tutors hired by their parents to help them improve their writing skills. Clear guidelines should be set to determine how writing center staff or a private tutor can provide needed help and still have the writing be the student's own work. Some of the questions to be addressed in the guidelines include:

- Should grammatical and spelling errors be pointed out?
- Should errors in interpretation or analysis be discussed?
- Should students be shown how to integrate direct quotes into their writing and cite their sources correctly?
- Should students be given practice learning to paraphrase?
- Should tutors suggest new questions to be considered or recommend additional references?
- Should tutors help with the proper organization and format of the bibliography?

The issue is whether a tutor, either in a lab or hired privately, should provide direct assistance that could improve a student's grade on a specific assignment. The teaching role is crossed when a skilled writer helps a less skilled student "write" a paper that would be well beyond the student's ability to do alone. Falcone described one case of a high school student who "dictated" his paper to a tutor hired by his parents; the tutor then wrote a paper that the student turned in as his own work. This clearly would be regarded as cheating (telephone interview).

Conway summarizes opinions from experts in the field regarding types of help considered to be acceptable: "questioning to help students arrive at their own meanings . . . exercises that are geared to build particular cognitive skills . . . modeling [and] teaching of specific content or form that the writer can incorporate in his text or writing process" (3).

> The writing lab is not a repair shop where broken papers get miraculously mended, without any sweat on the part of the student. The writing lab is a learning resource, a room full of teachers who have time, training, and inclination to guide students in improving their own writing processes. And we must allow these teachers to choose from a full range of strategies so they can effectively deal with any tutoring situation. (Conway 2–3)

Clark also recommends an active teaching role for writing center staff and expresses little concern about possible inappropriate help:

> Without excessive concern about plagiarism, writing center tutors would be able to experiment with imitation as a pedagogical method—showing students how to develop examples, write introductions, and vary sentence structure. Concerning the injunction against proofreading, I can see that at certain times it might be very helpful for a student, especially a foreign student, to observe how a tutor goes through a paper, noting and correcting errors, perhaps reading aloud to sense the melody of the prose or reading backwards to check for typos. Moreover, in this situation, it would not be unreasonable for the tutor to hold the pen and even use it occasionally to write on a student paper. With the student in attendance, the tutor could illustrate how text can be manipulated and moved, on the computer or with scissors and tape. Combing a text for one more example in a literary analysis, finding a model of a movie review in a newspaper—numerous writing techniques we have developed for ourselves can be acquired by students through the use of imitation and modeling. (10)

Parents and writing center staff can be questioned about a student's papers when those written outside the classroom are clearly superior to ones written during class time. The parents and the writing center staff need to know what levels and types of assistance are permitted and how much help is "too much."

A clear statement of school policy regarding the use of private tutors and writing centers can minimize such problems. It can be printed in the student writing handbook and published in parent newsletters.

Copyright Issues

A working rule of thumb is to treat every source as if it is copyrighted even when there is no copyright statement. *The Copyright Primer for Librarians and Educators* has a thorough discussion of copyright issues emphasizing library and educational applications. One section deals with the Internet and electronic databases:

> It is so easy to collect, compile, and modify information from the [Internet] searches that confusion concerning copyright is inevitable. . . . There are still users who believe that anything available over the Internet is fair game and public domain. They think that because the information is there and easy to manipulate, it has no copyright protection. Such is not the case. (Bruwelheide 85)

Information Power: Building Partnerships for Learning is an official publication of the American Association of School Librarians and the Association for Educational Communications and Technology. Principle 7 addresses legal and ethical issues related to plagiarism and copyright:

> As national and international groups draft and apply legal and ethical principles governing information access, intellectual property rights, and the responsible use of information technology, the learning community looks to the school library media program for guidance on these contemporary information concerns.
>
> By creating and communicating policies and procedures that reflect the highest legal and ethical standards, the school library media specialist leads in promoting the responsible use of information and information technology for learning. The school library media specialist fosters such use by modeling appropriate behavior and by collaborating with administrators and others to educate the school and local communities about the issues and about current national guidelines and district rules and interpretations.
>
> By providing intellectual and physical access to the full range of information, in a climate that invites learning, honors free inquiry, and respects legal and ethical principles regarding the uses of information and information technology, the program serves as a model for creative, effective, and responsible information use. (American 93–94)

Many students are convinced that all material on the Internet is free to copy. Stebelman's statement is a good discussion starter: "No difference exists between plagiarizing a printed essay and one that appears on the Web" (par. 5). Hardy makes a clear distinction between classroom use of online material and using it in a new publication:

> Fair use generally allows students and teachers to copy website material for use in their classrooms. But if they want to distribute the information—for example, by putting it on a web page—they are in effect publishing and must seek permission from the web

> site owner [and] if a school or a district wants to put a student's
> work on a web page, it needs to get permission from the student
> and his or her parents, if the student is under 18. (pars. 22, 25)

One difficulty students encounter when citing Internet sources is that expected elements of the citation might not be as obvious as they are in printed works, or can be missing entirely. Gresham explains that these elements, for example, title, author, volume, publication data, etc., might be harder to identify in electronic sources. The URL can present additional problems in citation due to its length and complexity, and to the fact that any given URL can change frequently. The copyright issue must be clarified for many students:

> In addition to the conceptual and physical differences of elec-
> tronic sources, confusion over the legal term "fair use," bandied
> about libraries and educational institutions, also contributes to in-
> cidents of plagiarism of Internet information. . . . Library users need
> to understand that information from the Internet is still a form of in-
> tellectual property, that ethical and legal conventions apply to elec-
> tronic information, and that the creation of a bibliographic citation
> for attribution of such information is possible. (49)

New editions of the American Psychological Association (APA) and Modern Language Association (MLA) style manuals have models for electronic citations. Several of the online sites dealing with plagiarism offer sample citations (Chapter 5). Students need specific instruction in learning to cite Internet sources correctly.

Copyright Basics, published by the United States Copyright Office, is available online at <http://lcweb.loc.gov/copyright/>. This eleven-page document defines "What Is Copyright?" and provides information on how to claim a copyright as well as how to register one. The Copyright Website at <http://www.benedict.com> is a nongovernmental site that "endeavors to provide real world, practical, and relevant copyright information." Both Web sites can provide useful information for students, teachers, and parents.

Explaining Collaboration and Plagiarism to Students from Other Cultures

Students new to American schools might have a very different perception of collaboration. Many have been taught that the greatest good is to work for the group and that it is selfish and wrong to refuse to share your work with others. These students often work together on class assignments and help anyone in the group who doesn't understand a concept. Many of their homework papers and reports have a very similar look and tone; the students have offered one another the expected assistance and see nothing wrong with the similarities.

These students often find the concept of plagiarism very difficult to understand. Some come from cultures where lessons are taught by having students repeat passages from important writers in the field. Copying the words of acknowledged authorities is viewed as being wise and appropriate, even an honor to the scholar whose work is being copied.

In the article following this chapter, Lenora Thompson and Portia Williams provide guidance to all teachers working with students who are learning English and coping with different instructional practices in our classrooms. Many of the suggestions in their article can be useful to any teacher trying to help students grasp the concepts of plagiarism.

Pointers

Electronic plagiarism and its detection are described in Chapters 3 and 5. Chapter 13 suggests ways to identify a plagiarized paper, addresses unintentional plagiarism, especially in the primary grades, and continues the discussion in an article following the chapter, "Dear Teacher, Johnny Copied." Lesson ideas in Chapter 15 cover topics that help students learn to recognize and avoid plagiarism.

COPY ME:
When Is Collaboration OK?

- Is it OK to form study groups and share notes, ask each other questions? What if some teachers prohibit study groups and others say study groups are fine?

- Can two or more students complete a lab assignment together? If this is OK, can they share their lab notes? Will their work be questioned if they report identical or almost identical data in their results?

- When a short, ungraded math homework assignment is required each day, is it fair for two students to take turns doing the problems and then copying from each other?

- Is it OK for students to review books together when there is an extensive list of assigned readings? What if one student in the group reads a specific assigned book or article and makes in-depth notes, then shares his notes and ideas with other students in the group who might not have read the book as carefully (if at all)? Is this collaboration or cheating?

- When students work together on a class presentation or report, how does the instructor assign a fair grade? How do the students identify the part of the presentation or report for which each is responsible?

- If the entire class has the same final assignment, are the students allowed to discuss the assignment among themselves? Is it OK to share resources they have located? What about sharing notes and drafts of their final report?

- Is it fair for a student to ask another student to read a paper and comment on it, suggest improvements, and perhaps edit the paper for grammar and spelling? What about help from a parent, tutor, or learning center?

COPY ME:
Are Any of These Cheating?

- copying someone else's homework
- copying someone else's assignment or report
- working on homework with one or two friends and then all handing in the same answers, essays, etc.
- working with one or more friends on homework or an assignment when the teacher told you to do the work independently
- copying another student's answers on a test
- letting someone copy answers from your test paper
- writing notes (or a formula, or dates) on something like a small piece of paper, or even on your arm, to look at during a test
- pretending you're sick so you can take a test later, then asking your friend to tell you the questions
- asking your friend who took the test first period to tell you the questions before you take the test fifth period
- reading a condensed version instead of the original book assigned for a report
- seeing the film or video of the book instead of reading a book assigned for a report
- using Cliff's Notes® when you are supposed to be reading an entire play or other literary work
- reading an English version of a literary work assigned to be read in a foreign language
- asking your parent or a friend to help you with a science or social science project
- asking your parent or a friend to do all or parts of your science or social science project for you
- looking in a file of old tests to study last year's final exam from the teacher you have for the same class
- brainstorming an assignment with other students and then each writing your own essay
- sharing lab experiment results with classmates, each changing some data to make your reports look different
- "fudging" the data on your lab report to get the results you want or need
- not telling your teacher that the score on your test is added wrong in your favor
- not telling your teacher when a wrong answer was not marked wrong on your test
- changing your score or grade in your teacher's print or electronic grade book

Reprinted with permission from Student Cheating and Plagiarism in the Internet Era: A Wake-Up Call *by Ann Lathrop and Kathleen Foss. Englewood, CO: Libraries Unlimited, 2000.*

COPY ME:
Are Any of These Plagiarizing?

- asking your parent or a friend to suggest changes or corrections in your written essay
- asking your parent or a friend to rewrite your essay, making all the changes or corrections for you
- asking your parents or a friend to help you search the Internet for information for a report
- asking your parents or a friend to search the Internet for you for the information you need
- reading someone else's term paper and then writing your own using some of his ideas and copying part or all of his bibliography
- listing books in your bibliography that you haven't read
- brainstorming an assignment with other students and then each writing your own essay
- taking a report or term paper you wrote for one class and rewriting it for another class
- taking a report or term paper you wrote for one class and handing it in for another class without rewriting it
- copying sentences or paragraphs from the encyclopedia for your report without using quotation marks or footnotes
- writing a report as a group and then each person writing a report that is just a little bit different to hand in
- copying a report or term paper from the Internet and editing it to be "yours"
- copying a report or term paper from the Internet and handing it in without any changes
- hiring a tutor to help you learn to write better
- hiring a tutor to rewrite your papers for you
- paying another person, or an editing service, to write your term paper

Reprinted with permission from Student Cheating and Plagiarism in the Internet Era: A Wake-Up Call *by Ann Lathrop and Kathleen Foss. Englewood, CO: Libraries Unlimited, 2000.*

But I Changed Three Words! Plagiarism in the ESL Classroom

Lenora C. Thompson and Portia G. Williams

As ESL writing teachers, we are confronted with the realization that many of our students not only are unfamiliar with the rules of plagiarism, but have, in fact, been taught in their home countries to appropriate the words of others without the use of proper citations. Indeed, many of these students believe such appropriation is not only needed but expected by their teachers of English.

We believe that these students can best be helped by having this topic introduced at the secondary level. Discussions of plagiarism will not only sensitize students but can help them to avoid potential problems, such as scoring poorly on international exams or being placed inappropriately in lower-level language classes.

In this article, we make several suggestions for combating the problem of plagiarism in the ESL classroom. These suggestions, however, need not be limited to ESL students, as we have found that they work with American students as well.

Looking at the Problem

For many ESL students, learning not to cheat is more than a difficult task; it is a cultural hurdle. In some Asian cultures, students are taught to memorize and copy well-respected authors and leaders in their societies to show intelligence and good judgment in their writing. This is particularly true of our Chinese students who have frequently defended this difference in class. Korean students, who say that their country shares similar "customs," argue that their educational system emphasizes the importance of grades more than the way in which one achieves those grades. Mexican students have remarked that this focus on grades is also true in their country, with one student arguing that there are only so many slots at the top.

What these students have in common is a general belief that to be the best, you have to copy the best. As teachers, we must address these cultural differences, as well as the general problems of plagiarism, if students are to succeed in their college careers.

Asking the Questions

When we first began teaching ESL students about the pitfalls of plagiarism, we spent several weeks preaching to our students on the various rules for citing, paraphrasing, and summarizing sources. Like many teachers who do not fully grasp the reasons and extent to which students "copy" others' work, we created sentence- and paragraph-level exercises that tested our students' ability to change important words and recognize blatant cases of theft. Unfortunately, however, these exercises tested little else.

A typical assignment began by having students read and discuss articles on plagiarism cases to have them think about the topic and about what their understanding of plagiarism already was. Then we put single lines and passages from a book on an overhead projector with proper citations. In small groups, students analyzed paraphrases of these quotations and decided whether plagiarism had taken place.

Not surprisingly, few students recognized the cases of appropriation unless the words were identical and lacking quotation marks. This led to both group and whole-class discussions of plagiarism and its multiple forms. Later, students practiced quoting, paraphrasing, and summarizing short passages or articles. After a few such exercises, we moved on to the next lesson—only to find that we had done so too soon.

It did not take long to learn that our students had not fully understood plagiarism or how not to do it. Indeed, by the ninth week, they were still plagiarizing extensively, albeit unintentionally. This caused us to reflect upon practices and to turn to our students for help.

Implementing Solutions

Through journals and class discussions, students helped us understand that we needed to expand our otherwise simple definition of plagiarism and go beyond teaching our students what quotes, paraphrases, and summaries are.

The first thing we did was throw out the old one- and two-liners in our original activities and replace them with authentic, discourse-level materials. We used entire papers and articles to illustrate the ways in which authors incorporate a broad range of sources within their own texts. In addition, we used actual ESL student papers to model successful and unsuccessful attempts at documenting sources. We found that using only well-documented examples forced students to see their own writing as either good or bad. Showing them a range also helped students grasp such gray areas as "common knowledge" within different academic disciplines.

Next, we created student-centered activities, asking our students to form mixed-culture groups to discuss differences between one another and the problems that might arise as a result of those differences. After one such activity, a Korean student said that learning not to plagiarize caused significant problems for her because of its very premise. Koreans, she said, believe in the group: "Our words are to be shared." Americans, she said, are so individual that they must own everything, even words and thoughts.

Finally, after hashing out many of our students' concerns, we had them practice paraphrasing or summarizing in class again. This time, however, we had them put away their sources before doing so, thereby forcing them to digest and present information in their own voices. If students continued to have problems, we had them write everything they knew about a subject before conducting research. This approach turned out to be effective in getting them to use sources as support, rather than the other way around.

Conclusion

When we began teaching the perils of plagiarism to our ESL students, we found that the typical textbook-type exercises simply did not work. Through journals and class discussions, we learned that it was insufficient to provide students with a list of rules and citation styles in order to show them how not to plagiarize. For many students, the concept itself was foreign (or "American")—a culturally different way of thinking and performing.

This meant we had to treat plagiarism as a technical, ethical, and cultural issue. In addition, we had to supply our students with more than a basic knowledge of writing strategies for acknowledging sources; we had to give them ample opportunity to practice their newfound skills. This extended immersion in training, followed by a semester of follow-up exercises and discussions, helped to reinforce that plagiarism is both a complex issue and one that is taken seriously in the United States.

Students who do not learn how to develop their own ideas and properly attribute the work of others can cheat themselves intellectually; they also risk ending their academic careers before the careers even get started.

[*Clearing House*, vol. 69, no. 1, pages 27–29, September/October 1995. Excerpts reprinted with permission of the Helen Dwight Reid Educational Foundation. Published by Heldref Publications, 1319 Eighteenth St., N.W., Washington, DC 20036-1802. Copyright 1995.]

Chapter 10

Dealing with Student Dishonesty

Question: If you have cheated, what happened?
6.2% I was caught and punished
6.4% I was caught but not punished
95.1% I was not caught
(Who's Who)

Chapter Overview

Cheating and plagiarism are unpleasant realities for teachers, especially in high schools and middle schools. The best preparation for dealing with these problems is to become familiar with the district or school Academic Integrity Policy or to help establish a policy if there is not one. Make sure students and parents understand the policy and know that it will be enforced. Work with teachers, students, administrators, and parents to create a school climate in which honesty is recognized as an important school goal.

This chapter begins with Dr. Rushworth Kidder's response to "Why Shouldn't I Cheat?" It suggests ways to identify and deal with suspected cheating and plagiarism. Teachers should be certain of the facts and give students the benefit of the doubt. Parents must be informed and involved in each step of the process when a student is accused of cheating or plagiarism. There is a list of possible penalties and a warning against penalties that teachers and parents might consider too harsh. An argument is made for requiring students to complete the test or assignment fairly with at least a grade of C, as well as accept a penalty, rather than being allowed to avoid the work entirely. A Copy-Me page describes the case of one student who plagiarized a paper from the Internet; questions are included as discussion starters for faculty or parent meetings. The article by Berk Moss has practical advice for teachers who must deal with a cheating incident.

Chapter subheadings:

- "Why Shouldn't I Cheat?"
- Dealing with Suspected Cheating or Plagiarism
- Suggestions for Informing Parents
- Fair and Effective Penalties
- Concern for Privacy Rights
- Requiring That an Assignment or Test Be Completed Fairly
- Copy Me: "A Case of High School Plagiarism"
- Moss: "Notes on Cheating for the Busy Classroom Teacher"

Why Shouldn't I Cheat?

The big question, of course, is "Why shouldn't I cheat? What's to keep me from doing it?" For a response, we turned to Dr. Rushworth M. Kidder, President of the Institute for Global Ethics in Camden, Maine, and author of *How Good People Make Tough Choices: Resolving the Dilemmas of Ethical Living.* Here's how he answered:

Why Shouldn't I Cheat?

Dr. Rushworth M. Kidder

"OK, so cheating on this one test may not make much difference. You probably won't get caught and, if you do, nothing much will happen to you. But let me sketch out four reasons why you might want to think more deeply about cheating.

1. How far do you plan to go with cheating? Where does it stop? This might be just a small step, just cheating on this one test. But let's look at your future. If you cheat on a test, will you then begin to cheat on the traffic laws while you're driving? Will you then cheat on your girlfriend? On your taxes? On the hours you work? On your bank? Where's it all heading, and where will it end? What kind of person are you learning to be? When you want to learn to do something well, you practice a lot. Maybe you want to learn to play basketball. You dribble, you learn to do layups, and you learn to avoid the defense so you can put the ball through the hoop. You practice and you practice and you practice. That's the way you learn anything. So your choice is simple. Are you going to practice doing the things that matter, things that can help you become the kind of person you want to be? Or are you going to practice being self-destructive?

(continued)

---

2. What kind of world do you want to live in? Do you want to live in a world where other people are trying to cheat you and everyone else? Or do you want to live in a world where you can trust others? We're building the life we want to live, and the world we want to live in. And we're showing others how to do it, too. There's nothing better than living in a situation where you're trusted, and where you trust others. It's really satisfying, and it's really efficient. And you don't build trust by cheating.

3. Are you happy when you're surrounded by phonies? You probably think of yourself as a pretty good judge of other people. You can tell when parents or teachers or other adults are phonies or hypocrites, right? You can read them like a book. Well, how do you suppose they got to be phonies? Remember, they were once teenagers, too. They could recognize phonies just the way you can. So what happened? How did they learn to be phonies? Pretty much the way you're learning it. They learned to look as though they were doing one thing when they were really doing something else. They learned how to cover stuff up. They learned how to look you right straight in the eye and lie. That's how you become a phony.

4. And you know what? They're not fooling anyone except themselves. Neither will you, if you become a phony. People will know. They'll be able to tell. Because that's the final secret about cheating: It hardly ever succeeds over the long term. Hardly anyone can keep lying and cheating without getting caught. Nobody's smart enough to remember all the different lies they told to different people and then keep them all straight when they have to tell them again.

Do you really think you won't ever get caught? Do you think you can get away with lying and cheating forever? Almost every liar and cheater gets caught eventually. Nobody gets away with it forever."

[Telephone interview by the author with Rushworth M. Kidder, September 27, 1999. The Institute for Global Ethics is at <http://www.globalethics.org/>.]

Dealing with Suspected Cheating or Plagiarism

Students do not want to be accused of lying and cheating. They do not want to consider the long-term consequences raised by Dr. Kidder. Yet they continue to cheat and plagiarize, apparently secure in the belief they won't be caught, or if caught, won't be faced with any meaningful penalty.

It is our responsibility to increase the odds that students *will* be caught whenever they cheat or plagiarize. We must convince them that significant penalties *will* be assigned and their parents *will* be notified. Student attitudes must be changed in order to establish an ethical school culture as described in Chapter 8.

Fairness and consistency are crucial when dealing with students suspected of cheating or plagiarizing. All students must know they will be held accountable, favoritism is not a factor, and teachers will not "look the other way" when they see suspicious behavior. The Academic Integrity Policy provides definitions and procedures to be followed and defines consequences. Navarro et al. cite four positive outcomes of consistency in reporting all instances of dishonest behavior. It

- Allows us to confront the student and with luck, stop the behavior.
- Allows us to record the student's name for future reference and to identify repeat offenders.
- Makes the community aware of the problem in general (all cases are strictly confidential; student's privacy is protected). Public reports can be published with the names removed or changed.
- Allows us to gauge the depth of the problem. (par. 17)

Sometimes a teacher lets an incident go with a warning when it cannot be proved legally. Other teachers just don't want the bother, especially if they have confronted a student in the past, proved that cheating occurred, and seen the student receive only trivial punishment.

It is best to discuss any suspected dishonesty with the student in private and in a factual way; for example, by saying, "I saw you looking in your notebook" rather than "I saw you cheating." Make it clear that cheating is unacceptable, but always listen to the student's explanation (Moss 8). Remember that a student sometimes can show exceptional improvement due to increased motivation, hard work and extra study, or a changed attitude toward school and learning. Such a student could be discouraged by any obvious doubt or distrust. In the absence of specific evidence it is better to give the student the benefit of the doubt.

In cases of suspected plagiarism, the following statement can be effective without being confrontational: "This sentence in your paper looks as though it is not yours. Please put quotes around it if it is not, even if you can not remember the source for a foot note." and later say "Now add quotes elsewhere if they are needed" (Fogg 330). It is important to be sure the student has made an error due to a lack of a clear understanding of what constitutes plagiarism.

The best way to identify cheating on a test is to catch the cheater in the act.

- Pick up a crib sheet or a bluebook full of notes and formulas.
- Pick up both tests when you see students talking and comparing answers.
- Pick up an unauthorized calculator and the test.
- Do not confront the student in class or discuss the incident at the time; schedule a private meeting.
- Immediately document the incident in writing and follow school policy for reporting dishonesty.

An unexpectedly high test score can be suspicious when it is well above former average performance on tests or much higher than would be expected based on class participation.

- Call the student in to discuss the test with you, compliment her on her high performance, and ask what she thinks has helped her to show such improvement.
- Use the discussion to probe for deeper understanding or even simple recall on questions answered correctly on the test.

- When appropriate, have the student complete the same test again in your presence; a substantially lower score might signal the need for a conference with a counselor or with parents.

Test answers that appear to be identical, or almost identical, can be suspicious.

- Several identical wrong answers on papers from students sitting beside each other or a number of identical correct answers from a poor student sitting beside an "A" student probably should be investigated.
- Call the student in to discuss the test.
- Give weekly quizzes and watch for a pattern.

When students in the first class of the day perform noticeably less well on the test than do students in later classes, especially after lunch, check whether test questions and answers are being passed from class to class.

- Call students in to discuss the test if they appear to have scored much higher than would be expected.
- Announce that some students might have given test questions and answers to friends in later classes, so all future tests will be different for each period.

Suggestions for Informing Parents

Parents can help only if they are aware of a problem; in many cases the parents never know a student has been accused of cheating or plagiarism. Failure to inform the parents is unfair to them and to the student. It lets the student "get away with it" and reinforces a belief that cheating is of little or no consequence. It deprives the parents of an opportunity to be involved in the ethical and moral growth of their child.

A carefully developed Academic Integrity Policy will include procedures for documenting and reporting cheating, and for informing parents about student dishonesty. The teacher and parents then can work together with the student to prevent future cheating or plagiarism.

Before contacting the parent:

- Be certain of your facts and proof; document the incident in writing.
- Discuss the situation with the student. When more than one student is involved, discuss it with each individually. It might be useful to have a counselor or administrator present to witness that procedures were followed fairly. Document the discussion in writing.
- Inform the principal or other designated administrator and the student's counselor in writing.

Contacting the parent:

- Discuss the cheating incident with the parent on the phone or by email depending on your personal preference or school policy. Keep notes on the phone conversation or a copy of the email. Make it clear that you have discussed cheating with the class and clarified exactly what you consider to be cheating. Send the parent a copy of the Academic Integrity Policy, your syllabus, or other policy materials.

- Arrange a meeting with the parent if requested or if it seems appropriate. Ask an administrator or counselor to be present at the meeting. Document the meeting in writing.
- Inform the parent of the penalty to be assigned and document the conversation in writing.
- When the parent is not supportive, or perhaps threatens legal action, request assistance from the administration before responding. Document any threatened actions in writing.

Fair and Effective Penalties

Penalties for dishonest behavior should be specified in the Academic Integrity Policy. They should be well-publicized, clearly understood, and fully supported by faculty, students, administrators, and parents. The following suggested penalties come from our own experience, from discussions with colleagues, and from our research. Ideas from the following authors were especially helpful: Fishbein, Moss, Schab, and Singhal and Johnson.

Discussing the incident

- Discuss the perceived cheating incident informally with the student.
- Issue a verbal warning if appropriate.
- Schedule a meeting with student and administrator or counselor.
- Meet with parents to discuss the incident.
- Meet with peer review board (if there is one at the school).

Assignment- and grade-related penalties

- Require that the student complete the assignment or take the test to achieve at least a grade of C, removing the cheating incentive of avoiding the work; then lower the grade according to the Academic Integrity Policy.
- Assign a failing grade for the specific assignment, test, or paper.
- Assign a failing grade for the class.

Activities-related penalties

- Remove from any elected or appointed student offices.
- Remove from athletic teams.
- Deny participation in any extracurricular activities.

Service penalties

- Complete a class in ethics.
- Write an essay on ethics, honesty, morality, the consequences of dishonesty, etc.
- Complete a specified number of community service hours.

More severe penalties, possibly for repeat offenders

- Be dropped from the class.
- Be placed on long-term probation.
- Be expelled from school.

Penalties associated with transcripts and recommendations

- Note incident on student's permanent record file (check that this does not violate state privacy laws or court rulings).
- Refuse to send letters of recommendation for college admission or cancel letters already sent.
- Refuse to recommend student for National Honor Society or National Merit Scholarship Program.

It is important that all faculty members agree on the definitions of dishonest behaviors and support the penalties to be imposed. Some teachers might hesitate to report students suspected of cheating or plagiarism when they regard the penalties as too harsh. This is most likely to occur if teachers were not involved in developing the Academic Integrity Policy.

Parents can be concerned that a penalty will impact too negatively on a student's education or career. They might deny that the cheating or plagiarism occurred, or argue for a lighter penalty. Some parents might hire a lawyer and threaten the school or district with a court battle. In no case should such threats result in the dismissal of charges when there is proof the student cheated.

The mutual trust required to control cheating will be damaged severely if school or district administrators decide not to pursue the incident because of parental threats. Teachers must be able to depend on strong support from their administrators when they report and document dishonesty; they deserve protection from vindictive or abusive parents. Parents and students must be confident that all instances of dishonesty will be treated fairly and according to the policy; pressure and threats cannot be allowed to impact decisions in these cases.

Such problems are less likely to arise when the entire community has been involved in developing and supporting the Academic Integrity Policy. Students and parents must understand the specific procedures to be followed, the definitions of offenses that are prohibited, and the penalties that will be assigned. They must believe there is absolute fairness in applying the Academic Integrity Policy to all students.

Concern for Privacy Rights

Negative information entered on transcripts can violate the privacy rights of students; district policy should be written clearly to conform to state laws and court decisions. School staff can, however, refuse to complete recommendations for college admission, scholarships, or jobs. Students can be excluded from the National Honor Society or the National Merit Scholarship Program. One new way to track student dishonesty is being explored at the University of California, San Diego (UCSD):

> UCSD is looking for fresh ways to root out problem students even before they come to campus. [They] may begin asking would-be transfer students if the school they are leaving would allow them to re-enroll. Depending on the answer, UCSD could follow up with the school to see if the student is transferring in good standing. Privacy laws prevent universities from detailing instances of academic dishonesty on school transcripts. (Schmidt, pars. 34–36)

Requiring that an Assignment or Test Be Completed Fairly

The penalty recommended most often for cheating or plagiarism is a failing grade. Fogg suggests such a penalty implies that learning the material covered in the test or assignment, or completing the research for the paper, was of little or no value to the student's education:

> [Assigning a failing grade as a penalty] rests on the assumption that learning the academic material is not important . . . the student decided in the first place that avoiding the work was worth more than the possibility of receiving a failing grade so [the make-up] work involved will probably be perceived by him as a punishment and a deterrent to cheating again. The time taken to discuss the consequences of cheating will also probably be perceived as a punishment. (331)

The student very likely cheated or plagiarized to avoid doing the required studying, research, or writing. When the grade is a relatively minor percentage of the total grade for the class, and there is little likelihood of being caught, the student perceives the risk to be small in relation to the benefit of avoiding the work.

A failing grade in such cases is an inadequate and inappropriate response. It would better serve instructional goals to require that the test or paper be completed satisfactorily. The student would continue to take the test (or a different version) until passing with at least a grade of C, or would research and write a paper to meet the original assignment for a grade of C or better. The final grade would then be reduced at the discretion of the teacher, or as specified in the Academic Integrity Policy.

The student in this case must put in the time and effort required to complete the work and receives the penalty of a lowered grade as well. This policy sends a strong message to students that cheating and plagiarizing will not result in avoiding the assigned work.

Pointers

Suggestions for identifying and dealing with various types of cheating and plagiarism in student work are in Chapters 5, 11, and 13. Additional information for parents who must deal with student dishonesty is in Chapter 6. Some of the sample online policies listed in Chapter 8 suggest penalties. Ideas for restructuring assignments to reduce plagiarism are in Chapters 14 and 16.

COPY ME:
A Case of High School Plagiarism

The assignment was to compare a book with the movie version. A close reading of one student's paper made it apparent to the teacher that the level of work was too advanced for that student. She decided to check her suspicions by comparing this paper with previous papers the student had submitted for the required portfolio maintained by the English department. These student portfolios were kept in each teacher's room in unlocked file cabinets while students worked on assignments. The portfolio for this student was missing.

When confronted, the student maintained that the paper in question was his original work. The parents told the teacher they had seen him working extremely hard on the paper. The teacher took the issue to the principal who asked if anyone on the staff had enough computer expertise to search the Internet for a source for the paper. She had read a newspaper article explaining that, if the paper had been plagiarized from the Internet, there were ways to locate the original source.

The librarian and several other staff members spent several days searching unsuccessfully. Finally, a records clerk who had been an Internet searcher for years found the online Siskel and Ebert review that clearly was the basis for the student's report. When confronted with the original printed review, the student confessed.

The student's punishment was the loss of a grade for the paper. He had to confess to his parents that he had cheated and that the teacher had been right. The whole process was highly confrontational.

In the opinion of the teacher involved, the student merited a stronger punishment. Considerable staff time had been involved. The situation had been highly unpleasant and she had been confronted with serious verbal abuse from the parents defending the student.

Discussion questions

- Would the teacher challenge another student in similar circumstances?
- Could the principal have acted differently?
- Would another punishment have been more appropriate for the student?
- What punishment, in the teacher's opinion, would be fair?
- Could future assignments be changed to avoid this type of plagiarism?
- Should the school re-examine the student code relating to cheating and plagiarism?

Reprinted with permission from Student Cheating and Plagiarism in the Internet Era: A Wake-Up Call *by Ann Lathrop and Kathleen Foss. Englewood, CO: Libraries Unlimited, 2000.*

Notes on Cheating for the Busy Classroom Teacher

Berk Moss

Thoughts on How to Confront a Student

It is never easy to confront a student when cheating is suspected. Make the contact in private. Be business-like and deal with the specifics of the situation first. When you've settled these you should clearly state that such behavior is unacceptable. Try to focus on the behavior that leads you to suspect cheating. Don't say, "I saw you cheating." Say, "I saw you looking in your notebook."

Confront the student in a reasonably timely manner after an incident, but don't act until you've thought through the matter:

- What evidence do I have? What did I see? What does the student's paper tell me?
- What do I know about this student?
- Were other students involved?

When you confront the student, give him/her a chance to explain. You must listen to the student's explanation if you take any disciplinary action. This is a matter of necessary due process expected of school personnel in dealing with disciplinary situations.

You must listen, but you don't have to agree or get involved in an argument. If a student becomes argumentative or repetitious, end the conversation by saying something like this: "I've heard your response. If there is nothing new you can say, we needn't go on. I'll let you know what I'm going to do about this when I've made a decision." (7)

Thoughts on Contacting Parents

In almost all cases of cheating it is best to contact the parents. Be ready to explain what behaviors indicate cheating has taken place. Ask them to deal with the moral aspect of cheating with the student. Tell the parent you are calling to get information about the student in general which might be useful in knowing how to deal with the academic aspect of the situation.

- Let them know that you will deal with the incident as a school discipline problem. If you don't know what you will do about the situation, don't feel you must decide while you are on the phone.
- Let them know that you've talked with the class prior to the incident about how you define cheating and how you will handle it.

The conversation might sound like this: "This is Mary Green of Sunset High School. We've had a problem during our math test. Ralph was using crib notes (or better, 'Ralph admits to using crib notes') on the test. We'll deal with the discipline aspect here at school, but I'd like to ask your help in two ways: Would you please deal with the moral aspects raised by the situation. I think it's better for the parent to deal with that. And can you tell me anything I should consider while I decide what to do here at school about this?"

If the conversation is anything but straightforward, if the parents are anything but supportive, if the potential for misunderstanding is too large, then ask the parents to come to school for a face-to-face conference. Don't try to handle a messy situation over the telephone.

It is also useful to inform the school counselor of problems with cheating. The counselor should help the student think about what caused the cheating and how to deal with those pressures in a positive way. Don't expect the counselor to make the first confrontation with the student, to contact the parents, or to administer a punishment. That's your responsibility as the teacher. Avoid the idea that you can "turn over" the incident to anyone. (8)

Thoughts on Responding to Cheating

Don't feel compelled to make a decision about a response to an incident of cheating until you've been able to gather information about the student and the situation.

- Ask the administrative vice-principal about any past problem with the student.
- Get ideas about appropriate responses from colleagues (other teachers of similar subjects or students, your department head, staff development people, administrators) and parents.
- Check with the counselor about information you might need in selecting a response.
- Consider the impact (both positive and negative) your reaction will have on other students.

Here is a partial list of some responses to cheating some staff members have used. In general they would be used in addition to the phone calls you make to the parents of students involved. They might or might not fit your needs. In many cases a combination of these can be used.

- Give the student a different test or a different type of test. Substitute an essay for an objective test. Give oral questions. Add questions to verify answers.
- Make the student do the assignment over with a slight difference: different questions, different problems, a different topic, etc. Have the student assigned to the prep room for the length of time it should take to finish the assignment.
- Lower the student's grade on that assignment or test. Average this grade in with his other grades for the quarter.
- Give the student a zero on the assignment or test and average this grade into the other grades for the quarter. If this causes a lowering of his quarter or semester grade, so be it.
- Assign the student to the prep room or to work for you after school for the time you had to put into detecting and dealing with the incident.
- If the student is a good writer or good verbally, ask him/her to do a report, either written or oral, on honesty, ethics, trust, or the implications when people can't be trusted. Have him/her present this to you after school and be ready to discuss it.
- Refuse to give recommendations for college or employment to students who cheat. But don't write in a recommendation that a student has been caught cheating. If you can't say anything nice, don't say anything. Give the form back to the student.
- Recommend suspension (in or out of school) to the vice-principal. (9–10)

[Excerpts from "Notes on Cheating for the Busy Classroom Teacher" by Berk Moss, Staff Development Specialist, Beaverton (OR) School District. Reprinted with permission of the author. Original document is available from ERIC (ED 243203).]

Chapter 11

Reducing Cheating on Tests and Assignments

The civil service examination system with its variations, established in China a millennium or more ago, was conducted in sealed individual cells from which candidates did not budge for three days. Before entering the examination room, the candidates were searched carefully for any aids they might have concealed on their persons. In spite of all the precautions, in spite of the death penalty for examiners and examinees when the cheaters were caught, there is live evidence of the circumvention of the rigid rules against external help [in the] Gest Oriental Library at Princeton University . . . a "cribbing garment" which was rented to those intending to cheat. When sewn into the coat, this garment could be smuggled into the cell and the candidate could copy, at leisure and without fear of detection, any number of the 722 essays based on the Confucian writings. (Brickman 412)

Chapter Overview

One of the strongest prevention strategies is to convince students that teachers and parents *do care* about student dishonesty and are determined to reduce it. Extra work will be required to establish new control measures and to restructure an already crowded curriculum to effectively address integrity and honesty. But without these efforts the students' grades can be so contaminated by cheating that they no longer represent a fair evaluation of work accomplished.

Specific techniques discussed in this chapter include security issues, test preparation and administration, correcting and returning tests, and working with parents. An emphasis on prevention includes changing the types of tests being given and replacing grading on a curve with mastery grading. Also discussed are suggestions for discouraging cheating on assignments and homework.

Chapter subheadings:

- "Smart-People" Tests
- Grading for Mastery vs. Grading on a Curve
- Teachers Who Care about Cheating
- Reducing Cheating on Tests
- Discouraging Cheating on Class Assignments, Homework, Lab Reports, Etc.

"Smart-People" Tests

Cheating on tests generally is regarded as the most serious cheating behavior. We probably cannot stop it completely but we can reduce it. Most of the strategies in this chapter are traditional or "low-tech" approaches; strategies to counter high-tech cheating are discussed in Chapter 5.

One researcher reports, "Copying answers from a nearby paper and using crib notes or cheat sheets are the two most frequently used methods of cheating . . . if students are going to cheat, one of these two methods will be used approximately 80% of the time" (Stephen Davis 11). Both can be reduced substantially by careful monitoring.

Changing the types of tests we give can reduce cheating significantly. Tests that emphasize rote memorization, generally multiple-choice and true-false questions, make cheating much easier than do essays, problem-solving, or other "smart-people" or "procedural" tests:

> It doesn't take a genius to do well on declarative tasks, you know. Almost anyone can memorize a few random facts and then regurgitate those facts on demand. . . . Procedural tests, on the other hand, are smart-people tests, asking students to apply information. . . . After all, which would you rather have: a physician who can solve health-related problems or one who can pass multiple-choice tests based on isolated facts? It is really pretty simple to tell which kind of test you are giving. A declarative test will ask students to prepare for the test by doing memory work and close readings of texts and notes; it asks students to know about a subject. A procedural test will ask students to prepare for the test by solving sample problems and applying textual information to personal and real-world situations; it asks students to know how to use information. That's the way smart people make tests. (K. Davis, pars. 7-9)

It is important to give "smart people" tests and monitor all test-taking situations carefully. Tell students you *will not* tolerate cheating; then be vigilant during the entire test.

Grading for Mastery vs. Grading on a Curve

"Often, the ways we teach invite students to treat our classes as hurdles to be cleared, one by one, on the way to a goal. . . . We fail to teach students that study, mastery, and knowledge are the prizes—not merely the means to success in the next class"

(Shropshire 24). Parents and teachers who place a strong emphasis on a student's grade rather than on the actual learning accomplished send this negative message. Too often we ask "What did you get on the test?" instead of "Tell me what you learned today."

Research with middle school science students suggests cheating could be reduced by putting less emphasis on grades or other performance goals:

> Indeed, why should a student be concerned about the inherent value of learning if, for example, the reward of getting on the honor roll is based purely on the grade that the student earns? If students perceive that success in school is defined in terms of grades and ability, then they may feel more justified to cheat. Data from the present study support this notion: Students who perceived that their schools emphasized performance goals were more likely to report engaging in cheating behaviors. (Anderman, Griesinger, and Westerfield 89)

A study of middle and high school students and teachers reported: "Students, more than teachers, voiced strong agreement that cheating is more likely to occur when large amounts of material are covered, where grading is on a curve, and where grades are based on just one or two exams or other products" (Evans and Craig 50).

Cheaters "steal" from the honest students when only a set percentage of A's can be earned in a class graded on a curve. Honest students can benefit from a policy of grading for mastery; grades are based directly on a student's work without reference to the level of work done by other students.

Teachers Who Care about Cheating

Students frequently comment "The teachers don't seem to care" when cheating is discussed. According to Whitley and Kite, "The perception that faculty are indifferent to cheating increases students' feelings of inequity . . . students who perceive faculty indifference to others' cheating may themselves cheat as a way to reduce the inequity. Hence, taking precautions against cheating is, in itself, an important deterrent" (46). It is our responsibility to convince students that we do care by taking such precautions.

Teachers who report suspicious student behavior whenever they observe it, and take action to stop it, help to reduce cheating in two ways. They have stopped a potential cheating incident and their prompt action helps convince students that teachers do care about cheating. Students in a math class, for example, can be seen preparing cheat sheets for a science test; the math teacher warns the science teacher and later confronts the students during math class by asking what they were doing. The students probably will reply "studying" but they will be aware that their teachers are vigilant.

When an important test is being given to an unusually large class, a teacher on a prep period can help by moving half of the class into an empty classroom. This makes it possible to separate students who are suspected of copying from each other and two teachers will be able to monitor the class more closely.

Teachers collaborate by providing a united front on student discipline. When all teachers and administrators enforce the school's Academic Integrity Policy fairly and consistently, the students and parents will hear a firm statement: *We do care, very much. Cheating is not tolerated in our classes.*

Reducing Cheating on Tests

The following suggestions emphasize "cheat-free testing" and focus on prevention rather than punishment. They come from our own experience, from suggestions of friends and colleagues, and from the authors cited. When the same suggestion was found in two or more articles, only the first is referenced.

Security Issues

- Do not leave rough drafts or hard-to-read copies of the test by the copy machine or in a wastebasket. Shred them or take them home to destroy (Singhal and Johnson 14).

- Do not leave exams in a faculty mailbox (Whitley and Kite 47).

- Do not allow student assistants to type, duplicate, or collate tests of any kind.

- Keep close track of teacher's manuals; many have been "lost from classrooms" and found their way into students' hands, yet teachers continue to use tests from those manuals.

- Keep the test answer key in a very secure location (Moss 2).

- Keep exams in a locked file cabinet in the department or faculty office before and after the test (Factor 59). Unlocked file cabinets take just a few minutes to access; tests or assignments will not be missed until they are needed.

- Teachers who are orderly about their filing can be especially vulnerable as students can locate their testing materials easily. Keep tests in unlabeled files as a precaution against theft (Fogg 330).

- The security of your desk materials and computer items is just as important as the security of your wallet or purse. Don't leave your room unlocked, even briefly. Students who wander into an open, empty room have immediate access to all the materials in that room (Moss 2).

- Don't allow students to be in your room unsupervised. Grades on computers and tests in file cabinets or on computers can be too tempting. This can create a moral dilemma for a student who sees another student hacking into the computer or going through your files, yet hesitates to report the incident.

- Check with campus security officers or supervisors, or with administrators, to find out how many teachers have reported items stolen from their rooms. This information isn't generally circulated, so faculty might be surprised at the extent of the problem.

Preparing the Test

- Never copy a test from the teacher's manual, from a book in the school library, or from any other source that students might know about, unless you make significant changes (Stephen Davis 12).

- Whenever possible, give essay tests rather than multiple-choice or true-false tests (Serafin. *Academic* 2).

- Try to avoid test items that force students to memorize a large number of historic dates, chemical or math formulas, biographical data, etc.; students might feel greater pressure to cheat on such tests (Singhal and Johnson 14).

- When using the same test for more than one class period, change at least some of the questions so each class has a different form of the test. For a multiple-choice test, rearrange both the questions and the letters of the correct answers (Fogg 330).

- If possible, always have two or more forms of a test for each class (Fowler 95–96).

- Consider printing the tests on different colors of paper for different periods so students can't pick up an extra copy for a friend to complete and hand in at a later period (Croucher 106). When two or more versions of a test are used, print each version on a different color.

- Never use exactly the same test you used the year or semester before; copies of old tests often are available somewhere on the campus (Baker 86). Change the order of the questions. Change at least some of the questions so the answers will be different. In math and science tests change the numbers in the equations, in history tests change true statements to false, etc. Make sure someone who memorized the correct answers for an old test will not pass based on that knowledge alone.

- Create and store the test on a computer that is neither on a school network nor on a dedicated line at your home in order to be protected from hackers (Benning, par. 22).

- Place a statement summarizing the official policy on cheating on every exam and require that students sign a statement verifying the exam work is their own. A sample statement from one university professor is reported by Graber:

  > At the bottom of each test are two statements, each followed by a line for the test-taker's signature: "I have not received nor given unauthorized aid during this exam. I have not observed any other students receiving or giving such aid." or "I cannot in good faith sign the above statement." Students must sign one of the two statements to receive credit for the exam. (pars. 24-25)

Scratch Paper and Bluebooks

- Provide the scratch paper for a test when students will need it; never let them bring or use their own paper (Singhal and Johnson 15).

- Require that all scratch paper be handed in with the test, stapling each student's scratch paper to the test. When convenient, staple adequate scratch paper to test papers before distributing them.

- If possible, provide colored paper, old printouts from the business office with one side blank, or any other paper that is not standard white paper and that can be varied from class to class and from period to period. Cheat sheets will be more obvious against colored paper.

- Bluebooks are designed to prevent cheating but sometimes they provide cover for cheaters when the student brings an extra blue book with notes, equations, dates, etc. (Wein 1).

- As a precaution, do not let students use the bluebooks they bring to class; collect and redistribute them (Navarro, par. 5).

- Collect all of the bluebooks from students in the first class, checking to be double sure no one has kept one with answers in it. Then distribute your own set, each marked with a colored pen or special stamp good for that day only—the simplest is a date stamp with a different color stamp pad for each class (Corbett 68). No one can guess which color will be used for which class. For the second class of the day, distribute bluebooks collected from the first class and stamped appropriately, etc. Any bluebook on any desk without the proper stamp is illegal and therefore suspect. You must have on hand enough bluebooks for your largest class in order to implement this plan.

Open-Book Exams

- For open-book tests, check students' books as you walk around the room to be sure that notes, Cliff's Notes®, have not been taped into a textbook unless you have told students these can be used (Corbett 114).
- One advantage of open-book exams is that they offer equal opportunity to the honest student who often must compete with dishonest students using illegal notes. Better yet, open-book exams that allow students to use notes in addition to the textbook encourage students to study ahead of time, to organize their notes (or copy and then study a friend's notes), and to become familiar enough with the textbook to be able to locate material quickly.
- Have students turn in their notes with the exam (Sharma, par. 33).
- The practicality of open-book exams can change, however, if students can use hand-held computers with a sophisticated search capacity that allows them to enter search words and find information without knowing the subject matter (Fishlock, par. 10).
- In a study of cheating by college students, Weber and McBee report: "It does not appear that cheating is more of a problem for open-book and take-home examinations than for closed-book types" (1).

Take-Home Exams

- There is a risk of penalizing the honest student who does the work at home independently and must compete with the dishonest student who gets help from friends or parents, or even pays someone to complete the test.
- A parent can be asked to sign that the work is the student's own, but in some cases the same parent who "helped" with the test also will sign the statement.
- One safeguard, after collecting all of the take-home exams, is to ask one question from the exam in class and have students write a short-answer essay from memory. Ask what section of the textbook or other references they used to answer that question on the exam. It should be obvious which students haven't a clue as to what answers they (or someone else) put on the original take-home exam or where their answers came from.

Classroom Arrangement

- Check desktops to be sure there are no notes, dates, formulas, etc., written on the desk, perhaps hidden in apparently innocent doodles (Corbett 53).
- Allow only materials required for the test to be on the desktop (Whitley and Kite 47).
- Check the floor for any information written on floor tiles under a desk (Baker 69).

- Collect all books, notebooks, calculators, headsets, coats, backpacks, etc., at the front of the room so students have only a pencil at the desk while taking the test (Graber, par. 22).
- Be able to see the face of every student.
- Sit at the back of the room (when you are not walking around) or consider having the desks turned around so all students face the back of the room; when you sit at your desk they will not be able to see you so will not know when you are watching them (Moss 3).
- Seat students in every other desk (Aiken 727).
- If possible, move to the cafeteria or a large auditorium, or use two rooms so students can spread out, but be sure to have one or more monitors in each room (Moss 3).
- Seat students alphabetically (Chidley, par. 23) or use some other scheme to mix the assigned seating up for the test so friends can't sit together and poor students can't plan to sit beside or behind good students.
- A seating chart lets you reconstruct the room if you suspect cheating and want to check whether two identical tests were turned in by students sitting near one another (Graber, par. 22). Number the tests to correspond to the seating chart so you will be able to check tests of students sitting beside, behind, or in front of one another if needed.
- Another way to reconstruct the room is to provide a space on the exam for the name or ID number of the student to their right. Before the exam begins, all students fill in their own name and ID first, then that of the student to their right.
- Check all chalkboards, bulletin boards, wall racks, or other display areas around the room to be sure students haven't posted any cheat sheets with dates, formulas, etc., on them (Moss 3).
- Be sure you have not overlooked any of your own large wall charts with chemical elements, historic time lines, etc., that inadvertently provide answers to test questions.

Distributing the Test

- In large classes a student might stay away and attempt to have someone else, a "ringer," take the test (Baker 118).
- Both the enrolled student and a "ringer" can take the test, then the "ringer" slips the completed test to the enrolled student to turn in. The student keeps the other test to throw away or contribute to a test bank (Orlans, par. 7).
- As a safeguard, require a picture ID (Croucher 6–7) and write the student ID number from the card onto the test.
- As an added precaution, require that the picture ID remain on the desk during the test (Nicosia).
- It might be a good idea, however, to turn over random ID cards as you walk around the room; some students write crib notes on the back of their ID card (*Cheaters*).
- A student can take an extra copy of a test for a friend or for a club or fraternity file if you pass tests out by handing a stack to the first student in each row. Either hand them out individually or count accurately, aloud, the number for each row (Baker 65).

- Hand out an alternate form of the test to every other row (Fogg 330).
- When handing out "scantron" forms or other answer sheets, number them with a stamp before the test and record the student's ID number beside the number of the answer sheet. This keeps a student from taking two answer sheets and filling out one for a friend (Stephen Davis 13).

Monitoring the Test

- Stay in the room and supervise the students carefully. Do not sit at your desk and read, grade papers, or do other work. Be unpredictable, walking up and down the rows and all around the room during a test (Fowler 95).
- In large classes, plan to use as many proctors as necessary to monitor all areas (Aiken 727).
- Try to use proctors who know the students by name (Chidley, par. 23).
- Have students cover their answers with a blank page to prevent copying (Sharma, par. 34).
- If you think you see someone copying from another student, but you aren't certain, remind the entire class that you are watching them and that "wandering eyes" or glancing at another student's test is forbidden (Fogg 330).
- Watch carefully so students don't have an opportunity to trade papers during a test to either compare answers or write answers for each other (Kindy, par. 7).
- If students have textbooks at their desks, be sure they don't sneak a look inside for an answer (Stephen Davis 12).
- When students are not allowed to use a calculator during the test, monitor the room for calculator watches or for calculators hidden in pockets, notebooks, or other accessible but not obvious places (Stephen Davis 12).
- Be on the lookout for body language signals from one student to another, for example, hand signals such as touching corners of the desk top or waving one or two fingers in the air (Stephen Davis 11), feet or legs placed in pre-arranged positions, tapping sounds made with a pencil on the desk, touching parts of the body, etc. (Orlans, par. 8).
- Coughs and nods can signal responses for a multiple-choice or true-false test (Fogg 331).
- Pay special attention to students sitting in the back rows; they might be there because they think that it will be easier to cheat, especially if the teacher sits at a desk in the front of the room during the test (Corbett 51). Again, walking around is the best deterrent.
- Don't allow students to use headsets (Stephen Davis 12).
- Notice anyone walking very slowly to the pencil sharpener and then back, perhaps glancing at other students' test papers along the way (Corbett 58). Wandering students can be passing cheat sheets (Baker 71). Walk toward a student who is wandering or catch the student's eye to make it clear that you are watching.
- Students might come to your desk one or more times to ask questions during the test, hoping to see another student's paper (Baker 64). Always turn completed tests facedown on your desk so students won't see the answers.

- Minimize student opportunities to come to your desk to ask individual questions by discussing any test questions that might be confusing before the test begins (Serafin. *Academic* 2). You can insist that students remain in their desks and raise their hands for assistance (Baker 127).
- A student who asks to leave the room during a test to go to the restroom might have cheat sheets, books, notes, etc., hidden there (Corbett 67).
- In a more contemporary scheme, a student with a cell phone might go to the restroom in order to call a friend who can supply a needed answer (Croucher xiv).
- Try to have someone check the restrooms close to the classroom if you have students who habitually ask to be excused during a test. Better yet, give the test in sections and announce ahead of time that breaks can be taken only after a student hands in one section of the test and before picking up the next section (Croucher xv).

Cheat Sheets

- A very small piece of paper can be folded and held in the palm or slipped into a pocket (Wein, par. 4).
- Folded up inside a gum wrapper, a cheat sheet can look like a piece of gum (Bushweller. *Generation* 29).
- Girls can hide thin strips of paper under long fingernails (Croucher 9).
- Watch for students who keep sliding their test papers around. They might have written notes on the desk top (Singhal and Johnson 15).
- Do a quick scan of the entire class, looking for students with their hand open and palm up on the desks; some students still write cheat notes on their palms (Chidley, par. 10).
- Students who cough or sneeze a great deal, requiring frequent use of tissues, might have made one or more tissues into a cheat sheet (Fogg 331).
- Cheat sheets can be pasted onto juice bottles or boxes, or onto water bottles, either replacing the label or written on the back of the label (*Cheaters*).
- A cheat sheet can be slipped behind a calculator in its case and then pulled out slightly to check a formula, fact, etc. (Corbett 14). It can be pasted inside the calculator instruction book (Croucher xiv). Either check all calculators being used, issue school-owned sets of calculators, design tests that do not require calculators, or let the class know in advance that you will be making random checks of calculator cases and instruction booklets.
- A small cheat sheet can be inserted into a watch face or hidden in the lead storage space of a mechanical pencil (*Cheaters*); it can be hidden inside a pen (Bushweller. *Generation* 29).
- Check large erasers students bring to the test—look on both sides for notes (Chidley, par. 10). Be sure students sharing an eraser are not writing notes on it as they pass it back and forth.
- A cheat sheet can be pasted onto the back of a ruler; two students sharing a ruler or a calculator can pass questions and answers back and forth (Baker 69).
- Information can be written or carved onto the sides of six-sided pencils (Carney, par. 31).

- Cheat sheets are best caught by wandering around the room continually during the test. Corbett advises students to eat the small piece of paper if caught so there is no evidence (16).

Cheater-Friendly Clothing

- Watch for information written on a student's arm and hidden by long baggy sleeves (Stephen Davis 12).
- Students can write notes on their legs and wear jeans with large tears or full skirts that can be pulled aside to let them see the notes; watch for anyone scratching their legs and looking down a lot (Corbett 66).
- Check boots for small papers attached to the soles with Velcro or glue to be viewed by a student who is crossing his legs frequently (Stephen Davis 12).
- Caps with long bills shade the eyes so it is more difficult to notice when eyes stray to another student's paper; ask that all caps be worn with the bills turned to the back of the head (Chidley, par. 11).
- Check a cap on a student's desk to be sure it isn't covering a cheat sheet or that notes haven't been written on the inside or bill of the cap (Graber, par. 23).
- Watch for notes in shirt pockets, in the large front pockets of sweatshirts, written on a belt buckle (Corbett 44), or on the underside of a long belt flap (*Cheaters*).
- One girl made a paper flower, wrote notes on it, then pinned it to her blouse (Stephen Davis 13).

Collecting Tests

- Have an orderly system for collecting tests. Students might take advantage of a brief period of chaos when students are turning in tests as they leave in order to glance at a cheat sheet or copy an answer from a friend (Baker 126).
- Always have students return the test, even if separate answer sheets are used, so a student cannot pass the test on to a friend or add it to a club or fraternity file (Factor 59).
- Don't leave completed tests visible on your desk; put them safely away in a folder or drawer, preferably locked. A student might try to pick up a completed test from the stack, either for a friend in a later period or for a club or fraternity file.
- Don't leave blank copies of a test on your desk.
- A student can return to class after "forgetting" to put her name on her test. Watch carefully that she doesn't use this opportunity to change one or more answers. Better yet, find the test and write her name on it yourself. Best of all, have students write their names and ID numbers on the tests as they are handed out or picked up at the beginning of the period and check each picture ID as tests are returned.

Correcting and Returning Tests

- If you have students correct each other's tests, never let them exchange with friends. Collect all of the tests and then hand them out in random order to be graded (Fowler 95).

- Warn students that you randomly select a number of exams to duplicate and will check these copies if a student brings in an exam to be regraded due to a supposed grading error (Navarro 1). In fact, the student might have changed an incorrect answer after hearing the test discussed or checking his notes (Chidley, par. 6).

- Always return tests to students in person. Never leave corrected tests in boxes or on a table where one can be picked up to study for the following semester or year (Baker 88). Some instructors have the reputation of using the same tests year after year, perhaps with minor changes, and students with an old test to study have a definite advantage over others in the class.

- Tell students that you will randomly select ten students on the day following the test and ask each one a question from the test. You will have each student's test paper in front of you and will expect the same oral answer that is on the test. Doing this regularly can help to identify students who have "forgotten" their answers from the day before. It also provides a good review of the test material.

Make-up Tests

- For any make-up test, be sure to change some, if not all, of the questions, rearrange the questions, or rearrange the answers on a multiple-choice test. Or tell students in advance that the make-up test for anyone who is absent probably will be an essay test (Fogg 330). In other words, make it impossible for a student to find out all about the test from a friend and come prepared after faking illness. Be sure your class knows that you will do this.

- Make-up tests should be given at your convenience, not the student's, and should be supervised closely.

- Never give a make-up test to a student left alone in the hall, in an office, or in an empty classroom (Corbett 28).

- Do not send a student to the library for a make-up test and expect the busy staff there to monitor for cheating.

Work with the Parents

- Before scheduling a make-up test, it can be useful to phone a parent to express your concern about the absent student's health, especially if the student frequently is ill on test days (Moss 3).

- Get to know your students' parents. If you have made contact with parents on Open House or Back-to-School nights, or just through phone calls or notes and postcards home, you have established a rapport that will allow the parent to be a part of their child's educational plan and a partner in discipline.

The bottom line is to be vigilant during all testing. A lack of vigilance can enable the cheaters, unfairly penalize honest students, and reinforce students' belief that "teachers don't care about cheating."

Discouraging Cheating on Class Assignments, Homework, Lab Reports, Etc.

The first preventive measure is to reassess and possibly revise all assignments. Be sure each assignment meets three criteria:

- The assignment is relevant to the course work, important, and unlikely to be perceived as "busywork." Students believe they have something to learn by completing the assignment.

- The degree of collaboration permissible on each assignment has been clarified, preferably in writing. Students allowed to work together understand clearly when the written work is to be completed individually and have standards explaining how to accomplish this. They also understand what will be considered evidence of unpermitted collaboration.

- Any "ungraded" assignment has very clear guidelines for how papers will be checked to determine whether students have done their own work. One approach is to grade a randomly selected 10% of the papers each day; tell students in advance this will be done. Again, it is important that students perceive the work to be useful and important in achieving course goals.

Students who do not understand an assignment might hesitate to ask questions in class. "Unfortunately, they might handle any confusion by inappropriately consulting peers or engaging in other forms of academic dishonesty. By communicating to the students that questions are allowed and encouraged, instructors might well discourage cheating" (Whitley and Kite 48–49).

To check that students have done their own homework or other assignments, occasionally give a brief, unannounced written test that repeats one of the items on the work handed in that day. Students should know this will be done and that their answer on the test will be expected to match their answer on the assignment just completed.

Singhal and Johnson recommend counting homework as only a small percentage of the final grade or not at all. As a standard precaution, they urge teachers not to give the teacher's manual containing answers to [student] graders under any circumstances (16).

Good teachers never relax their vigilance. They teach honesty along with their subject matter. They are dedicated to providing honest students with a level playing field where they can compete fairly based on hard work and intelligence, unhampered by other students who attempt to slide by with dishonesty. Honest students appreciate these good teachers.

Pointers ──────────────────────────────

Chapter 5 deals with high-tech defenses against cheating and plagiarism. Chapter 10 suggests ways to identify and deal with students suspected of cheating.

Chapter 12

The Librarian–Teacher Team

My vision is that we, as school librarians in cooperation with teachers, will find it imperative to make every library research project meaningful to students. We will examine each step of the project and figure out ways to help them grasp meaning in information, make sense of ideas, and learn more than a formula or a format. We will help students use their time in as productive a manner as possible, avoiding mindless activity. We will provide students experiences that teach them information skills they can transfer to real life. We will transform them from scribes to thinkers. (McGregor 7)

Chapter Overview

The librarian is an important team player who works with teachers and students during all steps of the research paper process. This team approach makes two teachers available to assist students and brings to the assignment a librarian's special expertise in identifying and locating all types of learning resources.

The importance of research in real life is explored with an emphasis on helping students to perceive the value of this life skill. Librarians provide valuable information about Internet resources, collaborate on research assignments, and make research materials easily accessible. A Copy Me page outlines a "Cyber-Plagiarism Faculty Workshop."

Chapter subheadings:

- The Librarian as Team Teacher
- Real-Life Importance of Research
- Librarians Are Sources of Information about the Internet
- Teachers and Librarians Collaborate on Research Assignments
- Librarians Make Research Materials Easily Accessible
- Copy Me: "Cyber-Plagiarism Faculty Workshop"

The Librarian as Team Teacher

At first glance reports and term papers appear to be the sole responsibility of the classroom teacher; they are the ones who do most of the work with their students. Librarians also have a vital role in the process. Working as a team, the librarian and teacher plan, design, and implement research projects that focus on the effective location, analysis, and use of information.

The librarian–teacher team approach means that two teachers are available to help individual students with each step of the assignment. Librarians are a sounding board and guide for students as the students work out the logistics of their research projects. Librarians offer suggestions on how to broaden or narrow a topic and how to design a search strategy.

Librarians and teachers both assist students in accessing information online, and in print, nonprint, or electronic formats. They help students determine the accuracy, relevance, and timeliness of the information they locate. They direct students toward appropriate information sources beyond the school walls. These all are important steps in learning to apply information skills to research assignments as well as to real-life problems.

Real-Life Importance of Research

Clarifying reasons why research skills are essential real-life skills can be just as important as teaching the actual mechanics of the research process. Information-literate students can move from writing a school report to gathering information upon which to base important life decisions: "How do I determine which bed is best, the $700 one or the $1,400 one?" "How do I find out about job requirements for a career I am considering?" "How do I evaluate a health plan?"

This real-life process for making decisions can be mapped to the research process being taught in class:

- determine what you need to know: "which bed is best?" (choose a topic);
- locate the information: "where do I find consumer information and reports?" (explore resources);
- evaluate the information for relevance to your needs: "determine how price compares with quality in selecting a bed" (analyze source material); and
- apply the decision: "buy a bed" (write the paper, make the speech, etc.).

Information Power: Building Partnerships for Learning, an official publication of the American Association of School Librarians and the Association for Educational Communications and Technology, defines information literacy as "the ability to find and use information" and describes it as "the keystone of lifelong learning" (American 1). Teachers and librarians use *Information Power* for help in planning new approaches to student research that emphasize the importance of these real-life skills.

Students who become personally and intensely involved in their search for information begin to understand that "cut and paste" is not research. They realize the research skills they are learning in order to complete an assignment also will serve them well in many areas of their life.

Librarians Are Sources of Information about the Internet

Librarians use a variety of techniques to make all faculty members aware of both useful and illicit Internet sites. They provide information for students and faculty to use in the library and in classrooms.

Document and illustrate plagiarism from Internet paper mills.

- Print the first pages of several term paper sites and several sample papers from each to make it very clear to the teachers just what is available to students.

- Copy a few pages that list the titles of available papers that match assignments given by teachers in your school. Circulate the list to the faculty to illustrate why they should not assign the same topics each year.

- Set up faculty bookmarks on library computers so teachers can investigate the term paper sites for themselves.

- Encourage teachers to browse the sites to get a feel for what is available in their subject area.

- Distribute an annotated list of term paper sites. Note that some papers are free and the rates charged for others.

- Set up bulletin-board displays on paper mills in the faculty lounge and cafeteria to get the attention of faculty and students. Let the students "know that we know" about the sites.

- Make selected suggestions from the online cheater sites available for teachers.

Develop effective workshops on the use of the Internet for teachers, perhaps one department at a time (see Farmer workshop at end of chapter).

- Demonstrate (1) interesting, legitimate sites their students might use for research, (2) apparently "safe" and legitimate sites that turn out to be questionable, and (3) sites that offer term papers and reports free or for sale.

- Demonstrate just how simple and fast it is to download a paper and quickly create a new title page with the student's name, current date, and class information.

- Demonstrate how easily a student could use a word processor to change the first paragraph or two and make the paper more difficult to recognize.

Disseminate information and documentation on the issues of cheating and plagiarism.

- Notice what is catching the attention of the news media and share these ideas and articles with faculty and staff.

- Search SIRS, ProQuest, NewsBank, etc., for articles on "plagiarism" and "cheating" and route them to faculty and staff.

- Provide information to be included in faculty announcements, the student newspaper, letters to parents, library files, etc.

Create three-ring binders to identify legitimate Internet sites on topics of general interest to faculty and students.

- Download one or more pages from each site selected, usually including the home page; be sure the URL can be read clearly.
- Put the page(s) in clear plastic three-ring covers, and then add the page(s) to a three-ring binder created for the specific topic. Printing the pages in color adds to their appeal.
- Binders can be used as indexes to the Internet just as print or electronic indexes are used for books or magazines. They can be checked out to teachers, or a teacher can copy pages for classroom use.
- Students and teachers can identify sites to be added to the binders.
- Pages in the binders can be updated easily as Webmasters redesign the sites or Web addresses change.
- Teachers can request binders to match specific classroom research assignments.
- Current topics and biographical sites are especially useful topics for binders.
- Sites in the binders can be bookmarked on the library computers or be saved to a disk for teachers or students.
- Sites for an entire department can be combined to create a CD-ROM to be checked out and easily loaded onto other computers.

Teachers and Librarians Collaborate on Research Assignments

As part of the librarian–teacher team, librarians provide support and resources for all phases of the research project. They work with students in class groups or individually as the students organize their search strategies and evaluate research materials.

Co-design assignments, identify adequate research topics, and explore alternative presentation ideas.

- Be available to brainstorm ideas with teachers.
- Teachers might have a general idea of what they would like their students to do as a research project, but are not sure it really is "doable." Help teachers avoid setting students up for frustration that can lead to cheating.
- Identify new topics or at least ones that have not been used recently.
- Suggest Internet sites for each topic; create bookmarks for teachers/departments.
- Be sure enough material will be available for the number of students/classes involved in the research project.
- Provide a variety of resource materials at appropriate reading levels.
- Help students focus their topics, clarify a topic for someone who was absent, or assist a shy student who didn't want to ask questions in class. Many times students select a topic that is either too broad or too narrow; help them adjust their focus.

Review the elements of a research paper, including outlining, note-taking, foot-notes, bibliographic format, etc.

- Design brief "Show-and-tell" lessons for classes based on immediate needs; offer refresher mini-lessons on new materials as appropriate.
- Provide MLA, APA, and other appropriate standards for citing sources. Post examples for frequently asked style questions in the library, distribute them on bookmarks, and add them to student writing handbooks.
- Provide multiple copies of the official school style guide(s) for student use in the library.
- Prepare oversized note cards showing the correct citation format for popular print reference sources and display them near the volumes referenced.
- Prepare oversized note cards or bookmarks showing the correct citation format for electronic resources, including SIRS, UMI ProQuest, NewsBank, Internet email or electronic articles, etc., and post these near the computers.

Encourage students to plan an alternative to a standard term paper, for example, plan multimedia presentations or publish papers and presentations online.

- Students developing a multimedia presentation cannot easily download a paper from the Internet and transform it.
- Multimedia reports often require more teacher–student interaction; this discourages blatant attempts at plagiarism.
- Publishing a paper online, or placing it on a class or school Web site, might require permission from the parents. If other students' pictures are included, their parents will have to give permission.
- Many students will need assistance in learning the software program(s) required.
- Careful attention is needed to schedule adequate access to school computers for all students.

Co-teach lessons when students come to the library as a class.

- Plan with teachers to make sure that students in each class scheduled into the library have specific goals to meet or tasks to accomplish that day. Require ten note cards due at the end of the period, a list of five new reference sources either to turn in or at least to show to the teacher, a revised outline, etc. This is more effective than simply telling students to "work on your paper" in the library.
- Help to break term paper assignments into manageable segments, check for completion, and assist with grading each step along the way.
- Collaborate with classroom teachers to develop assignments that fit each student's ability level.
- Teach research skills appropriate to the grade level and specific assignment.
- Teach with the teacher—word processing, presentation tools, CD-ROM or Internet searches, etc.
- Work with teachers so that assignments accept only photocopies of illustrations; this can reduce mutilation of original illustrations in library books and magazines.

- Alert teachers to students who seem to be copying or downloading an excessive number of pages, especially from an electronic encyclopedia, as this might be a sign of intentional or unintentional plagiarism.

Librarians Make Research Materials Easily Accessible

Librarians select print and electronic materials and provide access to appropriate online sites to support a wide range of research assignments for all departments in the school. They take special care to select resources to meet the needs of students at all ability levels.

Provide a wide variety of materials appropriate to each student's reading and ability levels so students can find needed information quickly and easily.

- Become familiar with students' needs by careful observation of their work in the library and through discussions with teachers and staff.
- Children's books and other "easy reads" can benefit all students seeking an overview of a topic or specific information in a brief format, even in high school. These books tend to be visually appealing and provide a welcome break for all students.
- Provide books from teachers' outside reading lists.

Assist students and teachers in locating and using appropriate outside sources.

- Librarians are familiar with local community library resources and can identify those helpful for students on specific assignments. As a courtesy, either the teacher or the librarian can notify college or public librarians of the upcoming assignment and request assistance.
- A school library that belongs to a cooperative library agency has access to material from surrounding libraries that can be requested as needed.
- Refer students to specialized or university libraries only if the materials are at a level they will comprehend.

Make materials accessible according to students' abilities and time constraints. Balance the need to provide individualized instruction in locating materials with a student's need to obtain the material quickly and easily.

- Help students locate the information they need, frequently working with them at the catalog or reference shelves, rather than making them locate all resources for themselves. Students have the same time pressures that adults do and appreciate assistance.
- When research time is at a premium and the library is scheduled heavily, put books, software, hardware, and other appropriate research materials on carts to send to the classroom.
- Place special collections of library materials on reserve as needed.
- Make reference materials available on overnight checkout.

- Borrow materials from public libraries to fill gaps in school collections for special assignments.
- Flyers and displays in the library can provide hints on locating specific types of resources and library services.
- When checking out special reference items or materials borrowed from other libraries or a teacher's personal library, consider holding the student's ID/library card overnight to assure that the materials are returned.

Create a friendly and welcoming atmosphere of assistance for research.

- Work at a desk in the library rather than in an office to be more accessible to students.
- Walk around the library periodically to notice students who need assistance.
- Provide brief, on-the-spot class lectures to remind students which sources and strategies are best.
- Make the library look less cluttered and more inviting.
- Rearrange the seating so it looks less institutional.
- Add plants, comfortable chairs, and low shelving to make the library more attractive.

Cyber-Plagiarism Faculty Workshop

The technology information in this workshop can be presented by the librarian or by a teacher–librarian team. It can be used with an entire faculty or the topics could be edited as appropriate for a single department. It would be an interesting program for parents.

Pointers

Chapter 14 stresses the importance of the research *process* as well as the *product* and suggests ways to structure writing assignments to reduce plagiarism. Chapter 16 describes alternative writing assignments that would be difficult to complete with a paper located online or in a file of old term papers.

COPY ME:
Cyber-Plagiarism Faculty Workshop

Dr. Lesley Farmer

Introduction

The Research Strategies Studies Group is working on improving the quality of student research. We believe that the temptation to plagiarize is one of the biggest hurdles students must overcome in conducting meaningful research. This activity is designed to familiarize teachers with the increasing number of Internet sites designed to assist students in the process of plagiarism. We believe that it is extremely important that teachers become aware of these sites in order to fully understand the scope of this problem.

The Assignment

It's 11:00 p.m. on Sunday evening and you have a term paper due tomorrow morning. Your teacher gave you class time to do library research, but you spent this time chatting with your friends. The paper is vital to your grade in the course and could even threaten your upcoming graduation. A friend told you about some Internet sites where you can essentially download a paper complete with bibliography. You decide that this is the path to take.

Work in groups of 2-3 (you can pick your own group). Choose one of the research topics from the list below. Find a computer in the library or computer lab. Your objective is to use the Internet to plagiarize a research paper. Your paper should be two to five pages in length, and include a bibliography. You can begin by using the list of web sites (URLs) listed below, or you can try using one of the search engines. Be certain to put the names of all group members on the top of the first page. Try to make your paper look as authentic as possible. The first group to hand in an acceptable paper will win a prize.

Time permitting, discuss as a group the questions for discussion. Written answers are appreciated.

Names of Group Members (Collaborating CyberScum):

Topics:

Helpful Web Sites Addresses: Start your research here.

- <http://www.chuckiii.com/>
- <http://www.collegepapers.com/>
- <http://www.members.tripod.com/%7ETexasTwister/>
- <http://www.researchpaper.com/>
- <http://www.schoolsucks.com/>
- <http://www.cheathouse.com/>
- <http://www.cyberessays.com/5>
- <http://www.nh.ultranet.com/~lmaccann/default_the_brain_trust.html>

Reprinted with permission from Student Cheating and Plagiarism in the Internet Era: A Wake-Up Call *by Ann Lathrop and Kathleen Foss. Englewood, CO: Libraries Unlimited, 2000.*

Topics: Choose a topic from the list below before you begin your research.

AIDS	Black Hole	Antibiotics
Brain	Carl Jung	Bronchitis
Light	Steroids	Nuclear Energy
UFOs	Daniel Webster	Hitler
The 1960's	Woodrow Wilson	Revolution in Cuba
Gandhi	Karl Marx	Lebanon
Henry Ford	Martin Luther King	Native Americans
King Henry VIII	*Catcher in the Rye*	*Glass Menagerie*
Brave New World	*Lord of the Flies*	Mark Twain
Censorship	*1984*	*The Great Gatsby*
Marijuana	African Art	History of Jazz and Classical Music
Johann Sebastian Bach	*Oedipus*	Leonardo DaVinci
Berkeley	The Beatles	

Questions for Discussion:

1. If the paper you just completed were turned in to you, would you be suspicious? Why or why not?

2. Describe the types of assignments that are most susceptible to plagiarism.

3. Describe the types of assignments that are least susceptible to plagiarism.

4. How could you change the assignment that you were just given to make it less susceptible to plagiarism?

5. Think about the research assignments that you currently give to students. What percent of these assignments are vulnerable to cybercheating? How could they be altered to make them less vulnerable?

[Developed for use in Tamalpais (CA) Union High School District. Reprinted with permission from Dr. Lesley S. J. Farmer, California State University, Long Beach.]

Reprinted with permission from Student Cheating and Plagiarism in the Internet Era: A Wake-Up Call *by Ann Lathrop and Kathleen Foss. Englewood, CO: Libraries Unlimited, 2000.*

Chapter 13

Identifying and Reducing Plagiarism

> *"Plagiarism" comes from the Latin plagiarius (a person who steals slaves), and was first used by the Roman poet Martial as a literary conceit for the stealing of servants of the imagination. Another poet, Fidentinus, had been borrowing Martial's poems and reading them as his own, and Martial mockingly and comically ridicules the weaker poet for trying to enslave those who serve the mind of a master.* (Kolich 143)

Chapter Overview

The easy availability of free papers from the Internet brings plagiarism forcefully to our attention. Many techniques to detect plagiarism are the same for a "high-tech" paper copied electronically as they are for a "low-tech" paper copied from a friend, book, or encyclopedia. Teachers familiar with their students' writing ability and style are most likely to recognize a paper that is "too good" and question the student about it.

A discussion of unintentional plagiarism is followed by lists of "Indicators of Possible Plagiarism." Two Copy-Me pages can be used as discussion starters in faculty or parent meetings. The first, "An Electronic Scavenger Hunt," is another example of the process of searching online for the original of a plagiarized paper. Bruce Leland's Copy-Me page urges teachers not to become "plagiarism cops" who spend excessive time and energy trying to locate a suspect paper online. Instead, he suggests bringing online paper mill sites into the classroom and building lessons around them. Students might be less inclined to turn in online papers when they have evaluated the papers as a class exercise and know their teachers are aware of the sites.

Chapter subheadings:

- "High-Tech" and "Low-Tech" Plagiarism
- Unintentional Plagiarism

- Indicators of Possible Plagiarism
- Copy Me: "An Electronic Scavenger Hunt"
- Copy Me: "Plagiarism and the Web"
- Jackson, Tway, and Frager: "Dear Teacher, Johnny Copied"

"High-Tech" and "Low-Tech" Plagiarism

Authors of "how to cheat" books and Web sites tell students to disguise their plagiarized papers in a variety of ways. Corbett advises them to "insert many new stupid, harmless errors on your own. The more menial correcting a teacher has to do (spelling, grammar, etc.), the less likely he is to think this paper was manufactured. Distract him; use grammatical errors as a decoy" (98). Croucher explains how to "doctor a paper" by using an electronic thesaurus to substitute synonyms for many words in the paper being copied (15).

We know that the techniques students use to revise a paper taken from the Internet are becoming more sophisticated. Many have learned to break up distinctive word strings and delete unique proper names. As described in Chapter 3, some use translation software to disguise a paper, for example, by translating a French paper into English. Other students use more traditional methods, copying paragraphs or entire articles from print encyclopedias. Still others copy a friend's paper or rework one of their own written for another class. All are guilty of plagiarism.

Students are in a learning mode as they write and we must keep this in mind. Spelling or grammatical errors and synonyms used in awkward ways are proof neither of plagiarism nor originality. A student whose word processor has an electronic thesaurus can pop in "ten-dollar" words that look suspicious but are innocent.

A brief discussion with the student usually clarifies the situation when there is a question of plagiarism. If a serious doubt remains, probably the best indicator of plagiarism is a comparison of the suspect paper with other work in the student's writing portfolio. These approaches work equally well for either "high-tech" or "low-tech" plagiarism.

Unintentional Plagiarism

In any discussion of plagiarism it is important to separate the issue of unintentional plagiarism, especially in the primary grades. Young children learn almost everything by copying the actions of those around them—walking, talking, drawing, singing, etc. It is not unusual for a student to read another student's story on the bulletin board or in a collection of class stories and then write an almost identical one. Rather than intentional plagiarism, this can be simply an extension of copying behavior that has been acceptable in the past. They might not be able to understand the concept of plagiarism fully until they are older, but we can help them begin to make a distinction between creating their own poem or story and "adopting" one written by another person.

Another form of unintentional plagiarism occurs when young children love a poem or story so much they internalize it to the extent that it becomes their own. Just as children can "become" Superman, the Lone Ranger, or Xena the Warrior Princess, the stories and poems they have made their own can become "theirs," and in their own minds no longer have another author. The difference between intentional and unintentional plagiarism by young children is explored more fully in the article following this chapter, "Dear Teacher, Johnny Copied."

Waltman makes a distinction between *intentional plagiarism* as "the wholesale copying of another's paper with the intention of representing it as one's own" and *unintentional plagiarism* as "careless paraphrasing and citing of source material such that improper or misleading credit is given" (37).

An important step to help older students avoid unintentional plagiarism is teaching research techniques and writing skills in the classroom. Many students need instruction on how to research a topic, outline it, paraphrase and quote selectively, summarize, make note cards, rewrite material in their own words, and cite sources in each instance. According to many authors, this instruction is necessary at each grade level whenever a research project is introduced. McGregor observed that effective teachers took three positive actions:

- provided students with ongoing instruction and guidance, taking them step-by-step through the process

- emphasized avoiding plagiarism on a regular basis, not just once the first day

- provided written information about how to avoid plagiarizing and talked about it in class. (McGregor 4)

Indicators of Possible Plagiarism

The three sections that follow describe fairly typical cases of student plagiarism and can be useful in identifying and dealing with plagiarism. A paper might appear to be too well written for that student, or it might sound familiar, or perhaps it does not quite fit the assignment. In each case plagiarism is possible but should not be assumed (with the exception of the paper handed in with the web address still evident printed at the top of the paper). Legitimate and reasonable explanations are possible.

Many authors writing about plagiarism agree the best defense is a caring, informed teacher who knows the writing ability level of the students. A second line of defense in many schools is a writing portfolio maintained for each student. Few students show sudden dramatic improvement in writing skills and the evidence represented by sample papers in the portfolio might be enough to encourage a student to admit to plagiarism. Once confronted in private, many students will confess and remediation can begin.

A Paper Seems to Be "Too Good"

A student's paper reads like an encyclopedia article.

- Ask your librarian for help in checking electronic encyclopedias and other sources.

- Pick an unusual string of four to six words or a proper name from the paper and search for that string on the Internet.

- Ask the student to explain why certain phrases were used or to identify the location of some specific fact.

A student turns in a paper that appears to be clearly above his research or writing capability (Fishlock, par. 19).

- Have him read aloud a few paragraphs from a paper in his portfolio, then read a long paragraph from the suspect paper; compare the fluency of reading and ask a few questions to check understanding.

- Give him a paragraph or two from the paper to rewrite in his own words in the classroom as you observe.
- Select five or ten big words in the report and ask him to explain them.
- Make a copy of a section of the report, cut the section into paragraphs, and have him reassemble it (if he wrote it, he should be able to organize it again).
- Ask what word processing program he used, which font and size he used, whether he used a computer at home or at school, and where he printed the report.
- Ask whether he used a spell checker; if so, ask him to explain why any misspelled words were not identified.
- Ask him to bring the outline and drafts to the interview; this is effective only if students have been told to save them to turn in with their papers.

A student's papers written at home consistently are better than papers written in class.

- Ask her if her parents or anyone else helps her with writing assignments at home. Does she have a private tutor? If so, discuss the problem of "too much help" with the parents and be certain she and her parents understand what is permissible.
- Ask her if she uses the writing lab at school. It can be helpful to clarify "permissible assistance" with the writing center staff.
- Explain the types of help that are acceptable and make it clear any help that goes beyond these limits is considered plagiarism.

A critical review of a play or film seems to be very professional in writing style and vocabulary (Benning, pars. 16–17).

- Check a few unique word strings on the Internet in search of the original review.
- Discuss the play or film in some detail with the student, asking her to explain and justify several of "her" opinions as expressed in the review.

A paper contains words you wouldn't expect the student to know, for example, unusual adjectives, archaic expressions, highly technical terms, etc. (Bjaaland and Lederman 203).

- Have the student read aloud a paragraph with unusual vocabulary or scholarly terms and note the fluency of his reading; students usually don't use unfamiliar sentence constructions or write words they don't know.
- Have him explain or paraphrase the paragraph.

A student's paper has a few poorly written paragraphs at the beginning, and perhaps a few at the end as well, but the rest of the paper is very well written (Benning, par. 6); *this could be a chapter copied from a book.*

- A good clue is whether the writing in the middle of the paper sounds too advanced for the student.
- Check for consistency of sentence length throughout the entire paper (Fogg 331).
- Check the bibliography for books and journal articles that actually exist; many book chapters do not have separate bibliographies.

- Ask the librarian to identify books in the school library that cover a broader topic than that of the suspect paper, but have a short chapter that might have been copied.
- Ask the student to read one or two difficult paragraphs and explain them.
- Ask where several items in the bibliography were located.

A paper has a journalistic sound, for example, short sentences, frequent quotes from experts in the field, snappy writing (Sanchez, par. 18).

- Pick an unusual phrase or two and search for that phrase on the Internet.
- Ask your librarian for help in checking CD-ROM and online sources of current news articles in your library such as ProQuest, SIRS, or NewsBank.
- Ask the student to discuss the paper with you and explain why he chose the experts he quoted.

A Paper Sounds Familiar

A student hands in a copy of a friend's paper from a previous semester, or one from a file of old papers from your class (or other sections of the same or a closely related class) that are available on campus.

- Keep all old papers filed in the department by topic; return a grade sheet with your comments to the student but don't return the paper. It's easy to spot a duplicate in the file and prove the student copied the paper. An alternative is to require that two copies be handed in; return one and file the other.
- Be sure to check the middle section of the paper; many students are savvy enough to have changed the beginning and ending sections as well as the title (Graber, par. 44).
- Avoid using the same assignment year after year; do not give students their choice of topics used in prior years (Bjaaland and Lederman 203).

Students in different sections/periods of the same class appear to have worked together on their papers and turned in very similar final versions.

- Check all papers on the same topic for conclusions that are too similar, or even for paragraphs that are the same in the middle of the paper.
- Check the papers for bibliographies that are identical or vary only slightly.
- Be sure you have explained to your students the degree of collaboration you consider to be fair.
- Ask the students, separately, for an explanation of the close similarity. Check their understanding of permissible collaboration on the assignment.

A Paper Appears to Be Just "A Little Bit Off"

The paper has an odd appearance.

- The title page is in a different font or typeface from the body of the paper (Navarro, par. 6) or printed on a different style of paper (Magney, par. 43).
- Gray or faded text in areas that were in color on the screen indicates a paper printed directly from the Internet.

- The layout seems strange and might appear to be a combination of two or more format styles.
- Links to Internet sites are embedded in the paper, there are strange headers or footers, or a web address from the Internet has been left on the printout (Bushweller. *Digital,* par. 11).
- Ask the student for an explanation of breaks in page numbers, a Web address, or other strange or "out-of-place" items.

The paper just doesn't match the assignment closely enough (Wentzel, par. 2).

- The paper is on the same general topic but perhaps has a different approach than the one assigned.
- The assigned topic is addressed to some extent but is not the focus of the paper.
- The actual topic is addressed only in a few paragraphs that don't seem to fit with the rest of the paper.
- Ask the student to clarify the treatment of the topic and have him explain several paragraphs to check his understanding of what "he" has written.

A quotation or a reference cited in the paper doesn't "sound right."

- Finish grading all of the papers before you return any; the suspect source might turn up cited correctly in another paper (Bjaaland and Lederman 205).
- Ask the student to discuss the quotation or reference, explain what it means to her, how it supports the topic, where she located the quotation or source, etc.
- Check that all citations in the paper actually are listed in the bibliography (Navarro, par. 6).

The bibliography is suspicious in some way, for example, it is unusually long, there are few if any references from the assigned readings for the class, many items are very scholarly, all or most of the copyright dates are three or four years old or more, the format is different from that required for the class or is in strict APA, MLA, or some other style the student would not be likely to know (Bjaaland and Lederman 203).

- Ask the student to explain why the bibliographic format differs from that required for the class and to show you the style manual she used.
- Have her demonstrate the format she used by writing new bibliographic citations for three new articles and books you provide; check whether they match the format used in the suspect paper.
- Ask where each reference was located; some, at least, should be from the school library. If not, ask why the school library was not used.
- Ask which print and electronic periodical indexes she used, and ask for a copy of the page from the index showing the reference cited.
- Ask her to explain how one specific reference influenced the research or is used in the paper.
- If no entries in the bibliography were published in the current or previous year, ask why there are no recent items.

- If there are one or more articles from highly specialized scholastic and academic journals, ones most students wouldn't normally know about or use in writing their papers, ask her to identify the library or online database where she located one of the journals. Ask her to discuss the article she referenced from that journal.

- As a precaution, require that the finished bibliography be turned in one week prior to the term paper, so you can look over the works cited and possibly check the online catalogs of your school library as well as local college and public libraries to see if some of the references actually exist and are cited correctly.

Pointers

The article following Chapter 5 explains in more detail how to search online to locate the original of a plagiarized paper. Chapter 14 recommends restructuring assignments to make plagiarism more difficult. The article by Robert Harris at the end of Chapter 15 suggests a variety of practical ideas for reducing plagiarism. Chapter 16 outlines alternative writing assignments that would be hard to locate online or in files of old papers.

COPY ME:
An Electronic Scavenger Hunt
Kathleen Foss

Like most educators, I was aware that sites on the Internet provided term papers to students. That was the extent of my experience until I overheard my son and a friend discussing how easy it would be to take a paper from the Internet and "fix it" to look like their own work. My interest was piqued because both of these students were in special education classes, and to my knowledge, had never been required to do a research or term paper—but they knew the process. When I had some time between classes scheduled in, I decided to see how easy it would be to create my own plagiarized report using one of our library computers.

Using Yahoo, I typed in "term papers" and the search began. Finding sites on the Internet can be compared to a complex treasure hunt. When one search engine has been exhausted, you switch to others or to a megasearch engine such as Dogpile. Usually you strike gold on the first or second citation. From then on it is a matter of going from link to link and in and out of sites. Occasionally you find a site with links to many other paper sites and the hunt expands in a hurry.

The Big Nerds site, one that offers free papers, was found late in my search. The paper I selected, "Medieval Castles," contained the distinctive name of a modern sultan who built his own castle in the 1980s, Sir Muda Hassanal Bolkiah Muizzaddin Waddaulah. This long and unusual name lent itself to the type of "string check" described by plagiarism detection specialists as a way to check suspect papers.

The writing in the paper on medieval castles was quite adequate to pass for acceptable student work so I decided to use it for my test case. There were, however, several problems with the bibliography: (1) The font did not match that used in the body of the paper; (2) The style was neither APA nor MLA; (3) Only four items were listed, none of them recent; and (4) A number in front of each entry in the bibliography appeared to reference a corresponding number in the text, but these numbered references did not appear in the text.

Next, pretending to be a teacher searching for this "plagiarized" paper online, I searched Yahoo using the name of the castle builder as my "string." The original, legitimate paper was listed among several other country profile sites that contained information on Sir Muda Hassanal Bolkiah Muizzaddin Waddaulah. As an added bonus, I also located the same paper on another term paper database. The paper available from this second paper mill had the bibliographic information in the same print font as the main body of the paper but still was not in MLA or APA style. I had now located the original paper and copies in two paper mills.

There are term papers available online to students on almost every conceivable topic. With just a little patience, a student probably could find two or three papers from different sites, then cut and paste sentences, paragraphs, etc., to create an "original" paper. An experienced student could remove any distinctive strings that a teacher could use to search online for a matching paper.

All of this can be accomplished with little real effort and without developing any true research or writing skills, thus defeating the entire purpose of the assignment. The student whose plagiarism is not detected has learned nothing of value and receives a false and totally undeserved grade.

Reprinted with permission from Student Cheating and Plagiarism in the Internet Era: A Wake-Up Call *by Ann Lathrop and Kathleen Foss. Englewood, CO: Libraries Unlimited, 2000.*

COPY ME:
Plagiarism and the Web
Bruce H. Leland

So what is a teacher to do? How do we cope with papers downloaded from the paper mills and turned in as the student's own work? Here are some suggestions, many of which also help with the much more common problem of papers borrowed or purchased from friends:

- Let students know that you know about these web sites. Then do actually check some of them out. Students will be less likely to submit a plagiarized paper if they think you might have seen it on the Internet, or that a classmate might submit the same paper.

- Take students to several of the sites. Have students look at a weak paper (there are plenty of these on the Internet!) and analyze its failures. They will learn something about writing and see that the papers available for downloading might not impress their teacher.

- Teach students to use the papers on the Internet as sources for their own papers (along with the multitude of other web sources). Show them how to correctly cite electronic sources.

- Regarding advice on avoiding plagiarism: it's best to approach it as an issue of fair use and intellectual property. A discussion about the ways people use (and acknowledge) one another's ideas is better than an *ex cathedra* "Don't Plagiarize" rule. When presented as a "rule," it gets relegated to the list of other rules (use one inch margins, put commas between items in a list) and students are genuinely surprised when violation carries a stiffer penalty than the other rules!

- Use the issues raised by the paper mill web sites as a writing assignment on ethics.

- Watch your students write. Ask them to bring notes or drafts to class, have short conferences about the assignment, use peer groups to comment on drafts, ask for drafts to be submitted with the final paper.

A word of advice: Do not write to the maintainers of the Web sites to complain or threaten. Kenny Sahr has turned such complaints into publicity for his site, letting the press know how he was being treated. In fact, he got enough publicity that he was able to sell advertising space at schoolsucks.com! He and the others have the same right to publish what they want on their web sites as do the rest of us (and the hate groups and the pornographers). And, as Kenny himself pointed out—at least these papers are available for teachers to access—unlike those collected in files around campus.

The fact is, I personally have very little problem with plagiarism. I rarely give exactly the same assignment from semester to semester, and I try to tie the assignments to the work we're doing in the course—both of which make it harder for students to find ready-made papers to submit. I assign one or two print or online sources that must be in the bibliography and worked into the paper. I also use group work or conferences on drafts of at least some course papers.

If there were one thing that I'd like to suggest it's that teachers not turn into plagiarism cops. I've seen teachers waste valuable time trying to track down a suspected plagiarism. It can become an obsession—and should be avoided. Most students will do their own work most of the time, and a teacher who has been paying attention to her/his students' work will readily spot cheating when it occurs.

[Excerpts printed with permission of the author. Bruce Leland can be emailed at <l@wiu.edu>. Article is online at <http://www.wiu.edu/users/mfbhl/wiu/plagiarism.htm>.]

Reprinted with permission from Student Cheating and Plagiarism in the Internet Era: A Wake-Up Call *by Ann Lathrop and Kathleen Foss. Englewood, CO: Libraries Unlimited, 2000.*

Dear Teacher, Johnny Copied

Louise A. Jackson, Eileen Tway, Alan Frager

It is Jason's turn to sit in the 1st grade Author's Chair. He chooses to share a piece of his writing that he finished at home. Even the teacher has not seen it. With great pride, conscious of his achievement in writing a whole book without teacher help, Jason announces: "This is my book. Its name is 'My Tree.' "

He begins to read in a clear voice. Before two pages are turned, Mrs. Turner, Jason's teacher, realizes that Jason is sharing a paraphrased version of Shel Silverstein's *The Giving Tree.*

Mrs. Turner wants Jason to continue to be enthusiastic about writing, but she is in a quandary. What should she do? Accept the writing and try to steer him into other avenues next time? Gently explain that she likes his story but has heard it before? Tell Jason firmly that it is not his story, show him *The Giving Tree,* and insist that all his writing be done at school from now on?

This is not an unusual problem. As editors of anthologies of children's writing, we have received letters from readers telling us as tactfully as possible that a particular poem in the latest edition of the anthology was not really written by that child.

We try to keep this from happening, and classroom teachers do, too. Yet, in spite of our best efforts, children still appropriate other authors' writing from time to time and submit it as their own. Why does this happen? What can teachers do to help prevent it?

Possible Causes

One possible cause is that a child, particularly a young child, might internalize a piece of writing so thoroughly as to be sincerely unaware some months later that it is not his or her own.

Larissa's example illustrates this. In 2nd grade, her basal reader included a fall poem that she loved. She read it over and over. Eventually, she memorized it and for several days said it to herself as she walked home from school. In the following October, when her teacher asked the 3rd graders to write poems, Larissa wrote the one she had memorized the previous year.

Not being familiar with the poem, but thinking it quite good, Larissa's teacher submitted it for consideration for publication. When it appeared in a collection of children's poetry, other teachers recognized and pointed out the source. When told she had copied this very honest, responsible student cried and really didn't seem to remember, until reminded, that the poem had been in her 2nd grade reader.

A second likely cause of naive plagiarism is competition for recognition, perhaps to win a contest or receive a good grade. Competitive conditions can drive an insecure young author to appropriate something already published, in a conscious or unconscious attempt to better the odds. Also, too much emphasis on the writing product often makes a child fear that his or her own work is unworthy.

The story of Harry, a 6th grader in a large city school, illustrates the relationship between self worth and ownership of a person's writing. Whenever it was writing time in his classroom, Harry would open a book and copy at random. His teacher knew that his selections were random that is, without meaning to him, because he always started at the beginning of any page where he happened to open the book, whether it was the beginning of a sentence or not. Harry just wrote because it was writing time and he evidently felt he had nothing of his own to say.

Harry's teacher tried to help him understand that he could write something of his own, something that mattered to him, but the few sentences that Harry could write must have seemed pale in comparison with the flowing sentences of his school books. Harry just would not write; he copied, until one day he was so full of the story and anguish of an accident that had happened to his brother that it spilled out of him—on paper. Harry wrote: "My brother hurt he hand. He had to go to the hospital. He alright now."

Harry's breakthrough was a long time in coming. His 6th grade teacher worked patiently to help Harry overcome his feelings of inadequacy. She received the account of his brother's accident with respect due to an important story. She asked Harry's permission to use the story in the class newspaper because it was "news."

Donald Graves (1983) says that, first, a teacher must receive a child's writing before commenting on it. The child needs to know that the teacher will focus on the information first, not the handwriting or spelling or other mechanics.

With the teacher's understanding, Harry finally found the power inherent in having something to say. Harry never copied again in that classroom.

A third possible cause of copying is that students might not understand how to synthesize book information with their own knowledge, experiences, and viewpoints. Such misunderstanding is frequently evident in the writing of research papers. According to Lee (1971) plagiarism starts with 2nd grade reports on topics such as plastics, in which many students might have little interest.

Geosits and Kirk (1983) suggest plagiarism is rooted in the many demands on elementary school teachers' time, which result in report writing being assigned but not guided through teacher modeling and conferencing.

A third culprit might be the high readability levels of encyclopedias, those universal sources for report writing. Children can easily find in encyclopedias the relevant information for reports, but they encounter so many difficult words that reporting often turns into verbatim copying (Dohrman, 1975).

Finally, we are painfully aware that the appearance of childhood plagiarism might happen by accident. Such an incident arose in the childhood of one of us. In this case, a verse enjoyed in a school reader was copied to share with the family. Thinking it was original and without waiting for an explanation, the grandmother carried on about how wonderful it was and promptly called an aunt to applaud the lovely poem the child had written.

In no time at all the situation was completely out of hand. The family kept exclaiming about the work and the child kept putting off the explanation until she was totally entangled and it seemed entirely too late to tell. What an agonizing experience! At last, a neighbor child recognized the poem, and told her own mother, who called the girl's parents. The relief that came when the unintentional deception was brought to an end completely outstripped the scolding that followed.

Suggested Remedies

Above all else, we feel that children are most likely to produce their own writing when the classroom environment provides lots of support and encouragement for writing, so that every child receives positive feedback about his or her writing. Making books of children's writing for the classroom library and encouraging the sharing of writing among classmates can add to children's positive feelings of owning their writing. When self-expression and self-growth aspects of writing are stressed, a child is less likely to be concerned whether or not someone else's writing is better.

Also, since successful writers compose from their own knowledge, whether acquired by experience or research, we need to help children understand that what they are interested in, what they have experienced, and what they want to know more about are the best bases for their writing.

Secondly, teachers should model the approaches we use in getting ideas for writing. As Graves and his associates so often point out, we need to go through the process out loud, to say "If I were going to write right now, here are some of the things I might write about and here's why."

For example, the idea for this article came as a result of a discussion about our own problems with children's submission of copied material without attribution. We realized that we were dealing with a common and puzzling problem, which might be valuable to share with others.

It is also helpful to explain explicitly why it is important not to use published ideas in exactly the same form. For older children, the term "plagiarism" can be presented. Because many children simply don't understand what the teachers are raising such a fuss about, they might have no sense of wrongdoing.

Teachers need to explain about "ownership" of writing to help children value their own compositions. The explanation might best include a demonstration in which the teacher models and guides students in how to use the ideas of another author. Take a short article, make copies for all the students, and then verbalize methods of paraphrasing, summarizing, and citing sources, which are used in adapting information for an original report.

Other types of direct instruction in report writing can also deter students from copying. Geosits and Kirk (1983) suggest the use of a who-what-where-why-how framework which requires more analysis and integration of the facts presented in encyclopedias. To help children see encyclopedias in a different way than just a repository for facts to be copied, Suid (1979) recommends asking children to write an encyclopedia-style article about a subject not found in an encyclopedia.

Students might also be given instruction in reviewing encyclopedia articles by upgrading them with new information, such as space flight articles prior to the Challenger disaster, or by combining the information in two encyclopedia articles on the same topic to produce a new, more complete article (p. 51).

Appropriate selections in children's literature, such as Karp's (1974) *Nothing Rhymes with April,* can be read during storytime to spark discussion about writing, ownership, and honesty. In this novel for intermediate grade children, a young girl's lie about her family convinces an adult judge of a poetry contest that the girl's well written poetry must have been plagiarized.

Similarly, the detrimental side effects of competition in the primary grades are well illustrated in McLenighan's (1977) book for children *I Know You Cheated,* which has an open ending to encourage children to think about and discuss the issue of owning one's work.

In summarizing, then, to remedy the copying syndrome teachers can:

1. Support the self expression and self discovery aspects of writing.

2. Model both the spontaneous generation of original ideas for writing and the integration of one's original ideas with information from published sources.

3. Use direct instruction to teach students how to write reports without copying.

4. Keep alive the discussion about writing, ownership, and honesty, using children's books where possible to spark new insights.

Can teachers, by following these suggestions, guarantee that children will never copy again? We doubt it. However, as in Harry's case, a classroom situation which is sensitive to the anxieties and rewards inherent in self expressive writing can help young writers avoid the jeopardy of copying and find the value in their own voices.

Jackson teaches at the University of Wyoming in Casper, Wyoming, and coedits *Pioneer Press,* a publication of children's writing. Tway is on the faculty of Miami University, Oxford, Ohio, and edits another magazine of children's writing, *The McGuffey Writer.* Frager teaches reading education at Miami University, Oxford, Ohio.

References

Dohrman, Mary H. "Stopping 'Copy-catting.' " *Elementary English* 52 (May 1975): 651–52.

Geosits, Margaret S., and William R. Kirk. "Sowing the Seeds of Plagiarism." *Principal* 62 (May 1983): 35–38.

Graves, Donald H. *Writing: Teachers and Children at Work.* London, England: Heinemann, 1983.

Karp, Naomi J. *Nothing Rhymes with April.* San Diego, CA: Harcourt Brace Jovanovich, 1974.

Lee, Nancy V. "Plagiarism Starts in Second Grade." *Grade Teacher* 88 (April 1971): 19–20.

McLenighan, Valjean. *I Know You Cheated.* Milwaukee, WI: Raintree, 1977.

Suid, Murray. "How to Take Copying out of Report Writing." *Learning* 8 (November 1979): 6–47, 51.

Chapter 14

Structuring Writing Assignments to Reduce Plagiarism

I don't believe there is any way in this rapidly changing environment that we can be sure that idea sources are being properly credited or that whole papers aren't being lifted. Yet we pay a high price when students feel we expect them to be dishonest. A good teaching and learning climate requires mutual trust and high expectations.

My approach would be to have students defend their ideas, not just hand in a written paper. If they can stand up to questions from peers, teachers and/or experts about where the evidence lies and its quality, or the connections of one idea to another, or the point of view of a cited author, then the worry about source diminishes, because the student has really worked hard enough to understand deeply the meaning of the ideas she/he is presenting.

If students know that as part of their paper's evaluation they will have to demonstrate not only the knowledge they have gained, but their facility with these habits of mind, there is much less value to them in simply handing in a copied paper. They have to go deeper so they can understand enough to defend the concepts, show evidence, and speculate about next questions.

Unfortunately, like everything else about technology, this requires often uncomfortable change both in the way teachers organize research and use class time. But the results for students are worth it.
(Mark W. Gordon, Library Consultant)

Chapter Overview

A student's grade for a research assignment should be based on an evaluation of all steps in the research *process* rather than only on the content and organization of the written report, or *product*. This can reduce plagiarism by requiring outlines, drafts, working bibliographies, etc., which are

174

not available from online sources. A student research portfolio can organize and document the research process.

A sample "Research Portfolio Cover Sheet" is formatted as a Copy-Me page. Suggested topics to be included in a school or district student writing handbook and extensive recommendations for structuring the writing assignment to deter plagiarism complete the chapter. A carefully documented model of the research process is provided in the article by Susan Davis.

Chapter subheadings:

- Evaluating Both the Research *Process* and the *Product*
- Copy Me: "Research Portfolio Cover Sheet"
- Student Writing Handbook
- Structuring an Effective Assignment for a Report or Research Paper
- Davis: "Teaching Practices that Encourage or Eliminate Student Plagiarism"

Evaluating Both the Research *Process* and the *Product*

Technology in the form of word processors, electronic databases, and the Internet makes it important that teachers reconsider how research papers are monitored for originality and how grades are assigned. Traditionally, the emphasis has been on grading the completed research paper for content and format, with little attention paid to how it was developed. Many teachers today grade each step of the research *process* and consider the process to be as important as the research paper, or *product*.

As Mark Gordon suggested, grading the research assignment can be expanded to include students' presentation of their conclusions in dialogue with classmates. An oral or multimedia presentation to the class becomes an addition to the formal written report. Students can publish their conclusions or entire papers on a class web site to initiate a dialog with students in other locales (see copyright issues in Chapter 9). Making these explanations and defenses a significant part of the grading rubric can reduce plagiarism as well. A student cannot meet the requirements of such an assignment with a paper downloaded from the Internet the night before it is due.

The impact of new technologies on research projects is another reason to revise grading rubrics to focus on the research *process* in addition to the written report, or *product*. Electronic search strategies speed the location of resources. Word processing software can format footnotes and bibliographies automatically. Evaluation, therefore, is best focused on an analysis of specific reference sources for accuracy and relevance, the quality of writing, the care with which conclusions are developed, and students' defense of their conclusions.

Specified parts of the paper should be submitted at stated intervals and supported with an outline, notes, note cards, drafts, photocopies of sources from books and magazines, copies of pages downloaded from the Internet, a working bibliography, etc. Students learn to organize these "bits and pieces" to provide documentation of the research process and proof of the originality of their papers. This type of material is not likely to be available for a paper from an online site.

A student research portfolio, set up as a separate section within the traditional student writing portfolio, is an effective way to evaluate each step of the research process. It provides a paper trail for work actually completed by the student and keeps the project from becoming a cut-and-paste word processing assignment.

A reflection segment can become an important feature of the research portfolio. Students record a personal account of the research process as they experienced it. This encourages them to review their research strategies thoughtfully (Harris, par. 14). Stripling suggests: "Students keep a research log during their whole process of research, noting in a brief entry at the end of each day what they learned, what questions they have, and where they need to go next" (168).

Student research journals are one of twelve strategies for developing information literacy in *From Library Skills to Information Literacy: A Handbook for the 21st Century:* "Students who are information literate must develop the ability to recognize what they are doing, analyze the results, and consider or reflect on how any learning based on these results might be applied to another situation" (California 73). Examples of several research journal formats are included in the discussion.

Student research portfolio cover sheets document the research process for each assignment; copies kept in the writing portfolio track a student's research topics over the years. The following Copy-Me page offers one design for a cover sheet.

Student Writing Handbook

A writing handbook developed by the district or school provides guidance for reports and research papers. The handbook can include:

- discussion of the research process and techniques for productive research in the library;
- suggestions for writing a research paper or reporting findings in another format, for example, publishing a paper online or developing a multimedia presentation;
- a list of community resources that can be helpful;
- an explicit statement of what is plagiarism and what is not, including the statement on plagiarism in the school Academic Integrity Policy;
- instructions for creating note cards;
- a sample outline for a research paper;
- models and clear examples of how to cite all types of print and nonprint sources, including Internet sources, community and family interviews, and original surveys
- a sample of a correctly formatted bibliography or list of works cited (MLA, APA, or other required style); and
- examples of various pages to show how a completed paper should look, including an outline of the various parts of the paper and the order in which they should be placed.

Evaluation criteria established in the school or district writing handbook should be followed unless students are informed otherwise and given written examples of the alternative criteria. Requiring that students adhere to specific criteria makes it more difficult to plagiarize; papers from online sites or other sources will not follow exactly the same style or conventions.

Some teachers might prefer a different style guide, for example, APA when examples in the school writing handbook use MLA. It is their responsibility to clarify the criteria and provide explicit examples of how the style they require differs from that in the writing handbook.

COPY ME:
Research Portfolio Cover Sheet

Student Name: _____

Teacher:_____ Period: _____

Topic:_____ Date Due:_____

This sheet and the following items are to be included with the final paper.

(any missing items will affect your cumulative final grade)

Prewrite due:_____

For five to ten minutes you will be writing what you know about your topic already and explaining what you would like to show or prove. Tell how you plan to investigate it.

Pre-search of available materials due:_____

Pre-search includes a check of the library holdings, a few searches on the Internet, and perhaps a call to the local public library to check on the amount and type of information available there. Documentation would be a list of several likely sources, note cards with titles and call numbers, photocopies of some materials found with call numbers and library location, printouts from the Internet, etc.

Note cards due:_____

First draft due:_____ Second draft due:_____

Rough drafts of the paper will be required throughout the process. Drafts are checked for style and format as well as content. Each new draft is expected to show significant progress in the work accomplished.

Draft of working bibliography due:_____

This is due prior to the actual due date of the paper in order to check for format and content.

Defending your paper:

After your paper has been turned in you might be called on to discuss it in class. Be prepared to explain your topic, defend your conclusions, and describe where you found your sources and where in the paper the sources were used.

Reflections on the research process:

This can be in the form of a diary or log and should document your search strategies, successes and frustrations, and the "ah-ha" moments in your research process. Turn it in with your paper.

Parent signature:_____ Date:_____

(for any questions about the assignment, please call or email me at:
_____)

Reprinted with permission from Student Cheating and Plagiarism in the Internet Era: A Wake-Up Call *by Ann Lathrop and Kathleen Foss. Englewood, CO: Libraries Unlimited, 2000.*

Structuring an Effective Assignment for a Report or Research Paper

"Simply assigning students to write a research paper on a general topic, then collecting the papers a few weeks later is an invitation to plagiarism" (Magney, par. 34). Yet this is, unfortunately, a very traditional approach to research assignments. The suggestions that follow can make such assignments more difficult to plagiarize and more effective learning activities for students. They come from our own experience, discussions with friends and colleagues, and from the authors cited.

Planning the Assignment to Discourage Plagiarism

- Plan to have several short papers of one or two pages during the semester rather than one long one; a shorter paper requires more summarization and makes it harder to incorporate lengthy, illicitly copied passages (Hall 7).

- Make the papers no more than three to five pages in length to discourage copying from the Internet; most of the online papers are six pages or longer (Galles, par. 9).

- Avoid student frustration that can lead to plagiarism by doing some preliminary research on new topics. Find out what sources are available at the reading levels your students need. This can usually be done in conjunction with the school library staff. It is helpful to call or fax the proposed assignment to nearby libraries the students can access; ask if students will find adequate research materials on their topics.

- If appropriate, plan to require that each student design and conduct an interview, survey, or experiment and report on it as part of the paper (Galles, par. 8). This individualizes the paper and makes it more difficult to substitute already written papers.

- Have students state their own opinion on the topic, and justify the opinion, as part of the paper (Fogg 330). This individualizes the paper.

Preparing Students for Honest Success

- Be certain all students have a clear understanding of acceptable collaboration, quoting, paraphrasing, and plagiarism, and what these differences mean in writing a paper (Fogg 330).

- Every student should have a copy of the writing handbook adopted by the school or district. Develop a student writing handbook if your school does not have one.

- Review the writing handbook with students and require adherence to this standard for footnotes, quotations, bibliographic format, etc. This is an important guard against the use of copied papers as they are unlikely to be written in the correct style.

Topics that Can Limit Plagiarism

- Use a new set of topics for each new class—never repeat topics (Bjaaland and Lederman 204).

- Develop a specific list of limited topics rather than letting students choose whatever catches their interest (Waltman 37).

- Assign very narrowly focused topics rather than broad general ones (Gonzalez A1).

- Use very, very current topics to lessen the chance of papers being available on the Internet (Wagner 4).

- Make writing assignments so unusual that papers probably aren't available on the Internet or from other sources (Galles, par. 9).

Managing the Research Process

- For a collaborative report, it is important that students have a clear concept of the whole project and understand exactly what their specific individual contributions will be.

- Structure the writing assignment as a series of steps with checkpoints. Require that a specific segment be handed in each week (Galles, par. 4). Respond to each of these with helpful comments—remember that teaching students to write better is one purpose of the assignment.

- Provide class time for research in the library and assign a specific task to be completed each period, for example, five note cards, two new reference citations, etc.

- Have students write one or more drafts, or the entire paper, in class.

- Have students read drafts of their papers aloud in both large and small groups, followed by discussion (Carroll 93). They should be able to state their main ideas orally without quoting directly from their sources.

Antiplagiarism Precautions

- Help students credit the sources of all ideas that are not their own by creating a "person-noting page" as a new category in addition to a formal bibliography. Here they acknowledge all the persons who have provided any type of assistance on their research project (Carroll 93).

- Keep a writing portfolio of each student's past written assignments for comparison with a "too good to be true" paper.

- Let students know you have their writing portfolios and are familiar with their general writing ability level. Tell them you will double-check any paper that appears to be well above that student's level. Keep the portfolios in a secure place so a student accused of plagiarism cannot remove papers.

- Monitor student work in the library. Students not doing any constructive work might be planning to hand in a plagiarized paper; be suspicious when told "I'm working on my paper at home."

- Periodically check specific parts of the paper to make certain students are doing their own work: title or statement of the focus of the paper, thesis statement, preliminary summary, outline, note cards, first draft, draft of bibliography, etc. (Wein, par. 23). The Student Research Portfolio Cover Sheet can be used to maintain a record of work completed.

- If possible, photocopy the handwritten drafts completed in class and initial each page, or date each page with colored ink or a stamp. Students then word process the paper at home or in the school computer lab. The handwritten work is turned in with the printed paper; a copy is available in case a student "loses" the original.

- Require that copies of at least two drafts, note cards, list of sources used, etc., be turned in with the finished paper; these are not available from online sources (Waltman 38).

- Use in-class writing assignments for a series of short papers rather than one long paper. Set the research topic and have students complete their research, bring note cards to class, and then write a paper in class based on a specific aspect of the topic that will be presented by the teacher in the class period when the paper is being written.

- For some classes, it might be appropriate to have students research a controversial topic and bring their notes to class; they will debate the topic, or write and document a paper, on one side of the issue or the other as assigned by the teacher (Galles, par. 7).

- Tell students in advance that you will select quotations at random and check them against the cited sources (Factor 59).

Creating the Bibliography

- Check the working bibliography early in the assignment. Continue to review it periodically and expect to see one or more new sources each time.

- Require that, in addition to being listed in the bibliography, print copies of all information located on the Internet be turned in with the report (Gonzalez A5).

- Have students photocopy one or more pages from each reference in the bibliography, highlighting relevant paragraphs, and turn these in with the paper (Galles, par. 6).

- It might be difficult for students to authenticate their sources by handing in copies of all materials used. Many copy services now require a copyright release for complete articles. Accept the first page and any pages that contain quotes referenced in the paper.

- Tell students in advance that you will select one bibliographic entry at random from each bibliography and the student will be required to produce that specific book, journal, etc., show you the online site, or tell you exactly where it was located.

- Set a due date for the finished bibliography a week before the paper is turned in so you can check it for anomalies. As time permits, check random entries with school and local libraries to see if the sources are really available.

- Require that all of the resources be current, most from the last two or three years unless there is a valid reason to use older materials (Waltman 38).

- Assign one or more specific references that must be integrated into the text of the paper and referenced in the bibliography; these should be ones not likely to be found in papers from the Internet (Galles, par. 9).

- Require an annotated bibliography with one or two sentences describing each source (Galles, par. 6). Tell where and how each source was located.

Presenting the Paper

- Abstracts for their papers can be written by students in class on the day they hand the papers in. Those who did their own work should be able to write a credible abstract (Galles, par. 6).

- As time permits, let each student read the abstract of the paper to the class, then lead a brief discussion (Serafin. *About* 3).

- Have students be prepared to present their papers orally, followed by class questions and discussion in which they must defend their conclusions (Galles, par. 7).

- On the day reports are due and after the papers have been collected, have each student write a letter to a prospective employer that describes the assignment and the research method used; include a summary of the conclusions as an abstract (Waltman 38). These letters could be posted online to share with others in the class or with students in other schools.

Security Issues

- Many departments set up a file of student papers arranged by topic so they can check suspected papers against the file (Wein, par. 40). Students turn in two copies, one for the file and one to be graded and returned.

- Keep papers handed in before the deadline in a safe place so other students cannot take them to copy.

- Do not put samples of students' papers on a course web site where other students might copy a paper for future use (Stebelman, par. 8).

- Do not leave graded papers in unsupervised areas where they could be picked up by someone expecting the same topics to be assigned again.

Pointers

Lesson ideas in Chapter 15 cover topics that can help students learn to write a research paper without plagiarizing. The article by Robert Harris at the end of Chapter 15 is an excellent summary of many of the antiplagiarism ideas developed throughout this book. Chapter 16 suggests alternative writing assignments that would be difficult to locate online or in files of old term papers.

Teaching Practices that Encourage
or Eliminate Student Plagiarism

Susan J. Davis

Middle school teachers have a love–hate relationship with research reports. They love to assign them, but they hate to grade them especially because they are so frequently plagiarized.

Student plagiarism of source texts has annoyed teachers for generations. Writing educators have gone through cycles of assigning reports, questioning their value, and assigning them again. In the early 1970s, Bjaaland and Lederman (1973) developed criteria to scrutinize each paper to detect plagiarism. Plagiarized papers, of course, were given failing grades. During the early 1980s, Schwegler and Shamoon (1982) bemoaned the continuation of plagiarized papers. The solutions they suggested were to abandon the research report, to spend more time training students to organize data, and to stress the argumentative nature of the research paper. Many teachers opted for the first idea and discontinued assigning reports. During the "back to basics" movement, research papers were not only reinstated in many schools, they moved further down the grades. Rather than staying in the domain of high school, reports became popular in middle schools and elementary classrooms and were assigned to children as early as first grade. Unfortunately, assigning student research papers in middle school does not guarantee that by high school students will be able to write reasoned accounts of a topic. Instead, plagiarism has become ingrained at earlier years and the resultant habits became more difficult for students to change.

Recently, however, researchers in the fields of reading, writing, and library science have begun investigating processes used in report writing. The findings of these researchers indicate that plagiarism is prevalent in middle schools for two reasons: (a) instruction on research is grounded on a faulty model of the research process, and (b) teachers unwittingly encourage plagiarized papers.

A Model of the Research Process

One of the reasons students plagiarize is because they are taught to do research under a faulty instructional model (Davis, 1992). Students have generally been taught to do research using a linear stage model that includes the stages of choosing a topic, narrowing that topic, locating information, taking notes, organizing the notes, and writing the paper (Kuhlthau, 1984). This model of research is based on the behaviorist philosophy of the best-match principle (Dervin and Dewdney, 1986). Best-match theory describes research as the formulation of a question that is then matched to existing texts that answer the question. The flaw in best-match theory is that it presumes that students can ask a question about an unfamiliar topic and that an answer to the research question exists in text that can be understood by middle school students.

Recent researchers have questioned the accuracy of using behaviorist philosophy for instruction on research (Davis, 1992; Kuhlthau, 1984). These researchers have hypothesized that writing a research report is an act of construction similar to reading and writing and that instruction should reflect that cognitive viewpoint.

Cognitive learning theories suggest that learning is an act of construction, an integration of what the student knows with new information. Because every student has different background knowledge, the construction of meaning from the same text will produce different meanings for different students. Furthermore, when new information is integrated into existing knowledge structures, students approach additional information differently than they would have in the past. Students are changed by new knowledge so that each interaction with information is a unique situation.

Viewing the research process from the cognitive view changes the complexion of research writing instruction. Rather than a behavioristic linear stage model for the research process, researchers operating under the cognitive viewpoint suggest that research is a recursive process (Davis, 1992; McGinley, 1992; Calkins, 1986). These researchers suggest that students are constantly setting goals for their research and using appropriate strategies to meet their goals. Students tend to move through the stages of research from initiation to writing (Davis, 1992; Kuhlthau, 1984), but they can move back and forth through the stages. Therefore the research process, like the writing process, has some linear elements, but it can be generally characterized as a recursive process (Davis, 1992; McGinley, 1992).

One result of the faulty instructional model of research is that by middle school, students have developed bad habits. During my research on student practices of writing reports in the content areas, I interviewed ten gifted eighth-grade students who had just completed a report on the causes of the Revolutionary War. During the interview, one student proudly explained how he wrote his social studies report. He said, "I just opened one encyclopedia on one side of my computer and laid another encyclopedia on the other side. I wrote one paragraph from the one on the left and then one from the one on the right. I always get A's that way."

What was more disturbing than the students' bad habits, was their attitude toward research. When I explained to the students that writing from source texts with minimal changes is plagiarism, they were amazed—and a little angry. The most common response was, "How come we can't plagiarize even a little? It's hard to write in our own words." Then the students came up with a most telling response, "Who cares if we plagiarize? It's only for school!"

Teachers Encourage Plagiarism

A second reason why students plagiarize is because teachers often encourage and reward plagiarism. One of the ways they encourage plagiarism is by assigning topics that are so broad that they could be the topic of an entire book (Applebee, 1981). When students are asked to find out about a broad subject such as marine animals, they feel that copying encyclopedia entries, which are highly synthesized accounts, is an acceptable response (Wray, 1985).

Not only are the topics assigned to students overly vague, teachers sometimes give higher grades for plagiarized work. Part of my job is to work with classroom teachers to implement the teaching of reading and writing strategies. I was working with a fifth-grade teacher who had assigned her students to write a report on explorers, a topic that set students up for failure. However, after I worked with them on gleaning information from source texts, charting and organizing the information, and writing in coherent paragraphs, I was pleased with the results. All of the students except two had struggled with the thinking processes necessary to abstract and synthesize information. The students had papers written in their own words.

Two of the students, however, resisted every effort I made, ignored my instruction, and refused to change their already bad habits. They copied entire paragraphs out of the source texts changing one word per sentence. As a result, their reports sounded more sophisticated than the real writing of the rest of the fifth graders. When the teacher graded the reports, she expressed dismay over the shorter paragraphs of the real researchers and gave the students who had plagiarized "A+s."

Teachers, then, often assign topics that are too general and reward plagiarized papers with higher grades. Because many teachers do not understand the processes involved in research, they even tell students they can plagiarize. I have had several students over the years tell me that their teachers have allowed them to plagiarize source texts for reports (sometimes under the rubric of paraphrasing). It is not often, however, that a teacher admits it. One fourth-grade teacher did. When I asked if she would like to learn some strategies for helping students write reports, she replied, "Oh, I let them copy out of the encyclopedia. After all, it's their first report."

If plagiarism is such a problem for middle school students and instructional materials and teacher practices do not ameliorate the problem, the question that has been troubling educators for decades needs to be recalled: Should middle school teachers continue to assign research reports? Recent research concerning reading–writing connections indicates that they should.

Research affirms what teachers have long believed: the reading–writing connection is a powerful learning combination (McGinley, 1992). Reading about a topic and synthesizing new information in a report is a valuable strategy for independent learning (Flack, 1986). Therefore, middle school teachers should not hesitate to assign research reports. To prevent plagiarism, however middle school teachers should consider the following educational recommendations.

Rethink Research Assignments

The most important responsibility of the teacher is to assign topics for research that are meaningful to students. Research reports should not be reports "about something," but an area that the student wants to investigate (Calkins, 1986). Reports should be an outgrowth of areas of student interest—"a topic should choose the writer" (Macrorie, 1984).

Because most middle school teachers also must teach an agreed upon curriculum, they need to strike a balance between student self-selection and the curriculum that needs to be covered. Such a balance is possible. The teacher can provide a broad framework for the assignment, but should also guide students into a section of that topic that is a personal search for meaning. For example, I was working with seventh-grade students who were studying Russian life and culture. The students were encouraged to find a part of that topic to investigate rather than to write about Russia in general. One student, whose family belonged to the Eastern Orthodox religion, investigated ways Russian Protestants celebrated Easter. The student then compared the Easter traditions of the Russians to those of his own family. Another student, who was taking ballet lessons, investigated famous Russian ballet dancers. Each student learned something about the Russian culture through the report, and most of the reports represented original student writing.

Another method of making report topics meaningful is to choose topics that are authentic problems. Renzulli (1982) defines authentic problems as those that do not have an existing solution that can contribute new information to any field of knowledge. Research reports should fall under that definition. They should be the ideas of the students combined with knowledge from source texts.

Middle school teachers can develop topics for research reports that would lend themselves to the creation of original work. One idea used in a literature class was for students to verify the accuracy of an historical novel (Davis and Hunter, 1990). Another possibility is for students to write for publication for a young adult or children's magazine (Davis and Johns, 1989). Teachers in any content area can develop ideas that would be authentic problems for students to investigate.

Build Background Knowledge

One reason middle school students have difficulty choosing research topics is because they lack the background knowledge needed to think of areas to investigate (Davis and Winek, 1989). Things that are common knowledge to adults, such as the expertise of Russian ballet dancers, might not be known to middle school students. Teachers tend to assume that students know more than they do. When assigning research reports, however, teachers should assume that their students know virtually nothing about the topic.

Middle school teachers can help students build background knowledge in a number of ways. First, they can use picture books for general information about the subject (Graves, 1989). Picture books are often highly informative and are written about many content areas.

A second way students can build background knowledge is by discussing what they have learned. Davis and Winek (1989) recommend discussion groups about similar topics for students to share what they have learned. Another strategy is for students to use peer-conference partners to question each other about their topic (Calkins, 1986).

A third important method to build background knowledge is by writing. Students who free write about their topic in a journal can begin to understand what they have learned already. The writing can be in first person (Today, I found out that . . .), or in third person (The Trojan Horse was . . .). Using either approach, students can learn what they know and do not know by writing. Murray (1985) suggests that writing can be a vehicle to express ideas that the writer cannot verbalize. "Why write? To be surprised. The writer sits down intending to say one thing and hears the writing saying something more, or less, or completely different" (Murray, 1985, p. 7). Therefore, asking students to write about the topic they are investigating helps them focus their thinking.

Keep Topic Selection Open During Research

As students learn about their topic through reading and writing, they should keep the topic of their papers an open choice. Topic selection is a compromise between the writer's own ideas and preferences, the source material available, and the time allowed for searching (Kuhlthau, 1984). Sometimes middle school students need to be given a deadline to force them to make a final decision about their topic, but generally students continue to revise their topic choice until they are actually in the writing stage of their research (Davis, 1992).

Provide Easy Source Texts

Providing easy reading source material is paramount to successful investigations by middle school students. Because comprehension of text is dependent on the existence of background knowledge, material written at grade level might be too difficult for students to comprehend. Encyclopedias are written at a level most middle school students can read, but the concept load is so dense that students cannot comprehend many of the passages. Teachers who insist upon middle level students reading articles from young adult or adult journals might be compounding the problem. Comprehending, selecting information, and synthesizing information written at reading levels and concept loads well above middle school level present an impossible situation for students. Students are unable to understand the material so they might again resort to plagiarism.

One way middle school teachers can determine the appropriateness of the source text is to have students read the text and explain the "gist" of the passage. If the reading level and concept load are appropriate for the students, they will be able to repeat a main point of the passage. If the text is too difficult, the students might have no response or they might repeat a detail or two from the passage.

Organize Data

Once students have begun to read, write, and discuss their topics, they need to start organizing their data. The methods they use to record their data should be left to student choice. Teachers can provide suggestions such as note cards and data charts, but students should be allowed to organize their data in the manner that best fits their topic. One very helpful strategy for organizing data is through graphic organizers. Students should brainstorm main ideas and examples from their reading and write them on the charts. After data is organized, the writing becomes easy.

Rethink Paper Length

Middle school teachers often assign reports that are a certain number of pages. In defense of that practice, most students feel more comfortable writing a research report if they understand the boundaries. However, in my interviews with seventh-grade students writing social studies reports, I found that most of them made the decision to end their search for information when they thought they had the designated number of pages, not the best reason for deciding to finish reading about a topic.

Perhaps an alternative to a five-page paper would be to assign a range of paragraphs the students should write. Ideally, that decision should be made by the teacher and individual student together as the student is organizing data. Clearly, some topics under investigation have a greater amount of source material available to students than others. If equity among students is important to the teacher, one recommendation is for students to think of three subheadings for their topic and to write from two to four paragraphs for each section.

Present Findings of Research

When students have gone through the time and effort to write a report, their findings should be made public in some manner. Teachers can think of a variety of ways for students to present their findings. One goal of the research, however, might be for students to think of two or three methods of presenting their material. The teachers can then choose which option would best fulfill their class requirements. Asking students to develop their own methods of presenting findings helps keep the idea of an audience forefront in their minds. The teacher can then guide the students in their final decisions and can balance the presentations between papers for the class to read and oral presentations for them to hear.

Conclusion

The research report has been misused for years because the research process has not been well understood. With the advent of cognitive learning theory, the research process is now being viewed from a different perspective, that is, a recursive process rather than the linear process that is most often followed in middle school instruction. If middle school teachers begin to understand the research process, they can tailor their instruction to better fit how students actually learn. With new instructional strategies, middle school students can learn the joys of writing research reports.

References

Applebee, A. N. *Writing in the Secondary School, English, and the Content Areas.* Urbana, IL: National Council of Teachers of English, 1981.

Bjaaland, P. C., and A. Lederman. "The Detection of Plagiarism." *Educational Forum* 37 (1973): 201–6.

Calkins, L. M. *The Art of Teaching Writing.* Portsmouth, NH: Heinemann, 1986.

Davis, S. J. "The Research Process of Middle School Students." Unpublished doctoral dissertation. DeKalb: Northern Illinois U, 1992.

Davis, S. J. and J. Hunter. "Historical Novels: A Context for Student Research." *Journal of Reading* 33 (1990): 602–7.

Davis, S. J., and J. J. Johns. "Students as Authors: Helping Gifted Students Get Published." *Gifted Child Today* 15 (1989): 20–22.

Davis, S. J., and J. Winek. "Improving Expository Writing by Increasing Background Knowledge." *Journal of Reading* 33 (1989): 178–81.

Dervin, B., and P. Dewdney. "Neutral Questioning: A New Approach to the Reference Interview." *Reference Quarterly* 25 (1986): 506–13.

Flack, J. (1986). "A New Look at a Valued Partnership: The Library Media Specialist and Gifted Students." *School Library Media Quarterly* 14 (1986): 174–79.

Graves, D. *Investigate Nonfiction.* Portsmouth, NH: Heinemann, 1989.

Kuhlthau, C. C. "The Library Research Process: Case Studies and Interventions with High School Seniors in Advanced Placement English Classes Using Kelly's Theory of Constructs." Doctoral diss., Rutgers U, 1983. *DAI* 44 (1961–1961A).

Macrorie, K. *Searching Writing.* Upper Montclair, NJ: Boynton/Cook, 1984.

McGinley, W. "The Role of Reading and Writing while Composing from Sources." *Reading Research Quarterly* 27 (1992): 226–48.

Murray, D. M. *A Writer Teaches Writing.* Boston, MA: Houghton Mifflin Company, 1985.

Renzulli, J. S. "What Makes a Problem Real: Stalking the Illusive Meaning of Qualitative Differences in Gifted Education." *Gifted Child Quarterly* 28 1982: 147–55.

Schwegler, R., and L. K. Shamoon. "The Aims and Process of the Research Paper." *College English* 44 (1982): 817–24.

Wray, D. *Teaching Information Skills through Project Work.* Kent, England: Hodder and Stoughton, 1985.

Susan J. Davis teaches at Illinois State University, Normal.

[Reprinted with permission from National Middle School Association. The information originally appeared in the January 1994 issue of *Middle School Journal*.]

Chapter 15

Tools for Writing without Plagiarizing

> *Whenever I introduce the subject of plagiarism to a writing class, I'm assailed by memories of my days in grades five through twelve when I wrote reports by copying information from the relevant* World Book *or* Encyclopedia Americana *article. Rather than chastise me, my teachers rewarded my efforts; one biology teacher complimented me by asking to keep the paper into which I had painstakingly copied details about the physiological systems of a representative from each phylum. As a result, I believed that length and relevance were the only criteria of acceptable scholarship [and] I continued to copy with an untroubled conscience unless asked to do otherwise.* (Dant 81)

Chapter Overview

Students who have learned the skills of paraphrasing, summarizing, and quoting selectively, with correct citations, will have a better understanding of plagiarism and how to avoid it. Mastering these skills can help students to achieve success independently, removing one reason to plagiarize.

The lesson ideas in this chapter are excerpts from journal articles or reports that suggest ways to teach the skills students need to avoid plagiarism. Complete citations to the original articles are provided for readers who want to explore a lesson in more detail. The article by Robert Harris at the end of the chapter is an excellent summary of much of the material presented here and in previous chapters.

Lessons:

- Brownlee: "Coping with Plagiarism Requires Several Strategies"
- Drum: "Responding to Plagiarism"
- Hall: "Decreasing Plagiarism Using Critical Thinking Skills"
- Kreis: "A Write Step in the Wrong Direction"

- Lasarenko: "Teaching Paraphrase, Summary, and Plagiarism: An Integrated Approach"
- Rankin: "Get Smart: The Crucial Link between Media Specialists and A+ Students"
- Whitaker: "A Pedagogy to Address Plagiarism"
- Harris: "Antiplagiarism Strategies for Research Papers"

Lessons

Brownlee, Bonnie J. "Coping with Plagiarism Requires Several Strategies." *Journalism Educator* 41.4 (1987): 25–29.

Brownlee identifies seven errors students make in citing their sources and emphasizes a need for class discussion of examples of each error. These discussions should go beyond the mechanics of proper citation to focus on the meaning and purpose of scholarship. Her seven types of errors are:

1. Out and out copying

2. Paraphrasing without attribution

3. Failing to quote a quote within a quote

4. Quoting the quote but not the author

5. Mixing the author's words with a person's own

6. Footnoting a paragraph

7. Failing to document interviews, speakers or videotapes. (26–27)

Drum, Alice. "Responding to Plagiarism." *College Composition and Communication* 37.2 (1986): 241–43.

Drum describes a series of assignments and a writing workshop designed to teach students how to avoid plagiarism.

> The preliminary assignments may include an abstract, a summary, a brief background paper. The writing workshops include sessions where the students analyze the style and the content of a selected passage and then attempt to put that passage in a different form. They can work on creating an effective paraphrase of a brief article; they can take a single sentence and rewrite it a number of times, making as many stylistic changes as possible without changing the content; they can rewrite a brief passage—an article from *Newsweek*—in the style of a well-known writer. The aim of these exercises is twofold: to help the students understand that writers do give an identity to their words; and to give students confidence in their own ability to create a style of their own in their writing. (242)

She stresses with her students that "avoiding plagiarism does not simply involve adhering to a formula, but, also, involves dealing carefully with the style and the content of the original" (242).

Hall, Ann W. *Decreasing Plagiarism Using Critical Thinking Skills.* A Practicum Report. Nova University, July 1986. ERIC (ED 323495).

This summarizing activity can be adapted for any grade level by changing the reading level of the material. For the first activity, Hall and the students read and discuss together each paragraph of a selection, restate the main idea in the students' own words, and write that sentence on the chalkboard. These sentences are condensed and combined as needed to create eight "main idea" sentences that summarize the selection. Students then write individual essays based on these eight sentences.

Hall introduced the second activity after the class had developed some proficiency in writing summaries:

> ... students were given a reading selection and instructed to write a 100 word summary. When they completed their summaries, the reading selection was taken from them and they were then asked to restate their 100 word summary in 75 words. A series of shorter and shorter summaries, based on their previous summaries of the same sketch, were required, forcing the students to put the summaries into their own words as they shortened each summary. (25–26)

The report describes other positive approaches to foster critical thinking in conjunction with the skills of report writing. According to Hall, "Simply defining and explaining plagiarism and the consequences therefore and using threats to prevent it is a negative approach and does not give students the skills they need to avoid plagiarizing" (13–14).

Kreis, Kathleen. "A Write Step in the Wrong Direction." *Teaching Pre K–8* 24.8 (1994): 66–67.

Kreis suggests six practical steps to help students understand the meaning of plagiarism and why it is wrong:

1. Define [plagiarism] as taking and using as a person's own the ideas or written work of someone else.

2. Equate plagiarism to stealing... bicycles, VCR's, sneakers or other items that are important to students.

3. Do not assume that all students understand the meaning of plagiarism.

4. Teach or review the use of quotation marks, footnotes, paraphrasing and other means of giving credit.

5. Ask every young writer to complete an application before his or her work will be considered [and] include a statement for the writer to sign that verifies the originality of his or her submission.

6. Have the student ask his or her teacher, parent or principal to sign a supporting statement [of originality]. (66–67)

The last two steps are appropriate for journalism classes or other situations when student work is to be published.

Lasarenko, Jane. "Teaching Paraphrase, Summary, and Plagiarism: An Integrated Approach." *Exercise Exchange* 41.2 (1996): 10–12.

Students learn to paraphrase and summarize correctly a short or well-known speech or essay; the example used is the "Gettysburg Address." They participate in seven carefully structured activities:

1. bring definitions of "summary," "paraphrase," and "plagiarize" to class [and] discuss the differences and relationships among the three terms.

2. paraphrase the first two sentences [then] examine each other's paraphrases and discuss the surface differences.

3. discuss in groups or in class as a whole the way(s) in which the paraphrase differs from the original text (what gets left out, what gets added, etc.)

4. summarize the text and compare summaries with one another.

5. [discuss] how paraphrase differs from summary—in length, in what gets included, and in what order.

6. review with the class the various ways that paraphrase and summary remain instances of plagiarism without citing the original text.

7. voice their remaining fears about plagiarism. (10–12)

Lasarenko prefers to have students work on a computer network so they can read each other's work and comment via email.

Rankin, Virginia. "Get Smart: The Crucial Link between Media Specialists and A+ Students." *School Library Journal* 42.8 (1996): 22–26.

Rankin has designed a model lesson to help middle school students present information without plagiarizing. The activity that follows is one step in the process.

> Thinking about it, I realized that students rarely, if ever, have a chance to practice examining information, reflecting on it, drawing conclusions, and then expressing themselves in their own words outside the pressure cooker environment of an assignment. So, by asking them to write an original five paragraph essay, we'd give them a chance to practice reporting on information without copying.

> To verify that they weren't copying, we would provide them all with the same information. To make sure the reading was generally accessible, I would choose fairly short, easy-to-read articles on high interest topics. There would have to be enough substance in the reading to allow for different slants and opinions so that the students' drafts would not all sound alike. The teacher would first demonstrate the process using one paragraph of text. The students, working in pairs, could then practice the process as a full class. (26)

The article includes suggestions for helping students create original visual presentations. A model grading rubric evaluates students' writing for purpose, organization, correctly documented information content, writing style, and mechanics.

Whitaker, Elaine E. "A Pedagogy to Address Plagiarism." *College Composition and Communication* 44.4 (1993): 509–14.

Whitaker first reviews correct techniques for quotations, citations, etc., with the class. She then assigns "a hands-on experience in which each student incorporates an aspect of a current magazine article into his or her own writing" (509). Each student has a different magazine article.

> Prior to class, I mark with a paperclip, a highlighter, and a marginal notation a sentence or phrase from one article in each copy. The passages that I select for highlighting include statistics, expert opinions, and memorable phrases that occur in contexts that do not require extensive reading of the articles or more than a general knowledge of world affairs. Attached to the paperclip-placemarker is a strip of paper on which the student completes the assignment given in my marginal notation, documents the assignment parenthetically, and writes a full citation for the article. (510)

The assignments written in the margin direct students to write an original short paper and insert the marked passage. They can be instructed to treat the insertion as a direct quote, a paraphrase, an authoritative quote to support a point being made, etc. Students exchange papers, with magazine article attached, and discuss each other's writing. "Any student who believes that another student's answer either lacks evidence of academic integrity or misrepresents the ideas in the periodical must discuss this conclusion with the writer" (510). Whitaker creates a handout of student responses for further analysis and discussion.

Pointers

A discussion of the defintion of plagiarism in Chapter 9 could be used as an introduction to these lessons. The writing assignments in Chapter 16 are suggested as ones that would be difficult to plagiarize; one or more could be integrated with a lesson from this chapter.

Antiplagiarism Strategies for Research Papers

Robert Harris

Here are some strategies that can be used to reduce the amount of wholesale plagiarism on research/term papers. By selecting a few of these, you can help encourage students to value the assignment and to do their own work.

Strategies of Awareness

Educate yourself about plagiarism.

First, understand why students cheat. Students are most tempted to copy a paper when they have planned poorly and run out of time near the due date for a paper. If you structure your research assignment so that intermediate parts of it (topic, early research, prospectus, outline) are due at regular intervals, students will be less likely to get in a time-pressure panic and look for an expedient shortcut. Second, learn about the various sites that give or sell research papers. There is a list of many of these sites at Termpapers.com.

Educate your students about plagiarism.

Do not assume that students know what plagiarism is, even if they nod their heads when you ask them. Provide an explicit definition for them. For example, "Plagiarism is using another person's words or ideas without giving credit to the other person. When you use someone else's words, you must put quotation marks around them and give the writer or speaker credit by revealing the source in a citation. Even if you revise or paraphrase the words of someone else or just use their ideas, you still must give the author credit in a note. Not giving due credit to the creator of an idea or writing is very much like lying."

In addition to a definition, though, you should discuss with your students the difference between appropriate, referenced use of ideas or quotations and inappropriate use. You might show them an example of a permissible paraphrase (with its citation) and an impermissible paraphrase (containing some paraphrasing and some copying), and discuss the difference. Discuss also quoting a passage and using quotation marks and a citation as opposed to quoting a passage with neither (in other words, merely copying without attribution). Such a discussion should educate those who truly do not understand citation issues ("But I put it in my own words, so I didn't think I had to cite it") and it will also warn the truly dishonest that you are watching.

Discuss the benefits of citing sources.

Many students do not seem to realize that whenever they cite a source, they are strengthening their writing. Citing a source, whether paraphrased or quoted, reveals that they have performed research work and synthesized the findings into their own argument. Using sources shows that the student is engaged in "the great conversation," the world of ideas, and that the student is aware of other thinkers' positions on the topic. By quoting (and citing) writers who support the student's position, the student gains strength for the position. By responding reasonably to those who oppose it, the student shows that there are valid counter arguments. In a nutshell, citing helps make the essay stronger and sounder.

Make the penalties clear.

If an institutional policy exists, quote it in your syllabus. If you have your own policy, specify the penalties involved. For example, "Cheating on a paper will result in an F on that paper with no possibility of a makeup. A second act of cheating will result in an F in the course regardless of the student's grade otherwise." If you teach at a university where the penalty for plagiarism is dismissal from the university, you should make that clear as well.

Strategies of Prevention

The overall goal of these specific strategies is to make the assignment and requirements unique enough that an off-the-shelf paper or a paper written for another class or a friend's paper will not fulfill the requirements. Only a newly written paper will.

Provide a list of specific topics and require students to choose one of them.

Change topics from semester to semester whenever possible. Unusual topics are good because there will be fewer papers already written on them. If you provide a substantial enough list of topics (say two dozen), most students will find something that can interest them. You can also allow for a custom topic if the student comes to discuss it with you first.

Require specific components in the paper.

For example, "The paper must make use of two Internet sources, two printed book sources, two printed journal sources, one personal interview, and one personally conducted survey." Or, "You must make use of Wells' article, 'Intelligent Design Principles,' and some material from either the Jones or Smith book." Or, "Include a graph that represents the data discussed in the first section." If a student begins with someone else's paper and has to work additional material into it, you'll probably be able to tell.

Require drafts of the paper well in advance of the due date.

A quick glance will reveal whether whole sections are appearing without citations. At the draft stage, you have the opportunity to educate the student further and discuss how proper citation works. You can also mark places and ask for more research material to be incorporated. Keep the drafts and let students know that you expect major revisions and improvements between drafts. (This is actually a great way to improve students' writing, quite apart from the prevention of plagiarism.)

Require oral reports of student papers.

Ask students questions about their research and writing process. (This can also be done in a one-on-one office meeting, if you prefer.) Many students have been caught by simple questions like, "What exactly do you mean here by 'dynamic equivalence'?" Few students use words they cannot pronounce, so having them read some of the paper aloud can be interesting as well (although you might be merely exposing the mindless use of a thesaurus). If you suspect a student has copied a whole paper, complete with citations, asking about the sources can be useful as well. "Where did you find the article by Edwards?" Or, "This quotation seems slightly out of context. What was Follett's main point in the chapter?"

Have students include an annotated bibliography.

The annotation should include a brief summary of the source, where it was located (including call number for books), and an evaluation about the usefulness of the source. The normal process of research makes completing this task easy, but it creates headaches for students who have copied a paper from someone (because few papers include annotated bibliographies like this). Another benefit of this assignment is that students must reflect on the reliability and quality of their sources.

Require most references to be up-to-date.

Many of the free term papers online (and many of the ones for sale) are quite old, with correspondingly old references. If you require all research material to be, say, less than five years old, you will automatically eliminate thousands of online papers.

Require a metalearning essay in class when the papers are turned in.

After you collect the papers, have students write an essay about what they learned from the assignment. What problems did they face and how did they overcome them? For most students, who actually did the research paper, this assignment will help them think about their own learning. It also provides you with information about the students' knowledge of their papers and it gives you a writing sample to compare with the papers. If a student's in-class essay ability diverges strikingly from the writing ability shown in the paper, further investigation is probably warranted.

Strategies of Detection

If you suspect a paper has been plagiarized in whole or in part, try some of these methods of detection.

Check for smoking guns.

Stories from other professors reveal that students occasionally turn in a paper that includes a line at the end such as, "Thank you for using TermpaperMania." If the paper has the look of being printed from a web browser (with dates in the corners, for example), it probably was.

If the paper includes some citations to Internet articles, visit those URLs to see if the whole paper is there. It is not uncommon for plagiarizing students to quote and cite a sentence or two and then continue to copy verbatim from the text.

Search for the paper online.

If you suspect the paper might have come from the Internet, go to a full-text search engine like Google, Northern Light, Fast Search, Alta Vista, or HotBot and perform an exact phrase search on a four-word phrase from the paper (find a phrase that has two or three relatively unusual words in it). If the paper is on the Internet, you can find it quickly this way. (You might need to try two or three engines, because they cover different content. See my *Search* page for links to these engines and more.)

Check the contents.

Look at the reference dates. Are they all very old? Are the references themselves unusual? Ask the student about these anomalies. Is the prose style remarkable? Are there two-page paragraphs that remind you of a nineteenth-century encyclopedia? Is there ornate rhetorical structure? Is the vocabulary a bit too sophisticated? Does the introduction get in its own way and stumble around, only to give way to glowing, flowing discourse? (None of these clues will provide courtroom proof, of course, but you might be able to use them profitably in a discussion with the student in your office.)

Use a plagiarism detector. For information on the commercial detection of plagiarism, go to plagiarism.com [Glatt Plagiarism Services] and plagiarism.org.

Chapter 16

Alternatives to Traditional Writing Assignments

IMHO, the most important technique is to assign REAL research. That is, don't assign a report on lions. If the child has any brains at all he will copy—after all, it has already been done so well by others far more informed and educated than he is. Rather assign a problem-based learning situation such as: You are an alien from Mars, assigned to collect two (a male and female, of course) specimens of the Earth animal known as a lion. You must research what the animal looks like (you will be in big trouble if you bring back tigers) and what kind of habitat, diet, etc., it needs. This report (and yes, this was a very simple example, but it can be expanded to any grade level) cannot be copied because it requires original thinking.
(Jamie Boston, Elementary School Librarian)

Chapter Overview

Many students do not write their own papers. Some go through the motions of producing a paper by copying material from one or more encyclopedias or other sources, then adding a few sentences or paragraphs of their own. Others, without guilt or apology, copy an entire paper from the Internet or a friend. No real learning takes place, teachers waste time grading work that is not the student's own, and the grade is meaningless as a measure of the student's ability.

The assignments suggested in this chapter encourage original student writing and are unlikely to be satisfied by papers available online or from any other source. Some are complete lessons reprinted with permission. Others are excerpts from conference sessions or journal articles, bare bones of good ideas that creative teachers and librarians will flesh out appropriately. Complete citations to the original article are provided for readers who want to explore a lesson in more detail.

197

Permission has been granted by Lesley Farmer and George Peterman to reproduce their lessons for classroom use.

Lessons:

- Brand: "Controlled Research: Putting Text to the Test"
- Dick: "Avoiding a Plagiarized Report"
- Farmer: "Beyond Research Reports"
- Fuchs: "Mona Lisa Writes a Letter: An Alternative to the Research Paper"
- Geosits and Kirk: "Sowing the Seeds of Plagiarism"
- Peterman: "Dinner with a Famous American Author"
- Wagner: "Outfoxing Fraud: Research Papers without Repression"
- White: "Too Many Campuses Want to Sweep Student Plagiarism under the Rug"
- Worthen: "A Way to Break Down Writing Research Papers into Steps that Emphasize the Discovery Aspect of Research"

Lessons

Brand, Alice G. "Controlled Research: Putting Text to the Test." Annual Conference on Writing across the Curriculum. Charlotte, SC. 2-3 Feb. 1995. ERIC (ED 377519).

One activity in this paper is designed to help students learn to write an abstract. They receive an article from which the abstract has been removed, write their own abstract, and then compare their work with the original abstract written by the author. In a second lesson, students are given two articles that take opposite positions on a controversial issue. Students write a brief essay to defend the position taken by one article or the other, explain why that article presents the more convincing argument, and document their position with information from both articles. They must include in the essay two or three direct quotes, two paraphrases, and three secondary sources—all cited correctly. For the bibliography, students convert APA references into MLA format, or vice versa (2–4).

Dick, Dwight D. "Avoiding a Plagiarized Report." *Journal of Reading* 27.8 (1984): 734–36.

If a junior high student is assigned a research paper by the science teacher, the result often looks like a photocopy of an encyclopedia article. In an effort to prevent plagiarized reports, try the following assignment. As an example, let's assume that the science teacher's goal is for students to (1) learn about a particular animal, and (2) practice research skills.

The Fact Sheet

Have each student choose the animal he/she is interested in and fill out a fact sheet using reference materials in the school or community library (see sample fact sheet). Require a reference for each fact on the form. Be sure students have copies of acceptable bibliography formats, so that they can list the books used in a bibliography on the reverse side of their sheets. Students should use a number to key each fact with the reference book it came from. (Have students note these numbers in front of each fact on their sheets.) This resembles a footnoting technique, yet is not as formalized.

The next step is for fellow students or the teacher to spot check these fact sheets. Is there enough information and is it written legibly? Do students cite each fact on the bibliography?

The First-Person Story

Using only their fact sheets, students then write a first-person story. Each student becomes the animal he/she chose and tells a creative story about him/herself. Tell students to try to include as many facts as possible from their sheets as they tell these stories. Emphasis should be on trying to write an entertaining story that "slips in" facts and, therefore, educates the reader in an enjoyable manner. Caution students not to give the animal human attributes as they write.

Variations could be for students to write the story for a young reader (and read it to the child), to include pictures, cartoons, or drawings, or to write the story as a script for a puppet show. Using measurements from their research, students could also draw or build full-size animals for display or use in the puppet show.

The value of this form of research assignment is that students find it necessary to use the reference material and record the standard bibliography information while in the library. Second, the finished product will not look like a photocopy from an encyclopedia because the final story is completed in a classroom away from reference books.

You can use this first-person approach to research in many subject areas and with various age levels. Using a similar approach you can have social studies students become figures from history or representatives of foreign governments. Construct your fact sheet according to the students' ability to locate data on people or subjects.

Just watch those next research papers unfold with no lengthy plagiarized sentences.

Sample Fact Sheet

Name:
Common name of animal:
Scientific name (genus & species):
Size:
Appearance:
Locomotion:
Track:
Senses:
Reproduction
Gestation period:
Average number of young:
Nest/den description:
Infant mortality:
Can infant stand/walk/fly at birth?
Length of time young stay with parents:
Normal habitat:
Food preferences:
Strength of current population (endangered? threatened species?):
Enemies:
Living relatives (species type):

Farmer, Lesley. "Beyond Research Reports." Unpublished paper, California State University, Long Beach, Long Beach, CA, 1999.

[Permission is granted by the author to reproduce this lesson for classroom use.]

Because students react to information in different ways and learn in different modes, it follows that we should look for ways to assess their research other than book reports. We also know that sharing research findings is a vital part of the process and needs to be encouraged. Finally, we know that thoughtful synthesis and reflection on research results in more meaningful learning. Yet we still receive possibly plagiarized research projects. What are some other ways that students can synthesize and share research and its impact?

Take World War II. Wouldn't it be more interesting to see Japan and England debating the merits of fascism than reading a three-page summary of the war? Or what about a story about a survivor of a concentration camp or Hiroshima? What would have happened if Hitler had survived? What would a photo album of a buck soldier look like? These are creative options that can excite both students and teachers. Here are some other novel approaches.

Change the Point of View

- Imagine that you are the parent in history. Describe an event and your reactions.

- Imagine that you are the child in history. How does a social upheaval affect you?

- Imagine that you are a sibling of a famous person. How are you influenced by that person's actions?

- Imagine that you are the enemy of the winning side. Justify your action within the story.

- Imagine that you are a teacher. How does an event affect your class? What happens if you interact with the social issues?

- Imagine that you represent a lobbying effort that either supports or opposes the majority's opinion. Give arguments relative to historical decisions and actions.

- Imagine that you are hiring the key person. What questions might you ask?

- Write a detailed resume for key historical figures.

- *YOU* are the significant figure. Explain what decisions you made along the way in the story, why you made those decisions, and the consequences thereof.

- *YOU* are the significant figure. If you had to do it all over again knowing what you know now, what would you have done differently in the story?

Focus on Time

- Describe a prequel to an event.

- Describe a sequel to an event.

- Describe a typical childhood relative to the time.

- Describe the daily life as a senior citizen relative to the time.

- Write an obituary for a civilization.

- Change one major decision that a key person made, and predict the probable consequences.

Reprinted with permission from Student Cheating and Plagiarism in the Internet Era: A Wake-Up Call *by Ann Lathrop and Kathleen Foss. Englewood, CO: Libraries Unlimited, 2000.*

- Imagine the same decisions made in another time frame. What would be the probable outcomes?
- Image the same decisions made in another culture at the same time. What would be the probable consequences?
- Create a timeline for a movement.
- Go backwards. Start at the end and point out what led to the outcome, and so on to the beginning.

Change the Format

- Create a skit or dramatic scene based on a key incident.
- Interview leading figures, either of the same period or in the same field over time.
- Hold a debate about a major decision.
- Write a diary based on an event.
- Develop a flowchart of an historical movement.
- Find "pull quotes" for the major shifts in an event.
- Write a movie "treatment" of history, choosing actors to play each part.
- Produce a newspaper for a climactic time.
- Set an historical decision as a trial.
- Write an editorial based on history.

Get "Arty"

- Make a diorama.
- Make an historical quilt.
- Create a storyboard.
- Make a simulated photo album.
- Develop a collection of artifacts that would represent the topic.
- Find artwork representing the topic, and caption them.
- Make the issue into a comic strip.
- Take photos representing an issue, localizing the story.
- Do "before" and "after" pictures for key points in the topic.
- Make a dollhouse to represent the issue.

Incorporate Technology

- Make a web page.
- Produce a brochure.
- Make a movie "leader."
- Develop a CAD-based environment.
- Create a hot-linked map.
- Shoot a video of a major turning point.

Reprinted with permission from Student Cheating and Plagiarism in the Internet Era: A Wake-Up Call *by Ann Lathrop and Kathleen Foss. Englewood, CO: Libraries Unlimited, 2000.*

- Produce a TV talk show about the topic.
- Create a hypermedia file.
- Complete a spreadsheet of an issue, making columns for Start, Middle and End of the book, and rows for Persons, Setting and Action.
- Do a PowerPoint presentation.

Make Comparisons

- Compare two viewpoints for the same issue.
- Compare two similar figures in different time periods.
- Compare two settings for the same issue.
- Compare two similar documents for the same issue.
- Compare two similar documents for different issues.
- Compare two decisions with the same issue.
- Compare two situations in two different cultures where the key figures made different decisions.
- Compare two similar situations in two different cultures set in different times.
- Compare two events within a movement: an early effort and a late effort.

Create a Game

- Create a Monopoly® type game based on the issue.
- Develop 20 Questions for the issue.
- Create a Trivia Pursuit® game based on the issue.
- Make a Jeopardy® game of the issue.
- Make author cards for the book: a suit for biographies, a suit for place, a suit for actions, a suit for time period.
- Create a snakes-and-ladders decision game based on the issue.
- Produce a video game based on the issue.
- Create a crossword based on the issue.
- Create a baseball type game where questions are used instead of hits, the harder the question resulting in more bases "run."
- Create a football type game where questions are used instead of plays.

Research the Book

- Get background information about the times, and relate it to the issue.
- Get background information about the culture, and relate it to the issue.
- Find out about women at that time, and relate it to the females affected by the issue.
- Find out about daily life at that time, and relate it to the issue.
- If the issue revolves around a significant decision of the times, compare that country's views to that of other contemporaries.

Reprinted with permission from Student Cheating and Plagiarism in the Internet Era: A Wake-Up Call *by Ann Lathrop and Kathleen Foss. Englewood, CO: Libraries Unlimited, 2000.*

- For a significant event of the times, compare the leading person's views to that of other contemporaries.
- If the issue has a definite setting (e.g., town or region), research the area and relate it to the issue.
- If the issue involves cultural clashes, research the situation of the time and compare the points of view.
- Research clothing of the time, and relate it to the issue.
- Research comparative housing of the time, and relate it to the issue.

Book Reading Survey

This activity can be done by teachers or students. The best part is the post-writing processing. It can also lead to exciting ideas for report alternatives.

Complete the following sentences:

- I like research that . . .
- When I enjoy research, I share it by . . .
- I think the most important aspect of research is . . .
- The way I decide on a research topic is . . .
- I think TV or movie versions of a research issue are . . .
- The purpose of research reports is . . .
- The way I can tell that someone has done good research is . . .
- Another way to assess research would be . . .
- The best way to encourage research is . . .
- The most important thing about research is . . .

[Developed for use in Tamalpais (CA) Union High School District. Reprinted with permission from Dr. Lesley S. J. Farmer, California State University, Long Beach.]

Reprinted with permission from Student Cheating and Plagiarism in the Internet Era: A Wake-Up Call *by Ann Lathrop and Kathleen Foss. Englewood, CO: Libraries Unlimited, 2000.*

Fuchs, Gaynell M. "Mona Lisa Writes a Letter: An Alternative to the Research Paper." Spring Conference of the National Council of Teachers of English. Louisville, KY. 26-28 Mar. 1987. ERIC (ED 282194).

Students write from the point of view of a person in a painting who is describing his or her life. They complete their research on the period and country of the painting and use their notes to write the paper; a bibliography is required but footnotes are not. Fuchs summarizes the results of the assignment:

> This time the students wrote better mechanically—the addition of "voice" or point of view added a freshness of expression; there was little evidence of plagiarism; students expanded on the topic as they became interested; from the standpoint of fostering writing as thinking, there was a much better synthesis of material. (1)

Geosits, Margaret S., and William R. Kirk. "Sowing the Seeds of Plagiarism." *Principal* 62.5 (1983): 35–38.

A "six questions" approach helps students learn to use their own words to present information from reference sources. They use the familiar "who, what, when, where, how, and why" of journalism. The lesson begins with a "dry run" at the chalkboard. Each student contributes a question, using complete sentences for both questions and answers in order to create "building blocks" for their papers. As an example, they suggest "movies."

1. The "who" category might pose these questions: who invented them, who makes them, and who sees them?

2. Under "what," what are some favorite movies that children remember?

3. Under "where," the questions could be where are they made, where does the money come from to make them, and where do ideas for stories come from?

4. Under "when," when was the first movie made, when was sound added, and when did color appear?

5. Under "why," why did Hollywood become its capital, why are movie scenes usually shot out of natural sequence, and why must a film be edited?

6. Under "how," how is a movie made, how is the sound track put in, and how does a film reach the local theater or television? (38)

The questions and answers on the board become the basic structure of the paper. Students use reference sources to find additional information to answer the six questions in their reports.

> But, instead of parroting what is found in these sources and understanding little of it, he or she can locate the information and then, as a response to the questions, restate it in words that are natural to the student's age-range. As this is happening, the youngster is sorting out facts and deciding which are most useful. (38)

Peterman, George. "Dinner with a Famous American Author." Unpublished paper, 1999.

[Permission is granted by the author to reproduce this lesson for classroom use.]

Dinner with a Famous American Author

Assignment: Choose a famous American author and fill out this fact sheet. Then imagine that you have had dinner and spent an evening with the author. Write a one- to two-page letter to tell a friend or someone in your family about the evening. Be sure to include all the information from your fact sheet in your letter.

Extra Credit: Draw a picture of the author, download and print a picture from the computer, or photocopy a picture from a book or magazine. Warning: an original picture cut from a book or magazine will not be accepted.

Fact Sheet:

Name (and pen name):

Date of birth: Date of death:

Birthplace:

Education:

Marriage, children:

Career information:

Why he/she is famous:

Type of writer (novels, short stories, plays, poetry, etc.):

Period or time of life:

Famous works:

Famous characters:

Famous quotes:

Other interesting or unusual information:

Reprinted with permission from Student Cheating and Plagiarism in the Internet Era: A Wake-Up Call *by Ann Lathrop and Kathleen Foss. Englewood, CO: Libraries Unlimited, 2000.*

Information Sources for Famous American Authors:

- Encyclopedia: If the author is famous enough, he or she will have an article in most encyclopedias. Less famous authors might be covered in more exhaustive encyclopedias. Don't forget about the index.

- Library catalog: A separate biography of a famous author might be in the general collection, possibly under 92, 921, or 809-813. Type in the last name of the author to find books about him or her.

- Online or CD-ROM encyclopedia: Again, type in the author's last name for information.

- Internet: Use the more popular search engines to find information and remember to capitalize the name when entering it as a keyword to search for.

- *American Heritage Magazine:* Check the 40-year cumulative index carefully. These magazines have a lot of valuable information about U.S. history.

- Reference books: The reference section is an invaluable source of information on people, places, and things. Try these particularly useful reference books:

>*American Authors and Books*
>*Biography Today*
>*Contemporary Authors*
>*Current Biography*
>*Cyclopedia of World Authors*
>*Dictionary of American Biography*
>*Encyclopedia of World Biography*
>*Major Writers of America, Vol. I and II*
>*The Oxford Companion to American Literature*
>*Something About the Author*
>*St. James Guide to Crime and Mystery Writers*
>*Twentieth Century Authors*

Reprinted with permission from Student Cheating and Plagiarism in the Internet Era: A Wake-Up Call *by Ann Lathrop and Kathleen Foss. Englewood, CO: Libraries Unlimited, 2000.*

Sample Letter:

Joe,

You won't believe who I ate dinner with last night! R. L. Stine came to my house. We spent the entire evening eating and talking. He was wearing a black cape, just like Dracula, and when I offered to take it for him, he refused. He wore it the entire time we talked. When he reached for his drink, his hand fell off onto the table. Well, not his real hand, but a fake one that looked pretty darn real to me, until I realized it was a joke. He likes to kid around a lot. When I brought out the potato soup, he even asked me if it was eyeball soup! Just like his books.

He told me that his real name is Robert Lawrence Stine, and he was born on October 8, 1943, in Columbus, Ohio. (Do you think it's a coincidence that his birthday is in the same month as Halloween?) In school he always read science fiction books and joke books. In fact, he actually wrote little stories and put them together into little magazines in high school. He attended Ohio State University and was editor of the school's humor magazine.

After college, he said, he worked for *Scholastic* magazine as an assistant editor. That was where he met his wife, Jane Waldorn. She helped him write funny books for a few years, then took his idea of *Fear Street* to a publisher she knew.

In 1986 he wrote his first scary book, *Blind Date,* while he was editor of *Bananas,* a humor magazine for children. In 1989 he wrote *The Babysitter,* one of his most popular books. Then came the *Fear Street* series for junior high kids and the *Goosebumps* series for elementary school kids.

He told me he writes two books a month and gets a lot of his ideas from his young son, Matthew, and his friends. His most popular book, *Welcome to Dead House,* has sold over 2 million copies! He even has a weekly TV show called "Goosebumps." With over 250 books to his credit, he has sold more books than any other author in history!

What a great night. Ghouls and monsters and zombies and tarantulas. It was so cool!

Stay in touch,

Bob

[Reprinted with permission from George R. Peterman, Anaheim Union High School District.]

Reprinted with permission from Student Cheating and Plagiarism in the Internet Era: A Wake-Up Call *by Ann Lathrop and Kathleen Foss. Englewood, CO: Libraries Unlimited, 2000.*

Wagner, Eileen N. "Outfoxing Fraud: Research Papers without Repression." Conference on College Composition and Communication. Kansas City, MO. 31 Mar. - 2 Apr. 1977. ERIC (ED 143015).

Wagner adds a new dimension to traditional research assignments by having students create their own primary source material. She presents this as one way to control plagiarism.

> His paper will have to exhibit at least one piece of *primary* evidence, exclusive evidence, evidence only he has and cannot be found in exactly the same form anywhere else. The principal way students accomplish this requirement of primary evidence is by interviewing scholars, experts . . . anyone else who might give an authoritative opinion [or] by constructing and implementing surveys. (8)

Students conduct their research for the paper either to support or to refute this original evidence. The combination of gathering exclusive primary evidence, combined with the specific focus of the research required to complete the paper, creates an assignment that becomes almost impossible to complete with a plagiarized paper.

White, Edward M. "Too Many Campuses Want to Sweep Student Plagiarism under the Rug." *Chronicle of Higher Education* 39.25 (1993): A44.

White suggests research assignments that require reflection and careful evaluation of source material:

> For example, instead of asking for a summary of one scholar's thought, an assignment could ask students to compare, contrast, and evaluate two different positions. Instead of asking for the causes of the Civil War or for the developments that gave rise to the theories of evolution or of postmodernism, an assignment could require students to consider several theses articulated by different writers, and to show the strengths and weaknesses of each argument. Perhaps most important, professors should discuss assignments in detail with students and explain why retelling of knowledge will be insufficient. (A44)

It would be difficult to find a paper online or an encyclopedia article to copy that would meet the requirements of such an assignment. It has the added advantage of developing both writing skills and critical thinking skills.

Worthen, Helena. "A Way to Break Down Writing Research Papers into Steps that Emphasize the Discovery Aspect of Research." Intersegmental Faculty Seminar. California Assn. of Community Colleges. Bass Lake, CA. 20 July 1990. ERIC (ED 331064).

I teach English 1–A, the transfer reading and composition course, in a PACE (Program for Adult Continuing Education) program at Vista Community College in Berkeley [CA] . . . . I have made a fuss about trying to get students to write what I call a "real" research paper.

For nearly all of my students, this is the first time they've ever written a research paper; for many of them, it's the first time they've written anything more than four or five pages long. I try to make it clear that a research paper differs from a theme, an essay, a term paper, or a report in this way: writing the research paper involves doing research; that means finding out something you didn't know previously. This has consequences. A change of perspective, a transformation, a re-casting of experience happens as a result of finding out something. Sometimes, if you think about something differently, you might even have to act differently.

Problem:

How do you get students to distinguish between what they already know and what they find out? Also: avoiding cut-and-paste, redeye, and plagiarized research papers.

> *First step of writing:* In class, have them write a description of everything they know about the topic already. Lean heavily on the word "description"— the student has an image, a picture, in his or her mind of what this topic means, looks like, feels like, etc.: every detail is important (like associating to a dream). Take at least an hour to get this description on paper. Teacher needs to understand what kind of investment, what past experience, draws each student to his or her topic.

> *Second step:* Students develop questions based on difference between what they already know and what they want to know. Lots of class input here on how to formulate strong questions.

> *Third step:* Make lists of possible ways to shed light on this question: resources, class suggestions.

> *Fourth step:* Go out and investigate these resources until they find out something they didn't know before. (This is the minimum; most students go far beyond this.)

> *Fifth step:* Write a first draft, show to teacher and class. (Length is irrelevant; message from teacher is "Make it as long as necessary.") Students will be using the narrative of their discovery as structural spine of the paper. Costs of xeroxing for entire class can affect class response opportunity at this point.

> *Sixth step:* Teacher will usually recommend some additional resource, a book or experience the student hadn't thought of. Student writes another draft, integrating this new resource. (This is a very hard step; teacher usually recommends something from left field!)

Seventh step: Final drafts, two or three of them, as students get a grip on writing evaluative conclusions instead of just summaries, as well as footnoting and citing.

Time span: Entire semester; other assignments happen concurrently. Final paper is usually 20–30 pages [with] at least 4 (sometimes 15) items in bibliography.

Unacceptable papers: One kind of paper that I get that does not count as research paper (and therefore can't get better than a B, no matter how tidy, well-constructed, and well-documented) is the paper that reads like a stack of index cards written up into paragraphs.

Another unacceptable paper is the one that expresses a student's opinion, however eloquently, but shows no sign of that opinion having been tested against empirical data in the recent past. Such papers tend to be against Darwin, against homosexuality, against racism, against oppression, against drug use, etc. Some of these are powerfully written and on the side of the angels; therefore, unless the teacher has explicitly required that the student show signs of having learned something because he or she started writing the paper, they're hard to challenge.

Aspects of Research that My Students Need to Hear About:

- Research takes time. That's why the assignment is spread out over the whole semester. You can't do research in one night, even if you drink a lot of coffee. You can't re-think something unless you have time to mull it over. The grass has to grow.

- Don't lie to yourself about what you're interested in. This lie will catch up with you; you'll get bored.

- Don't choose a topic because you're already an expert in it; research isn't about showing off what you already know, it's about finding out new stuff.

- Research exposes you to the possibility that you might have to change your mind about something. There is no guarantee you will like what you find out. It has consequences, often in action.

- Don't compromise on your question; if you're really doing research, there will be times when your question will be your only friend, so choose it carefully.

Discussion:

The first step—the one in which students write down everything that they already know about their topic before they start doing any research—is the key step. Those pages, often full of errors or misapprehensions, provide a benchmark against which new understandings can be measured, creating a story about how the student moved from one way of thinking to another way of thinking.

The student who wasn't sure if her mother had Alzheimer's investigated enough health care services to get her mother into a program researching Alzheimer's; the student who wanted to know why utopias didn't last learned about Tahiti and the history of exploration in the 18th century, but balked at taking on anthropology; the student who asked about the women in the Civil Rights movement traced the connection between the Civil Rights movement and the last 20 years of the feminist movement.

The successful papers—and a surprisingly high number of students were able to generate long, successful papers—were those that displayed a real development of thought. They also displayed a degree of familiarity with the language of the subject matter and a consciousness of the extent to which this language was particular to that subject matter. Because they stayed close to the writer's own perspective, they contained little, if any, plagiarism. And finally, despite being much longer than anything these students had written before, they hung together, so that the reader was never lost; the overall organization of the papers was the simplest organization there is, a narrative of something that happened over time.

A Few Final Comments:

- The topics must be generated by the students. A topic laid on from above won't have the same effect.

- Deadlines for the various drafts must be firm; even good students will try to write the whole thing the night before, thereby missing the point.

- The class, not the teacher, should be the audience. The class is the culture in which the student lives. A topic a teacher might be bored with can be a live topic for a class. Class time must be set aside for getting class reactions to various drafts. Think of Aristotle's four categories of criticism: something might be challenged because it is inconsistent, inaccurate, incomplete, or morally harmful. The only one the teacher is likely to be better at spotting than the other students is the third.

[Excerpts reprinted with permission from Helena Worthen, Assistant Professor of Labor Studies, University of Illinois, Chicago.]

Pointers ————————————————————————————

The specific lessons in Chapter 15 could be integrated into one or more of these assignments.

Chapter 17

Online Sites for Reports and Research Papers

Does the Internet help college students learn? Enthusiasts proclaim that it has made a world of information available to any freshman with a computer. Skeptics warn that cyberspace is so full of junk that research in it will never amount to anything more than garbage collecting. . . . [My] students have taught me that, if handled with care, the Internet can be an effective tool. Instead of turning our backs on cyberspace, we need to take control of it—to set standards, develop quality controls and direct traffic. Our students will learn to navigate the Internet successfully if we set up warning signals and teach them to obey: "Proceed with caution. Danger lies ahead." (Darnton A17)

Chapter Overview

The fifty online sites listed here were online in March 2000 and the factual information for each site was accurate at that time. Of the fifty, only twenty-one offer some or all of their papers without charge. No effort has been made to provide qualitative evaluations of the sites. Within days or weeks, some undoubtedly will have vanished, changed their URL, or become an entirely different type of site. Rapid change is a widely acknowledged hallmark of the Internet that certainly holds true for online sites for reports and research papers.

1-800 TERMPAPER ACADEMIC AND BUSINESS RESEARCH SOURCE
<www.al-termpaper.com>
Disclaimer: One line in capital letters states "all work offered is for research purposes only."

Description: Offers 20,000 on-file papers and custom papers for students and the business community. Has a subject index for broad categories with subindexes for prewritten papers.

Pricing: Each on-file paper is individually priced. Custom papers are from $19.95 to $35 per page.

4RESEARCH'99
<www.4research.com>

Disclaimer: Simply states that their product may be used for research purposes only.

Description: Offers more than 7,000 term papers and class notes "from Anthropology to Zoology."

Pricing: Free.

12,000 PAPERS.COM
<www.12000papers.com>

Disclaimer: Warns students that these "example" term papers must be cited and to consult their professors prior to using their papers as a source.

Description: Claims 12,000 fully researched current papers. The database of prewritten papers can be searched by keyword or by subject. Can preview first page of any paper prior to buying. Custom paper service available. Also includes a "how to cite" link.

Pricing: Each on-file paper is $8.95 per page. Custom papers are $18.95 per page.

ABCRESEARCH.COM
<www.abcresearch.com>

Disclaimer: "Our service is strictly for research and reference purposes only. Do not submit our research work for academic credit in your own name! Plagiarism is a CRIME!"

Description: They are a custom term paper service. Users are invited to make an appointment and visit their offices.

Pricing: Custom papers are $25 per page.

ACADEMIC TERM PAPERS
<www.academictermpapers.com>

Disclaimer: Warns students that these papers "may not be submitted either in whole or in part for academic credit."

Description: Has over 30,000 research papers. Will custom write a report.

Pricing: Each on-file paper is $7 per page with a maximum charge of $120. There is no charge for bibliographies, footnotes, or partial pages. Custom papers are $19 and up per page.

ACADEMIC WRITING
<www.cyberhighway.net/~gailmae>

Disclaimer: None.

Description: Offers to provide part or all of a master's thesis, doctoral proposal, seminar paper, or survey. They will finish a draft written by the user.

Pricing: Fee varies with request; call for pricing.

ACI WRITING ASSISTANCE CENTER
<www.aci-plus.com>

> Disclaimer: States in several places that they "do not provide custom research to individuals who give us reason to believe that they intend to claim the ACI's work for their own and submit it for academic credit."

> Description: Custom writing service for high school and college as well as for the business community. They suggest ESL students may benefit from their expertise. They will edit or write a paper, train for tests and college applications, or provide a scholarship referral service.

> Pricing: Fee varies with each project, but a standard rate for custom papers is $40 per page with a minimum of $500.

BIGNERDS.COM
<www.bignerds.com>

> Disclaimer: None.

> Description: Has over 800 free essays, term papers, and book reports on a wide variety of topics or will have a custom paper written through its partnership with Collegiate Care. Anyone ordering a custom paper is asked to "Please describe the research you need compiled: Include title, topics, length requirement, citation style, and time frame for completion of the report." Also will supply college admission applications and essays. Has links to fifty-plus additional paper sites.

> Pricing: Free on-file papers. Custom papers from Collegiate Care are $16.95 per page with a five-page minimum. Rush requests cost more.

CHEATER.COM
<www.cheater.com>

> Disclaimer: "Who we are, who we aren't," states that "we provide a service for students, like anything it can be abused if used improperly. Like any Library, we offer lots of information that can be used for facts only. Plagiarism is illegal and Cheater.com does not support it in any way, shape or form." and "For once and for all, all you should gain from this site is other peoples' ideas. We are not here to promote plagiarism. If you turn in a paper from this site as your own you are hurting yourself. Cheater.com is meant to be used as a resource."

> Description: Term papers can be accessed by keyword using a Boolean search or by browsing general categories. Custom papers are referred to School Sucks. Claims 72,000 members.

> Pricing: Free. Must submit a paper for membership.

CHEATHOUSE—THE EVIL HOUSE OF CHEAT
<www.cheathouse.com>

> Disclaimer: No disclaimer is listed on the main page, but a copyright link is at the bottom of the page.

Description: Claims over 2,000 essays or 9,500 for their members who have a password. Search strategy offers students who submit papers the opportunity to list the title and summary length of their paper, their grade level, school system, author information, and the original grade with comments on the papers in the database. Offers links and tips on how to cheat on exams.

Pricing: Free, but must register for password.

CHUCKIII.COM
<www.chuckiii.com>

Disclaimer: On the page listing the reports, essays, and book reports available is a statement that says, "Please use the following papers for informational purposes only. Please do not turn these papers in as your own." There is a link to a definition of plagiarism and how to properly cite a source.

Description: Lists free term papers, essays, and book reports written by others and also a section of papers written by ChuckIII himself. There are links to a multitude of sites of interest to students in high school and college.

Pricing: Free. Must either submit a paper or add a link to their page.

COLLEGE TERM PAPERS.COM
<www.collegetermpapers.com>

Disclaimer: Above the list of titles of papers to choose from is a statement: "Putting your name on someone else's paper is against the law."

Description: Free papers are accessed from over fifty categories listed on the main page. A sidebar lists the very limited segment of term papers, research reports, book reports, and essays available without membership.

Pricing: Free access to a limited number of papers. Must submit a paper for membership to access most of the papers.

COLLEGIATE CARE RESEARCH ASSISTANCE
<www.paper-online.com>

Disclaimer: Disclaimer quotes a Washington State statute and says they will not supply a paper to anyone who they think will use the paper illegally.

Description: Database of 3,000 papers and essays.

Pricing: Each on-file paper is $5.95 per page. Custom papers are $16.95 per page with a five-page minimum.

CYBER ESSAYS
<www.cyberessays.com>
Disclaimer: None.

Description: A free service that depends on student submissions. Can search for an essay by keyword or by general category.

Pricing: Free.

DOWNCRAP
<www.members.xoom.com/_XOOM/downcrap>
> Disclaimer: None.

> Description: Claims to have over 1,000 essays that can be searched by categories and subcategories or by subject using a Boolean search. Lists the title of the essay, the date it was added, and the number of times it has been downloaded.

> Pricing: Free.

ESSAY DEPOT
<www.essayDepot.com>
> Disclaimer: Disclaimer is at bottom of the first page with an added warning that (1) the papers are submitted by students so the quality varies, and (2) your teacher knows about this site.

> Description: Can browse curricular categories for essays. Custom papers are referred to The Paper Store. A sidebar gives the steps to downloading an essay, with number 5 stating "Open your word processing program and your [sic] done!"

> Pricing: Free.

ESSAYBANK
<www.essaybank.com>
> Disclaimer: None.

> Description: Index of essays gives the word count and subject area. You can preview the first few lines or the first paragraph.

> Pricing: $15 membership fee or send six essays for a year's free membership.

GP GENIUS PAPERS
<www.geniuspapers.com>
> Disclaimer: Disclaimer is several pages in length and states that these papers are to be used for research purposes only and that plagiarism is a serious offense and "not, by any means condoned or encouraged by Genius Papers."

> Description: Offers term papers, essays, and book reports.

> Pricing: Membership.

HIREDPENS
<www.hiredpens.com>
> Disclaimer: None.

> Description: Hiredpens will provide a customized paper or resume written by professionals in their fields. They offer a regular service which will deliver a paper in five days or more; an urgent request will be delivered in three days. Three question boxes ask for: the topic/author/book, the writing format/manner of the pages, and any other instructions. A secured server to process credit card information is available.

> Pricing: Regular service is $10 per page and Urgent service is $14 per page.

HOMEWORK'S DONE
<www.members.aol.com/oohalooo/index2.html>

Disclaimer: "As a student I know how hard writing a report can be but, all the papers here are to be used as examples only. Do yourself a favor and don't turn them in. Besides you found this site, how do you know your teacher hasn't found it too?"

Description: "Homework's Done is a web site that will give you a chance to look at what other people have done on projects similar to yours." Papers are divided into five subject categories with subheadings: English, Humanities, History, Law, and Science. There is no indication of the size of the database.

Pricing: Free.

IVYESSAYS PAPERS
<www.ivyessays.com>

Disclaimer: States that their sample essays are for your guidance and inspiration.

Description: Offers an editing service for applications to college, business school, law school, medical school, etc. A prepackaged group of essays covering all possible interview questions is available.

Pricing: Fee varies with type of service required.

JUNGLE PAGE
<www.junglepage.com/asp/index.asp>
Disclaimer: None.

Description: Offers prewritten essays, custom essays, book reports, college entrance essays, resumes, and professional proofreading of original student papers. Also has a book exchange, teacher rating service, and tutor listings.

Pricing: Each on-file paper is $19.95.

KILLER ESSAYS
<www.freeessays.com/killer/>

Disclaimer: "Welcome to killer essays! We're not going to lie to you and tell you that our essays are for reference use only; they're here for you to copy, steal, plagiarize; whatever you want to do with them."

Description: Essays can be retrieved by typing in a term or subject, or by browsing through the general categories listed on the main screen.

Pricing: Free.

KNOWLEDGE REPORTS
<www.knowledge-reports.com>

Disclaimer: Copyright statement says that students should "never turn in [papers from their service] as their own work" and they do not "want you to violate policies concerning academic dishonesty." Knowledge Reports is described as a "time management tool" for students who must "balance work, study, class, research and writing." One paragraph later they say it "provides students with excellent research materials without spending long hours in the library wading through information that does not apply to their topics" and that the information supplied can "be cited and incorporated into the student's own work."

Description: Offers reports and essays, and also provides statistical processing and analysis.

Pricing: Prices vary for on-file papers. Custom papers are $20 and up per page.

MAD PAPERS
<www.madpapers.com>

Disclaimer: "Mad Papers is not responsible for what its members do with the information or materials found on their site. Plagiarism is a serious crime and anyone found doing it can be prosecuted to the full extent of the law."

Description: Claims to have more than 8,000 papers. If they don't have the paper requested on hand, they will try to find it.

Pricing: Required subscription fee is $7.95 per year.

NET ESSAYS
<www.netessays.net>

Disclaimer: States prominently on the main page: "feel free to read our papers to gain ideas, then you can develop your own essay."

Description: Claims to have 4,332 free essays and over 3,000 term papers. Custom papers are referred to The Paper Store. Papers and essays are indexed and can be searched by curricular department or by subject. Includes the title of the paper and the date it was added to the database.

Pricing: Free. Must submit a paper for membership.

OPPAPERS.COM
<www.oppapers.com>

Disclaimer: Featured on the first page is a box with the disclaimer: "We are against plagiarism 100%. These materials are for research purposes only. Use of these papers for any other purpose is not the responsibility of OPPapers.com. By viewing any pages on this site in any way, you agree to these terms. Please hit your browser's back button if you do not agree to these terms."

Description: OPPapers.com has 2,277 papers and lists for each paper the date it was accepted into the database and the number of words in the essay.

Pricing: Free.

PAPER MASTERS
<www.papermasters.com>
> Disclaimer: Papers are referred to as "model papers" and there is a legal resources link on the main page.

> Description: All papers are custom written by professionals upon request and delivered within one week. Papers are not resold. "Study, relax, enjoy and GRADUATE" is step four in the ordering process.

> Pricing: Custom papers are from $15.95 to $18.95 per page. Rush orders needed within five days or less are $24.95 per page.

PAPER STORE
<www.paperstore.net>
> Disclaimer: They state that "the intended purpose of our example term papers is that they be used as study aids or as models of what a term paper should be like."

> Description: "Since 1994, The Paper Store has helped tens of thousands of college & graduate students overcome their greatest fear: WRITING PAPERS." They offer examples of term papers and custom research. Can preview an excerpt of their 15,000 on-file research papers.

> Pricing: Each on-file paper is $8.95. Custom papers are $14.95 per page.

PAPERCAMP.COM
<www.papercamp.com>
> Disclaimer: Papers are to be used as "models for creating your own work—no plagiarizing!"

> Description: Offers free quality essays, reports, term papers, college admission essays, and research papers. Also has a custom writing service.

> Pricing: Free on-file papers. Custom papers are $16.95 per page with a five-page minimum.

PAPERS 24-7
<www.papers24-7.com>
> Disclaimer: "The intended purpose of our example term papers is that they be used as models to assist you in the preparation of your own work."

> Description: Can preview any of their "thousands of example term papers: Visitors may request a free full-page excerpt from any report before purchasing it."

> Pricing: Each on-file paper is $8.95 per page; bibliography pages are free. Custom papers are $18.95 per page.

PAPERS INN
<www.papersinn.com>
> Disclaimer: None.

> Description: Custom and free papers. Offers to "write for students of all levels...college term papers...term papers for high school students, or essays for junior high and primary school students."

Pricing: Custom papers are $9.95 per page.

PAPERSURE: THE RESEARCH PAPER CENTER
<www.papershack.com>

Disclaimer: Disclaimer states that their papers are to be used as an information source only.

Description: All papers are custom written.

Pricing: Custom papers are $15 per page.

PENQUEST.COM
<www.ezwriters.net>

Disclaimer: Disclaimer on the bottom of each order page gives the standard warning against plagiarism and states that the papers are to "help provide you with a new look of ideas and information for your use, as a source of research."

Description: Provides both file copy reports and custom papers. Stresses that they have professionals who will assist you to access new ideas and information.

Pricing: Each on-file paper is $20. Custom papers start at $20 for the first page and $10 for each page after that. Rush orders are charged an extra $5 per page.

PLANET PAPERS
<www.planetpapers.com>

Disclaimer: Disclaimer posted on the FAQ page is listed as an acceptable use policy.

Description: Select from 850+ essays listed on the main page by subject headings: Art and Music, Biographies, Creative Writing, Film, etc. Custom papers are referred to Collegiate Care Research Assistance.

Pricing: Free.

POETRY PAPERS.COM
<www.poetrypapers.com>

Disclaimer: "These papers are not designed and must not be used for submission for credit as if they were the work of the student who has purchased them. . . . Poetry Papers (the company) and its staff members disclaim any responsibility and/or liability for any wrongful or unlawful acts committed by the purchaser with items ordered from this site and misused as such."

Description: Only papers that deal with poets or poetry. You can view a sample of three entries. Authors treated include: Eliot, Donne, Shakespeare, Yeats, Dickinson, Hughes, Plath, Frost, Wordsworth, Auden, Herbert, Blake, Hopkins, Keats, Lawrence, Whitman, Walcott, Lowell, Larkin, Browning, Coleridge, Hardy, Heaney, Thomas, Williams, Wright, Harrison, Rich.

Pricing: Each on-file paper is $9 per page.

RESEARCH ASSISTANCE
<www.research-assistance.com>
> Disclaimer: None.

>> Description: Offers an indexed database of over 25,000 papers. Advertise that they have been providing library research reports to academic and business communities since 1969. Offers a custom service too.

>> Pricing: Each on-file paper is $7.50 per page plus shipping and tax up to seventeen pages, with a flat fee of $127 for any single report that is longer than seventeen pages. Custom papers are from $20 to $35 per page.

RESEARCH PAPERS ON-LINE A+
<www.ezwrite.com>
>> Disclaimer: "Research Papers On-Line intends their products to be used as RESEARCH MATERIAL ONLY and are not intended to be submitted for educational, business or private credit. It is the sole responsibility of the buyer (not the seller) to ascertain through competent legal counsel how any law or laws may apply to the use of each item purchased through this catalogue and act accordingly."

>> Description: Offers never-been-circulated papers that can be searched for by subject. The actual papers under the various department headings list the title, cost, and number of pages you will receive. A sample paper is available to view.

>> Pricing: Each on-file paper is $4.95 per page.

SCHOOL PAPER.COM
<www.schoolpaper.com>
>> Disclaimer: "Our research papers are to be used only as references for your paper. We refuse to sell a research paper to any student whom we have reason to believe will submit our work, either in whole or part, for academic credit in their own name. If you choose to quote from our work you must cite our paper as one of your sources."

>> Description: A database of thousands of prewritten "reference papers" and literary summaries for those "who do not wish to waste the time reading all of the novels, plays, and other pieces of literature for your classes."

>> Pricing: Each on-file paper is $20 per paper regardless of length. Membership fee required.

SCHOOL SUCKS
<www.schoolsucks.com>
>> Disclaimer: "School Sucks is 100% against plagiarism. If we wanted to encourage plagiarism, we would a) charge even $1 per paper and thereby deny educators the right to see them and b) rate or grade the papers."

>> Description: "School Sucks is the largest collection of free, but awful homework." Can search by word, word string, or topic/subtopic categories. For example, there are 125 papers on the subtopic of "History—European."

>> Pricing: Free.

SCHOOL SUX
> Disclaimer: None.

> Description: "Welcome to SchoolSux.com. The 1999-2000 School year is upon us!! Well Big Daddy SchoolSux.com will lead the Students in to the Y2K!!!" Provides links to thirty-six term paper sites but does not offer any papers directly to students.

> Pricing: n/a

SCHOOLBYTES.COM
<www.schoolbytes.com>
> Disclaimer: None.

> Description: Offers free book plot summaries, short story plot summaries and free term papers.

> Pricing: Free.

SCREW ESSAYS
<www.screw-essays.com>
> Disclaimer: There is no disclaimer listed on the main page, but the following sentence appears under each essay title: "This essay was found at www.screw-essays.com and should not be plagiarized."

> Description: Screw-Essays is divided into five categories of reports: English papers, Acceptance essays, Shakespeare papers, Book Reports and History papers. They also have a section on Class Notes, Citing Essays and then a link to other essay sites.

> Pricing: Free.

SMART ESSAYS
<www.FreeEssays.com/smart/>
> Disclaimer: Long and very detailed disclaimer fills one page with all legal possibilities.

> Description: Essays can be accessed from a general index on the first page or user can request a customized search. The index will tell how many words are in the essay and the approximate number of pages. Downloading is more complicated than just highlighting and hitting the print button.

> Pricing: Free.

SPECIALTY RESEARCH
<www.papermasters.org>
> Disclaimer: Refers to their products as "model papers" and has standard disclaimer.

> Description: Offers 20,000 prewritten papers or will write custom papers for students and the business community. Has a subject index for broad categories and then subindexes for prewritten papers.

Pricing: Each on-file paper is individually priced. Custom papers are from $19.95 to $35 per page.

STUDENT ESSAYS
<www.freeessay.com/student/get_essays>

Disclaimer: One of the questions in the FAQ section is titled Acceptable Use. "The essays on this site are put there as an educational resource. The essays can be used for research purposes, e.g., finding an interesting topic, different point of view or relevant resources. However, we do not support the plagiarizing of other people's work. You must never submit an essay from this site as your own work, or repost the essay anywhere else on the Internet."

Description: The essays in this database are divided into twelve broad annotated categories: Art and Music, Biographies, Creative Writing, Film, Geography, History, Literature, Miscellaneous, Politics, Religion, Science and Technology, and Social Issues. There is no description of the essays or indication of the extent of the database.

Pricing: Free.

STUDENTCENTRAL
<www.studentcentral.co.uk>

Disclaimer: No disclaimer is listed on the main page, but this European site lists itself as an educational link.

Description: "Every page and link on studentcentral is available in Spanish, Italian, German, Portuguese and a few more obscure European languages." They claim to list 500 essays and provide links to 500 other resources dealing with test preparation, essay sites, and academic links that can access an additional 4,000 essays. A site of the day and an essay of the day are listed on the main page.

Pricing: Free.

SUPERIOR TERMPAPERS
<www.superior-termpapers.com>

Disclaimer: "All written material sold through our company is for research purposes only and may not be submitted, in whole or in part, for academic credit. By ordering a paper through our company you agree that it is legal to do so in your city, state/province, and country."

Description: Custom papers only. There are three samples of their work and testimonials online. Orders are accepted by phone or email.

Pricing: Custom papers are $18 per page for all subjects, all levels.

TERMS N PAPERS
<www.termsnpapers.com>

Disclaimer: "These papers are to be used for research purposes only. Use of these papers for any other purpose is not the responsibility of TERMS n PAPERS.Com."

Description: "TERMS n PAPERS is your own personalized Custom Term Paper Site. TERMS n PAPERS offers Term Papers, Book Reports, and Essays for students of all academic levels. TERMS n PAPERS is like having your own personal tutor at your service twenty-four hours a day. Whenever you are in trouble, you can call on the tutor for help."

Pricing: Custom papers are $18.95 per page delivered in five days or $34.95 per page delivered in two days.

THOUSANDS OF PAPERS
<www.termpapers-on-file.com>

Disclaimer: "The intended purpose of our example term papers is that they be used as study aids or as models of what a term paper should look like. We encourage students to use our reports to help them in quickening their research. Pursuant to New Jersey Statutes 2A: 170-17.16-18 and similar statutes that exist in other states, The Paper Store Enterprises, Inc. will NEVER offer its services to ANY person giving ANY reason to believe that he or she intends to either wholly or partially submit our work for academic credit in their own name... Plagiarism is a CRIME!"

Description: "Welcome to the Largest Catalog of Expertly-Researched Model Term Papers—All Written By Our Company after 1995!!! We are the ONLY Site With Enough Confidence in our Work to Let You View Full Page Excerpts of ANY Paper Before You Buy it !!!" All papers are digitized and can be delivered in "any word processor format." Search by keyword or use index on the main page. Offers a "how to cite" link.

Pricing: Each on-file paper is $8.95 per page with free reference pages and bibliographies. Custom papers are $18.95 per page.

Pointers

A representative list of ten sites, formatted as a Copy-Me page, is in Chapter 3.

References Cited

Aiken, Lewis R. "Detecting, Understanding, and Controlling for Cheating on Tests." *Research in Higher Education* 32.6 (1991): 725–36.

Akins, Bill. Telephone interview. 29 Sep. 1999.

Albrecht, Larry. Letter. *Des Moines Register* [IA] 3 June 1999: 8. Bell & Howell Information and Learning-ProQuest. Los Alamitos High School Lib., Los Alamitos, CA. 10 Aug. 1999 <http://proquest.umi.com>.

Alschuler, Alfred S., and Gregory S. Blimling. "Curbing Epidemic Cheating Through Systemic Change." *College Teaching* 43.4 (1995): 123–26.

American Assn. of School Librarians and Asso. for Educational Communications and Technology. *Information Power: Building Partnerships for Learning.* Chicago: ALA, 1998.

Anderman, Eric M., Tripp Griesinger, and Gloria Westerfield. "Motivation and Cheating During Early Adolescence." *Journal of Educational Psychology* 90.1 (1998): 84–93.

Anderson, Nick. "Line Between Cheating and Teamwork Trips Students." *Los Angeles Times* 11 Apr. 1997: A3. Bell & Howell Information and Learning-ProQuest. Los Alamitos High School Lib., Los Alamitos, CA. 10 Aug. 1999 <http://proquest.umi.com>.

Asch, Kim. "Emphasis on Winning Can Mean Losing." *Washington Times* [DC] 17 Mar. 1998: E3. Bell & Howell Information and Learning-ProQuest. Los Alamitos High School Lib., Los Alamitos, CA. 15 Sep. 1999 <http://proquest.umi.com>.

Baker, Howard, Jr. *And the Cheat Goes On: An Expose on How Students Are Cheating in School.* Salem, OR: Forum, 1989.

Barnett, Cynthia. "Is Cheating Becoming a Way of Life?" *News & Observer* [Raleigh, NC] 2 Nov. 1997: A25. NewsBank. Los Alamitos High School Lib., Los Alamitos, CA. 4 May 1999 <http://infoweb.newsbank.com>.

Bell, Alison. "Cheating Minds." *Teen Magazine* 42.8 (1998): 96–98. InfoTrac. Long Beach Public Library, Long Beach, CA. 16 Sep. 1999 <http://web.infotrac.gale-group.com>.

Benning, Victoria. "High-Tech Cheating Hits the Campus: Computers Make It Easy for College Students to Break Rules." *Washington Post* [DC] 4 Oct. 1998: A1. Bell & Howell Information and Learning-ProQuest. Los Alamitos High School Lib., Los Alamitos, CA. 8 Apr. 1999 <http://proquest.umi.com>.

Bjaaland, Patricia C., and Arthur Lederman. "The Detection of Plagiarism." *Educational Forum* 37.2 (1973): 201–06.

Boston, Jamie. Email to the author. 19 May 1999.

Brand, Alice G. "Controlled Research: Putting Text to the Test." Annual Conference on Writing across the Curriculum. Charlotte, SC. 2-3 Feb. 1995. ERIC (ED 377519).

Brickman, William W. "Ethics, Examinations, and Education." *School and Society* 89.4 (1961): 412–15.

Brownlee, Bonnie J. "Coping with Plagiarism Requires Several Strategies." *Journalism Educator* 41.4 (1987): 25–29.

Bruwelheide, Janis H. *Copyright Primer for Librarians and Educators.* 2nd ed. Chicago: ALA, 1995.

Bushweller, Kevin. "Digital Deception." *Electronic School* March 1999. 23 Apr. 1999 <http://www.electronic-school.com>.

———. "Generation of Cheaters." *American School Board Journal* 186.4 (1999): 24–32.

California School Library Assn. *From Library Skills to Information Literacy.* 2nd ed. San Jose, CA: Hi Willow, 1997.

Carnevale, Dan. "How to Proctor from a Distance." *Chronicle of Higher Education* 46.12 (1999): A47-48.

Carney, Tom. "High School Cheating on the Rise, Reports Say." *Des Moines Register* [IA] 24 May 1999: 1. Bell & Howell Information and Learning-ProQuest. Los Alamitos High School Lib., Los Alamitos, CA. 14 July 1999 <http://proquest. umi.com>.

Carroll, Joyce Armstrong. "Plagiarism: The Unfun Game." *English Journal* 71.5 (1982): 92–94.

Center for Academic Integrity. "The Fundamental Values of Academic Integrity: Honesty, Trust, Fairness, Respect, Responsibility." Durham, NC: Center for Academic Integrity, 1999.

———. "Research Highlights." Center for Academic Integrity, Duke U, 1999. 21 Aug. 1999 <http://www.academicintegrity.org/activities/highlights.html>.

———. "Ten Principles of Academic Integrity for Faculty." *AAHE Bulletin* 50.4 (1997): 2.

Chang, Jane. "Exams on Laptops: Breaking New Ground with Xmn8r." *USC Law Library Newsletter* 23.2 (1998). 29 Aug. 1999 <http://www.usc.edu/dept/law-lib/libadmin/newsletters/mar98.html#Xmn8r>.

Cheaters Paradise. 24 Aug. 1999 <http://www.jaberwocky.com/cheat/index2.html>.

Chidley, Joe. "Tales Out of School." *Maclean's* [Toronto, ON] 24 Nov. 1997: 76–79. Bell & Howell Information and Learning-ProQuest. Los Alamitos High School Lib., Los Alamitos, CA. 10 Mar. 1999 <http://proquest.umi.com>.

Clark, Irene Lurkis. "Collaboration and Ethics in Writing Center Pedagogy." *Writing Center Journal* 9.1 (1988): 3–12.

Clayton, Mark. "Term Papers at the Click of a Mouse Cheat Sheets." *Christian Science Monitor* 27 Oct. 1997: 1+. Bell & Howell Information and Learning-ProQuest. Los Alamitos High School Lib., Los Alamitos, CA. 25 Sep. 1999 <http://proquest. umi.com>.

Cobbs, Lewis. "Honor Codes: Teaching Integrity and Interdependence." *Education Week.* 3 Apr. 1991: 31.

Conway, Kathleen. "Prescriptive Teaching: An Rx for the Writing Lab." Conference on College Composition and Communication. Phoenix, AZ. 12-15 Mar. 1997. ERIC (ED 413615).

Corbett, Bob. *Cheater's Handbook: The Naughty Student's Bible.* New York: Harper, 1999.

Croucher, John. *Exam Scams: Best Cheating Stories and Excuses from Around the World.* St. Leonard's, Australia: Allen and Unwin, 1996.

Dant, Doris R. "Plagiarism in High School: A Survey." *English Journal* 75.2 (1986): 81–84.

Darnton, Robert. "Web Can Dull the Learning Experience." *Seattle Post-Intelligencer* [WA] 16 June 1999: A17.

Davis, Kevin. "Student Cheating: A Defensive Essay." *English Journal* 81.6 (1992): 72–74.

Davis, Stephen F. "Cheating in College Is for a Career: Academic Dishonesty in the 1990s." Southeastern Psychological Assn. Atlanta, GA. 24-27 May 1993. ERIC (ED 358382).

Davis, Susan J. "Teaching Practices that Encourage or Eliminate Student Plagiarism." *Middle School Journal* 25.3 (1994): 55–58.

DeBoer, Vicki. Email to the author. 27 May 1999.

Dick, Dwight D. "Avoiding a Plagiarized Report." *Journal of Reading* 27.8 (1984): 734–36.

Drum, Alice. "Responding to Plagiarism." *College Composition and Communication* 37.2 (1986): 241–43.

Dunn, Ashley. "Welcome to the Evil House of Cheat." *Los Angeles Times Magazine* 7 Feb. 1999: 30+.

Educational Testing Service. "Academic Cheating Background." 12 Oct. 1999 <http://www.nocheating.org/adcouncil/research.cheatingbackgrounder.html>.

———. "Academic Cheating Fact Sheet." 12 Oct. 1999 <http://www.nocheating.org/adcouncil/research.cheatingfactsheet.html>.

———. "ETS and the Advertising Council Launch a National Campaign to Discourage Academic Cheating." 12 Oct. 1999 <http://www.nocheating.org/adcouncil/news/launchrelease.html>.

Evans, Ellis D., and Delores Craig. "Teacher and Student Perceptions of Academic Cheating in Middle and Senior High Schools." *Journal of Educational Research* 84.1 (1990): 44–52.

Factor, Sidney, et al. "Students' Ethics Require New Ways to Cope With Cheating." *Journalism Educator* 44.4 (1990): 57–59.

Falcone, Stephen V. "One Principal's Commitment to Ethics." Email to the author. 18 Sep. 1999.

———. Telephone interview. 19 Aug. 1999.

Farmer, Lesley. "Beyond Research Reports." Unpublished paper, California State University, Long Beach, Long Beach, CA, 1999.

————. "Cyber-Plagiarism Faculty Workshop." Unpublished paper, California State University, Long Beach, Long Beach, CA, 1999.

Fishbein, Leslie. "We Can Curb College Cheating." *Education Digest* 59.7 (1994): 58–60.

Fishlock, Diana. "Technology and Cheating." *Express-Times* [Easton, PA] 20 Sep. 1996. NewsBank. Los Alamitos High School Lib., Los Alamitos, CA. 11 Mar. 1999 <http://infoweb.newsbank.com>.

Fogg, Richard. "Discouraging Cheating." *Clearing House* 49.7 (1976): 329–31.

Fowler, Delbert H. "Cheating: A Bigger Problem Than Meets the Eye." *NASSP Bulletin* 70.493 (1986): 93–96.

Fritz, Mark. "Redefining Research, Plagiarism." *Los Angeles Times* 25 Feb. 1999: A1. NewsBank. Los Alamitos High School Lib., Los Alamitos, CA. 4 May 1999 <http://infoweb.newsbank.com>.

Fuchs, Gaynell M. "Mona Lisa Writes a Letter: An Alternative to the Research Paper." Spring Conference of the Natl. Council of Teachers of English. Louisville, KY. 26-28 Mar. 1987. ERIC (ED 282194).

Galles, Gary M. "Copy These Strategies to Stop Plagiarism by Students." *Houston Chronicle* [TX] 29 Sep. 1997. 22 July 1999 <http://www.chron.com/content/chronicle/editorial/97/09/29/galles.0-0.html>.

Geosits, Margaret S., and William R. Kirk. "Sowing the Seeds of Plagiarism." *Principal* 62.5 (1983): 35–38.

Gladden, Craig A. *A Funny Thing Happened on the Way to My Diploma.* Philadelphia: Dorrance, 1973.

Gordon, Mark. Telephone interview. 21 Sep. 1999.

Gonzalez, Zenaida A. "How-to Web Sites on Cheating Spur Alarm." *Marin Independent Journal* [Marin County, CA] 29 Mar. 1999: A1, A5.

Graber, Debra. "Test of Character." *The University of Kansas Report* Fall 1995. <http://www.urc.ukans.edu/report/fall95/cover.html>.

Gresham, Keith. "Preventing Plagiarism of the Internet: Teaching Library Researchers How and Why to Cite Electronic Sources." *Colorado Libraries* 22.2 (1996): 48–50.

Guernsey, Lisa. "Web Site Will Check Papers against Database to Detect Plagiarism." *Chronicle of Higher Education* 45.16 (1998): A.38+. Bell & Howell Information and Learning-ProQuest. Los Alamitos High School Lib., Los Alamitos, CA. 10 Mar. 1999 <http://proquest.umi.com>.

Hall, Ann W. "Decreasing Plagiarism Using Critical Thinking Skills. A Practicum Report." Nova U. July 1986. ERIC (ED 323495).

Hardy, Lawrence. "Copyright in the Cyber Age." *Electronic School* June 1998. 21 Sep. 1999 <http://www.electronic-school.com>.

Harris, Robert. "Anti-Plagiarism Strategies for Research Papers." 1999. 28 Aug. 1999 <http://www.vanguard.edu/rharris/antiplag.htm>.

Hickman, John N. "Cybercheats." *New Republic* 23 Mar. 1998: 14–15. Bell & Howell Information and Learning-ProQuest. Los Alamitos High School Lib., Los Alamitos, CA. 10 Mar. 1999 <http://proquest.umi.com>.

Hinman, Lawrence M. "Download Your Workload, Offload Your Integrity." *Los Angeles Times* 15 Nov. 1999: B7.

Horovitz, Bruce. "Wired on Campus E-life." *USA Today* 19 Aug. 1999: 1B–2B.

Jackson, Louise A., Eileen Tway, and Alan Frager. "Dear Teacher, Johnny Copied." *Reading Teacher* 41.1 (1987): 22–25.

Jones, Emily Nielsen, Kevin Ryan, and Karen E. Bohlin. *Teachers as Educators of Character: Are the Nation's Schools of Education Coming Up Short?* Washington, DC: Character Education Partnership, 1999.

Josephson, Michael. "1998 Report Card on the Ethics of American Youth." 19 Oct. 1998 <http://www.josephsoninstitute.org>.

———. "Cheating Leads to Cheating." Radio address KNX, Los Angeles. 22 Oct. 1998. Transcript. 8 Sep. 1999 <http://www.charactercounts.org/knxwk67.htm>.

———. "Willful Blindness about Cheating." Radio address KNX, Los Angeles. 16 Aug. 1999. Transcript. 8 Sep. 1999 <http://www.charactercounts.org/knxwk110.htm>.

Keith-Spiegel, Patricia. "Multi-Media Integrity Teaching Tool: A Demonstration of the MITT." Center for Academic Integrity 9th Annual Conference. Durham, NC. 15-17 Oct. 1999.

Kibler, William L. "Cheating." *Chronicle of Higher Education* 39.12 (1992): B1–2.

Kidder, Rushworth M. "Why Shouldn't I Cheat?" Telephone interview. 27 Sep. 1999.

Kilpatrick, William, et al. *Books That Build Character: A Guide to Teaching Your Child Moral Values through Stories.* New York: Simon & Schuster, 1994.

Kindy, Kimberly. "UCI Sees Cheating Reports Increase." *Orange County Register* [Santa Ana, CA] 21 Oct. 1998: A1+. Bell & Howell Information and Learning-ProQuest. Los Alamitos High School Lib., Los Alamitos, CA. 10 Mar. 1999 <http://proquest.umi.com>.

Kleiner, Carolyn, and Mary Lord. "The Cheating Game." *U.S. News and World Report* 22 Nov. 1999: 54–66.

Kolich, Augustus M. "Plagiarism: The Worm of Reason." *College English* 45.2 (1983): 141–48.

Kongshem, Lars. "Censorware." *Electronic School* January 1998. 21 Sep. 1999 <http://www.electronic-school.com>.

Kreis, Kathleen. "A Write Step in the Wrong Direction." *Teaching PreK–8* 24.8 (1994): 66–67.

Krouse, Paul C. "Honoring Tomorrow's Leaders Today." Email to the author. 14 June 1999.

Lasarenko, Jane. "Teaching Paraphrase, Summary, and Plagiarism: An Integrated Approach." *Exercise Exchange* 41.2 (1996): 10–12.

Leland, Bruce. "Plagiarism and the Web." Email to the author. 29 Aug. 1999 <http://www.wiu.edu/users/mfbhl/wiu/plagiarism.htm>.

Levine, Judith. "What to Do When Your Child Cheats." *Family Life* Oct. 1997: 56–58.

Lickona, Thomas. "Educating for Character: A Comprehensive Approach." *The Construction of Children's Character: Ninety-sixth Yearbook of the National Society for the Study of Education. Part II.* Ed. Alex Molnar. Chicago: Natl. Society for the Study of Education, 1997. 45–62.

Lipsett, Judith. "How Parents Can Help With Homework." Family.com: Our Kids San Antonio Sep. 1998. 29 Aug. 1999 <http://www.family.go.com/Features/family_1998_90/sano/sano98homework/sano98homework.html>.

Los Alamitos High School. "Academic Honesty Code." Los Alamitos High School, 1997. Unpublished paper, 1999.

Love, Dennis. "Civics Students Discuss Cheating, Reasons for It." *Orange County Register* [Santa Ana, CA] 20 Oct. 1998: A6. Bell & Howell Information and Learning-ProQuest. Los Alamitos High School Lib., Los Alamitos, CA. 10 Aug. 1999 <http://proquest.umi.com>.

Magney, Reid. "Caught in a Web of Plagiarism." *LaCrosse Tribune* [WI] 21 Feb. 1999. NewsBank. Los Alamitos High School Lib., Los Alamitos, CA. 4 May 1999 <http://infoweb.newsbank.com>.

Mahoney, Bert. Personal interview. 4 Aug. 1999.

Maramark, Sheilah, and Mindi Barth Maline. "Academic Dishonesty among College Students." *Issues in Education* Aug. 1992: 3–14.

Marshall, Eliot. "The Internet: A Powerful Tool for Plagiarism Sleuths." *Science* 279.5350 (23 Jan. 1998): 474. 6 Sep. 1999 <http://www.sciencemag.org>.

Martelle, Scott. "Cheating Is Seen as Widespread." *Los Angeles Times Orange County* 21 Nov. 1999: B1, 7.

Martz, Ron. "News for Kids: If It's Someone Else's Story, It's Not Yours." *Atlanta Journal/Constitution* [GA] 10 Jan. 1998: A.3. Bell & Howell Information and Learning-ProQuest. Los Alamitos High School Lib., Los Alamitos, CA. 10 Mar. 1999 <http://proquest.umi.com>.

McCabe, Donald L. "Academic Dishonesty among High School Students." *Adolescence* 34.136 (1999): 681–87.

———. "Faculty Responses to Academic Dishonesty: The Influence of Student Honor Codes." *Research in Higher Education* 34.5 (1993): 647–58.

McCabe, Donald L., and Sally Cole. "Student Collaboration: Not Always What the Instructor Wants." *AAHE Bulletin* 48.3 (1995): 3–6.

McCabe, Donald L., and Patrick Drinan. "Toward a Culture of Academic Integrity." *Chronicle of Higher Education* 46.8 (1999): B7.

McCabe, Donald L., and Gary M. Pavela. "The Effect of Institutional Policies and Procedures on Academic Integrity." *Academic Integrity Matters.* Ed. Dana D. Burnett, et al. Washington, DC: Natl. Assn. of Student Personnel Administrators, Inc., 1998. 93–108.

McCabe, Donald L., and Linda Klebe Trevino. "What We Know About Cheating in College." *Change* 28.1 (1996): 29–33.

McCabe, Donald L., Linda Klebe Trevino, and Kenneth D. Butterfield. "Academic Integrity in Honor Code and Non-Honor Code Environments." *Journal of Higher Education* 70.2 (1999): 211–34.

McEwan, Elaine K. *I Didn't Do It: Dealing with Dishonesty.* Wheaton, IL: Shaw, 1996.

McGregor, Joy. "Student Research: Productive or Counterproductive?" Intl. Assn. of School Librarianship. Ocho Rios, Jamaica. 28 July-2 Aug. 1996. ERIC (ED 414906).

McKay, Gretchen. "Taking a Peek at Classroom Cheating: Surveys Report Rising Trend of Students Who Take the Easy Way Out." *Pittsburgh Post-Gazette* [PA] 7 June 1999: A13. Bell & Howell Information and Learning-ProQuest. Los Alamitos High School Lib., Los Alamitos, CA. 14 July 1999 <http://proquest.umi.com>.

Molnar, Alex, ed. *The Construction of Children's Character: Ninety-sixth Yearbook of the National Society for the Study of Education. Part II.* Chicago: Natl. Society for the Study of Education, 1997.

Monsour, Theresa. "No-Honor System: More Kids Admit Cheating." *Saint Paul Pioneer Press* [MN] 7 Feb. 1999:1A. NewsBank. Los Alamitos High School Lib., Los Alamitos, CA. 4 May 1999 <http://infoweb.newsbank.com>.

Mosholder, Karen Sandusky. "Cheating and the Internet." Online posting. 17 June 1998. NCTE-Talk. 25 Aug. 1999 <http://www.ncte.org/lists/ncte-talk/jun98/msg00874.html>.

Moss, Berk. "Notes on Cheating for the Busy Classroom Teacher." Sunset High School Workshop. Beaverton, OR. 7 Mar. 1984. ERIC (ED 243203).

Navarro, Joseph., et al. "Strategies to Promote Academic Integrity." U of California, Santa Barbara. Online. 15 Mar. 1999 <http://www.id.ucsb.edu/IC/Resources/Teaching/Integrity.html>.

Netherton, Ginnie. "Cheatin' Hearts: Survey Says Students Still Trying to Beat the System." *Tulsa World* [OK] 11 Feb. 1997: D1. NewsBank. Los Alamitos High School Lib., Los Alamitos, CA. 4 May 1999 <http://infoweb.newsbank.com>.

Nicosia, Ray. Telephone interview. 27 July 1999.

Orlans, Harold. "How to Cheat on Exams." *Change* 28.5 (1996): 10.

Osinski, Bill. "The Kids Aren't All Right." *Detroit Free Press* [MI] 25 Nov. 1990: 1F+. SIRS 1990 Ethics, Vol. 3 Article 78. Los Alamitos High School Lib., Los Alamitos, CA. 10 Aug. 1999 <http://sks.sirs.com>.

Partello, Peggie. "First-Year Students and Cheating: A Study at Keene State College." *Research Strategies* 11.3 (1993): 174–79.

Peterman, George. "Dinner with a Famous American Author." Unpublished paper, Anaheim Union High School District, Anaheim, CA, 1999.

Peterson, Lorna. "Teaching Academic Integrity: Opportunities in Bibliographic Instruction." *Research Strategies* 6.4 (1988): 168–76.

Posnick-Goodwin, Sherry. "Truth or Consequences." *California Educator* 4.2 (1999): 7–8.

———. "Catching Cheaters in the Net Requires Computer Literacy." *California Educator* 4.2 (1999): 10–11.

Pownell, David, and Gerald Bailey. "Electronic Fences or Free-Range Students? Should Schools Use Internet Filtering Software?" *Learning & Leading with Technology* 27.1 (1999): 50–57.

Preston, Elisa. Letter. *Indianapolis Star* [IN] 26 Mar. 1999: 8. Bell & Howell Information and Learning-ProQuest. Los Alamitos High School Lib., Los Alamitos, CA. 10 Aug. 1999 <http://proquest.umi.com>.

Raffetto, William G. "The Cheat." *Community and Junior College Journal* 56.2 (1985): 26–27.

Rankin, Virginia. "Get Smart: The Crucial Link between Media Specialists and A+ Students." *School Library Journal* 42.8 (1996): 22–26.

Roach, Ronald. "High-Tech Cheating." *Black Issues in Higher Education.* 24 Dec. 1998: 26. Bell & Howell Information and Learning-ProQuest. Los Alamitos High School Lib., Los Alamitos, CA. 15 July 1999 <http://proquest.umi.com>.

Rocklin, Tom. "Downloadable Term Papers: What's a Prof to Do?" Email to the author. 4 Sep. 1999.

Ropp, Thomas. "The Odyssey of Teacher's Term Paper." *Arizona Republic* [Phoenix, AZ] 20 Oct. 1997: C.1. Bell & Howell Information and Learning-ProQuest. Los Alamitos High School Lib., Los Alamitos, CA. 10 Mar. 1999 <http://proquest.umi.com>.

Rudolph, Lynn, and Linda Timm. "A Comprehensive Approach for Creating a Campus Climate That Promotes Academic Integrity." *Academic Integrity Matters.* Ed. Dana D. Burnett, et al. Washington, DC: Natl. Assn. of Student Personnel Administrators, Inc., 1998. 57–75.

Ryan, Julie J. C. H. "Student Plagiarism in an Online World." *ASEE Prism* (December 1998). 11 Mar. 1999 <http://www.asee.org/prism/december/html/student_plagiarism>.

Ryan, Kevin. "The Six E's of Character Education: Practical Ways to Bring Moral Instruction to Life for Your Students." 10 Aug. 1999 <http://www.education.bu.edu/CharacterEd/6Es.html>.

Saenger, Elizabeth Baird. *Exploring Ethics through Children's Literature, Book 1.* Pacific Grove, CA: Critical Thinking, 1993.

Sanchez, Roberto. "Students Are Casting the Net to Plagiarize Papers." *Sacramento Bee* [CA] 30 Dec. 1998: H3+. Bell & Howell Information and Learning-ProQuest. Los Alamitos High School Lib., Los Alamitos, CA. 10 Mar. 1999 <http://proquest.umi.com>.

Schab, Fred. "Schooling without Learning: Thirty Years of Cheating in High School." *Adolescence* 26.104 (1991): 839–48.

Scheinin, Richard. "From College to High School to Elementary School, Students Learn Life Lessons about Ethics." *San Jose Mercury News* [CA] 16 June 1998. NewsBank. Los Alamitos High School Lib., Los Alamitos, CA. 5 June 1999 <http://infoweb.newsbank.com>.

Schmidt, Steve. "Cheatin' Arts May be Rising at UCSD." *San Diego Union-Tribune* [CA] 2 May 1994: B1. NewsBank. Los Alamitos High School Lib., Los Alamitos, CA. 11 Mar. 1999 <http://infoweb.newsbank.com>.

Schubert, William H. "Character Education from Four Perspectives on Curriculum." *The Construction of Children's Character: Ninety-sixth Yearbook of the National Society for the Study of Education. Part II.* Ed. Alex Molnar. Chicago: Natl. Society for the Study of Education, 1997. 17–30.

Serafin, Ana Gil, ed. "About Plagiarism." *Instructional Exchange* 2.1 (1990): 3–4.

———. "Academic Dishonesty in Our Classrooms." *Instructional Exchange* 2.2 (1990): 1–4.

Sharma, Amita. "School Cheating Study Finds Hole in 'Moral Ozone' Bigger." *Press-Enterprise* [Riverside, CA] 5 Dec. 1998: A1. Bell & Howell Information and Learning-ProQuest. Los Alamitos High School Lib., Los Alamitos, CA. 14 July 1999 <http://proquest.umi.com>.

Shropshire, William O. "Of Being and Getting: Academic Honesty." *Liberal Education* 83.4 (1997): 24–31.

Singhal, Avinash C., and Patti Johnson. "How to Halt Student Dishonesty." *College Student Journal* 17.1 (1983): 13–19.

Sommers, Christina Hoff. "Teaching the Virtues." *Public Interest* No. 111 (Spring 1993): 3–13.

Stansbury, Robin. "For Many of the Brightest Students, Honest Is Academic." *Hartford Courant* [CT] 2 Mar. 1997: A1+. Bell & Howell Information and Learning-ProQuest. Los Alamitos High School Lib., Los Alamitos, CA. 17 Apr. 1999 <http://proquest.umi.com>.

———. "Popular Get Tough Policies Don't Extend to Cheating in Schools." *Hartford Courant* [CT] 4 Mar. 1997: A1+. Bell & Howell Information and Learning-ProQuest. Los Alamitos High School Lib., Los Alamitos, CA. 17 Apr. 1999 <http://proquest.umi.com>.

———. "Technology, Internet Powerful Tests of Student Integrity." *Hartford Courant* [CT] 3 Mar. 1997: A1+. Bell & Howell Information and Learning-ProQuest. Los Alamitos High School Lib., Los Alamitos, CA. 17 Apr. 1999 <http://proquest.umi.com>.

Stebelman, Scott. "Cybercheating: Dishonesty Goes Digital." *American Libraries* 29.8 (1998): 48–50. Bell & Howell Information and Learning-ProQuest. Los Alamitos High School Lib., Los Alamitos, CA. 15 July 1999 <http://proquest.umi.com>.

Sterling, Gary. "Plagiarism and the Worms of Accountability." *Reading Improvement* 28.3 (1991): 138–40. Bell & Howell Information and Learning-ProQuest. Los Alamitos High School Lib., Los Alamitos, CA. 19 Mar. 1999 <http://proquest.umi.com>.

Strickland, Leif B. "Term Papers from the Web Spark Debate." *Star Tribune* [Minneapolis, MN] 12 Sep. 1997: 23E. Bell & Howell Information and Learning-ProQuest. Los Alamitos High School Lib., Los Alamitos, CA. 10 Mar. 1999 <http://proquest.umi.com>.

Stripling, Barbara K. "Learning-Centered Libraries: Implications from Research." *School Library Media Quarterly* 23.3 (1995): 163–170.

Summergrad, David. "Calling It What It Is." *Education Week* 18.43 (1999): 46.

Thompson, Lenora C., and Portia G. Williams. "But I Changed Three Words! Plagiarism in the ESL Classroom." *Clearing House* 69.1 (1995): 27–29.

Tom, Darielle. Personal interview. 8 Aug. 1999.

Wagner, Eileen N. "Outfoxing Fraud: Research Papers without Repression." Conference on College Composition and Communication. Kansas City, MO. 31 Mar.-2 Apr. 1977. ERIC (ED 143015).

Waltman, John L. "Plagiarism: (2) Preventing It in Formal Research Reports." *ABCA Bulletin* 43.2 (1980): 37–38.

Weber, Larry J., and Janice K. McBee. "Cheating: A Problem with Take-Home Exams?" Annual Meeting of the Natl. Council on Measurement in Education. Montreal, PQ. 11-15 Apr. 1983. ERIC (ED 242730).

Webster's Third New International Dictionary of the English Language, Unabridged. Ed. Philip Babcock Gove. Springfield, MA: Merriam-Webster, 1981.

Wein, Eric. "Cheating: Risking It All for Grades." *Arizona Daily Wildcat* [Tucson, AZ] 2 Dec. 1994: 3. 15 Mar. 1999 <http://www.wildcat.arizona.edu/papers>.

Wentzel, Michael. "Internet Makes Cheating Easy." *Democrat and Chronicle* [Rochester, NY] 20 Apr. 1999. NewsBank. Los Alamitos High School Lib., Los Alamitos, CA. 5 June 1999 <http://infoweb.newsbank.com>.

Whitaker, Elaine E. "A Pedagogy to Address Plagiarism." *College Composition and Communication* 44.4 (1993): 509–14.

White, Edward M. "Too Many Campuses Want to Sweep Student Plagiarism under the Rug." *Chronicle of Higher Education* 39.25 (1993): A44.

Whitley, Bernard E., Jr., and Mary E. Kite. "The Classroom Environment and Academic Integrity." *Academic Integrity Matters.* Ed. Dana D. Burnett, et al. Washington, DC: Natl. Assn. of Student Personnel Administrators, Inc., 1998. 39–55.

Who's Who Among American High School Students. "Cheating and Succeeding: Record Number of Top High School Students Take Ethical Shortcuts." 1998 annual survey. 20 June 1999 <http://www.honoring.com/highschool/annualsurveys/29.shtml>.

Worthen, Helena. "A Way to Break Down Writing Research Papers into Steps That Emphasize the Discovery Aspect of Research." Intersegmental Faculty Seminar. California Assn. of Community Colleges. Bass Lake, CA. 20 July 1990. ERIC (ED 331064).

Further Readings

Anderson, Judy. *Plagiarism, Copyright Violation, and Other Thefts of Intellectual Property: An Annotated Bibliography with a Lengthy Introduction.* Jefferson, NC: McFarland, 1998.

Beall, Elizabeth. "Mapping the Way to the Land of Good Grades." *Teaching PreK–8* 25.4 (1995): 68–69.

Bowden, Darsie. "Coming to Terms: Plagiarism." *English Journal* 85.4 (1996): 82–83.

Bowers, William J. *Student Dishonesty and Its Control in College.* New York: Bureau of Applied Social Research. Columbia U, 1964.

Brandes, Barbara. *Academic Dishonesty: A Special Study of California Students.* Sacramento, CA: California Dept. of Education, 1986.

Broz, Nancy D. "Writing or Plagiarizing?" Leadership Conference. New Jersey Council of Teachers of English. Lawrenceville, NJ. 5 May 1977. ERIC (ED 146619).

Bushweller, Kevin. "Student Cheating: A Morality Moratorium?" *Education Digest* 65.3 (1999) 4–11.

Diekhoff, George M., et al. "College Cheating: Ten Years Later." *Research in Higher Education* 37.4 (1996): 487–502.

Ede, Lisa S., and Andrea Lunsford. *Singular Texts/Plural Authors: Perspectives on Collaborative Writing.* Carbondale, IL: Southern Illinois U, 1990.

Evans, Ellis D., et al. "Adolescents' Cognitions and Attributions for Academic Cheating: A Cross-National Study." Society for Research in Child Development. Seattle, WA. 18-20 Apr. 1991. ERIC (ED 335612).

Fey, Charles J., and Kenneth E. Kelly. "Integrating Ethics into the Curriculum and Co-curriculum: Model Comprehensive Approaches." National Assn. of Student Personnel Administrators. Atlanta, GA. 13-16 Mar. 1996. ERIC (ED 397385).

Heyboer, Kelly. "Honor Codes Really Work in Colleges." *San Diego Union-Tribune* [CA] 22 Jan. 1999: E6. Bell & Howell Information and Learning-ProQuest. Los Alamitos High School Lib., Los Alamitos, CA. 10 Aug. 1999 <http://proquest.umi.com>.

Houser, Betsy Bosak. "Student Cheating and Attitude: A Function of Classroom Control Technique." *Contemporary Educational Psychology* 7.2 (1982): 113–123.

Kidder, Rushworth M. "Children's Moral Compass Wavers." *Christian Science Monitor* 16 May 1990: 12.

———. "Ethics Is Not a Luxury; It's Essential to Our Survival." *Education Week on the Web* 10.28 (1991). 15 July 1999 <http:///www.edweek.org/ew/>

———. "What Ever Happened to Honesty?" *Boston Globe* 20 Nov. 1998: A27. Bell & Howell Information and Learning-ProQuest. Los Alamitos High School Lib., Los Alamitos, CA. 14 Aug. 1999 <http://proquest.umi.com>.

237

McCabe, Donald L., and William J. Bowers. "Academic Dishonesty among Males in College: A Thirty Year Perspective." *Journal of College Student Development* 35.1 (1994): 5–10.

Murphy, Richard. "Anorexia: The Cheating Disorder." *College English* 52.8 (1990): 898–903.

Newstead, Stephen E., Arlene Franklyn-Stokes, and Penny Armstead. "Individual Differences in Student Cheating." *Journal of Educational Psychology* 88.2 (1996): 229–241.

Nienhuis, Terry. "The Quick Fix: Curing Plagiarism with a Note-Taking Exercise." *College Teaching* 37.3 (1989): 100.

O'Neill, Michael T. "Plagiarism: (1) Writing Responsibly." *ABCA Bulletin* 43.2 (1980): 34–36.

Payne, Stephen L., and Karen S. Nantz. "Social Accounts and Metaphors about Cheating." *College Teaching* 42.3 (1994): 90–96.

Sharkey, Paulette Bochnig. "What to Tell Your Students about Copyright." *Clearing House* 65.5 (1992): 213–14.

Stahl, Norman, and James R. King. "Open to Suggestion: Using Paraphrasing Cards to Reduce Unintentional Plagiarism." *Journal of Reading* 34.7 (1991): 562–63.

Who's Who Among American High School Students. "Top Teens and Teachers Suggest Back to School Lessons for Parents." 1997 annual survey. 20 June 1999 <http://www.honoring.com/highschool/annualsurveys/lessons.shtml>.

Who's Who Among American High School Students. "What Parents of Top Teens Don't Know about Their Kids Confirms Parents' Worst Fears." 1996 annual survey. 20 June 1999 <http://www.honoring.com/highschool/annualsurveys/parent.shtml>.

Summary List of Web Addresses

Web Sites with Resources for Countering Plagiarism

(Chapter 5)
About Plagiarism, Pixels and Platitudes
   <http://www.svsu.edu/~dboehm/pixels.htm#NextStep>
Avoiding Plagiarism
   <http://www.hamilton.edu/academic/resource/wc/wc.html>
Combating Cybercheating: Resources for Teachers
   <http://www.epcc.edu/library/>
Plagiarism
   <http://webware.princeton.edu/Writing/wc4g.htm>
Plagiarism and Anti-Plagiarism
   <http://newark.rutgers.edu/>
Plagiarism: Definitions, Examples and Penalties
   <http://www.chem.uky.edu/courses/common/plagiarism.html>
Plagiarism: What It Is and How to Recognize and Avoid It
   <http://www.Indiana.edu/~wts/wts/plagiarism.html>
Policy on Plagiarism and Outside Help
   <http://www.ualberta.ca/~german/plagiar.htm>

Software Tools to Combat Cheating and Plagiarism

(Chapter 5)
ExamSoft Xmn8r Examination Security Software
   <http://www.examsoft.com>
Glatt Plagiarism Services
   <http://www.plagiarism.com>
IntegriGuard
   <http://www.integriguard.com>
Intelligent Essay Assessor
   <http://www.lsa.colorado.edu/essay>
MOSS (Measure Of Software Similarity)
   <http://www.cs.berkeley.edu/~aiken/moss.html>
Plagiarism.org
   <http://www.plagiarism.org/>

Institutes and Centers that Support Ethics, Integrity, and Character Education

(Chapter 7)
The Center for Academic Integrity
    <http://www.academicintegrity.org>
Center for the Advancement of Ethics and Character [Boston University]
    <http://education.bu.edu/CharacterEd/>
The Center for the 4th and 5th Rs
    <http://www.cortland.edu/www/c4n5rs/>
CHARACTER COUNTS!
    <http://www.charactercounts.org/>
Character Education Partnership
    <http://www.character.org/>
The Heartwood Institute
    <http://www.enviroweb.org/heartwood/about.html>
The Institute for Global Ethics
    <http://www.globalethics.org/>
International Center for Character Education (ICCE)
    <http://www.teachvalues.org/icce/>
Josephson Institute of Ethics
    <http://www.josephsoninstitute.org/>
Markkula Center for Applied Ethics
    <http://www.scu.edu/SCU/Centers/Ethics/>
The Values Institute: The Place for the Thoughtful Discussion of Moral Issues
    <http://www.ethics.acusd.edu/values/>

Academic Integrity Policies Online

(Chapter 8)
Middle Schools
Blocker Middle School (TX): Honor Code and Academic Honesty
    <http://www.texascity.isd.tenet.edu/Academic.html>
H. E. Huntington Middle School (CA): Cheating Policy
    <http://www.san-marino.k12.ca.us/~heh/binderreminder/cheatpolic.html>
St. Patricks School (NY): Discipline
    <http://www.stpatrick-school.org/Discipline/discipline.html>
Webb School of Knoxville (TN): Middle School Honor Code
    <http://www.webbschool.org/info/enrollment/Honor.html>

High Schools
Citizens' High School (FL): CHS Honor System
    <http://www.citizenschool.com/40.html#honor>
El Toro High School (CA): Ethics and Cheating Policy
    <http://www.svusd.k12.ca.us/schools/eths/ethcspol.htm>
Langley High School (VA): Honor Code
    <http://www.fcps.k12.va.us/LangleyHS/saxon/honor.html>

Providence High School (CA): Academic Dishonesty
  <http://www.providencehigh.org/hb/hb. htm>
Webb School of Knoxville (TN): Upper School Honor Code and Procedures
  <http://www.webbschool.org/info/enrollment/Honor.html>
West Springfield High School (VA): Honor Code
  <http://www.wshs.fcps.k12.va.us/info/hcode.htm>

Universities and Colleges
Queen's University Policies: Policy on Academic Dishonesty
  <http://www.queensu.ca/secretariat/senate/policies/acaddish.html>
State University of West Georgia: Cheating and Plagiarism
  <http://www.westga.edu/~vpaa/handbook/207.html>
University of Arizona: Code of Academic Integrity
  <http://w3.arizona.edu/~uhap/appendg.html>
University of Kansas: Academic Misconduct
  <http://www.cc.ukans.edu/cwis/units/safacts/codes.html#AcademicMisconduct>
University of Maryland, College Park: Code of Academic Integrity
  <http://www.inform.umd.edu/JPO/AcInteg/code_acinteg2a.html>
University of Virginia: The Honor System
  <http://www.virginia.edu/%7eregist/ugradrec/chapter5/uchap5-3.2.html>
University of Washington College of Engineering: Academic Misconduct
  <http://www.ee.washington.edu/undergrad/handbook/misconduct.html>

Online Sites for Reports and Research Papers

(Chapter 17)
Abcresearch.com
  <www.abcresearch.com>
Academic Term Papers
  <www.academictermpapers.com>
Academic Writing
  <www.cyberhighway.net/~gailmae>
ACI Writing Assistance Center
  <www.aci-plus.com>
Bignerds.com
  <www.bignerds.com>
Cheater.com
  <www.cheater.com>
Cheathouse—The Evil House of Cheat
  <www.cheathouse.com>
Chuckiii.com
  <www.chuckiii.com>
College Term Papers.com
  <www.collegetermpapers.com>
Collegiate Care Research Assistance
  <www.paper-online.com>
Cyber Essays
  <www.cyberessays.com>

Downcrap
 <www.members.xoom.com/_XOOM/downcrap>
Essay Depot
 <www.essayDepot.com>
Essaybank
 <www.essaybank.com>
4research'99
 <www.4research.com>
GP Genius Papers
 <www.geniuspapers.com>
Hiredpens
 <www.hiredpens.com>
Homework's Done
 <www.members.aol.com/oohalooo/index2.html>
Ivyessays Papers
 <www.ivyessays.com>
Jungle Page
 <www.junglepage.com/asp/index.asp>
Killer Essays
 <www.freeessays.com/killer/>
Knowledge Reports
 <www.knowledge-reports.com>
Mad Papers
 <www.madpapers.com>
Net Essays
 <www.netessays.net>
1-800 Termpaper Academic and Business Research Source
 <www.al-termpaper.com>
OPPapers.com
 <www.oppapers.com>
Paper Masters
 <www.papermasters.com>
Paper Store
 <www.paperstore.net>
Papercamp.com
 <www.papercamp.com>
Papers 24-7
 <www.papers24-7.com>
Papers Inn
 <www.papersinn.com>
Papersure: The Research Paper Center
 <www.papershack.com>
Penquest.com
 <www.ezwriters.net>
Planet Papers
 <www.planetpapers.com>
Poetry Papers.com
 <www.poetrypapers.com>
Research Assistance
 <www.research-assistance.com>

Research Papers Online A+
    <www.ezwrite.com>
School Paper.com
    <www.schoolpaper.com>
School Sucks
    <www.schoolsucks.com>
School Sux
    <www.schoolsux.com/>
Schoolbytes.com
    <www.schoolbytes.com>
Screw Essays
    <www.screw-essays.com>
Smart Essays
    <www.FreeEssays.com/smart/>
Specialty Research
    <www.papermasters.org>
Student Essays
    <www.freeessay.com/student/get_essays>
Studentcentral
    <www.studentcentral.co.uk>
Superior Termpapers
    <www.superior-termpapers.com>
Terms n Papers
    <www.termsnpapers.com>
Thousands of Papers
    <www.termpapers-on-file.com>
12,000 Papers.com
    <www.12000papers.com>

Miscellaneous Sites

3Com Corporation PalmPilot (Chapter 2)
    <http://palmpilot.3com.com/prodsoft.htm>
Arizona Daily Wildcat [Tucson, AZ] (References Cited)
    <http://www.wildcat.arizona.edu/papers>
Center for Applied and Professional Ethics (Chapter 7)
    <http://cape.cmsu.edu/>
Character Education Manifesto (Chapter 7)
    <http://education.bu.edu/Charactered/manifesto.html>
The Character Education Pages (Chapter 7)
    <http://cuip.uchicago.edu/~cac/chared>
Cheaters Paradise (Chapter 2)
    <http://www.jaberwocky.com/cheat/index2.html>
Copyright Basics (Chapter 9)
    <http://lcweb.loc.gov/copyright/>
The Copyright Website (Chapter 9)
    <http://www.benedict.com/>

Cyber Classics (Chapter 3)
  <http://www.cyberclassics.com>
Education Week on the Web (Further Readings)
  <http:///www.edweek.org/ew/>
Educational Testing Service (ETS) "Academic Cheating Background." (Chapter 5)
  <http://www.nocheating.org/adcouncil/research/>
Educational Testing Service (ETS) "Academic Cheating Fact Sheet." (Chapter 5)
  <http://www.nocheating.org/adcouncil/research/>
Educational Testing Service (ETS) "Cheating is a personal foul" Ad Campaign (Chapter 1)
  <http://www.nocheating.org/adcouncil/news/launchrelease.html>
Electronic School (Chapter 5)
  <http://www.electronic-school.com>
Homework Helper (Chapter 6)
  <http://family.go.com/Features/family_1997_07/dony/dony77lesupervise/>
Motorola Corporation Beepwear pager (Chapter 2)
  <http://www.beepwear.com/html/index.html>
Multimedia Integrity Teaching Tool (MITT) (Chapter 7)
  <http://www.bsu.edu/csh/mitt/>
National Council of Teachers of English (NCTE) (References Cited)
  <http://www.ncte.org/lists/ncte-talk/jun98/msg00874.html>
Professional Code of Ethics for Teacher Educators (Chapter 7)
  <http://www.teachvalues.org/icce/CodeTE9.htm>
PubMed (Chapter 5)
  <http://www.ncbi.nlm.nih.gov/PubMed/>
Science (References Cited)
  <http://www.sciencemag.org>
Texas Instruments TI-92 electronic calculator (Chapter 2)
  <http://www.ti.com/calc/docs/news/cg-418t.htm>
United States Copyright Office (Chapter 9)
  <http://lcweb.loc.gov/copyright/>
University of California, Santa Barbara (References Cited)
  <http://www.id.ucsb.edu/IC/Resources/Teaching/Integrity.html>
Versity.com (Chapter 3)
  <http://www.versity.com>
Who's Who Among American High School Students (Chapter 4)
  <http://www.honoring.com/highschool/annualsurveys/>

Articles Online

Harris, Robert A. "Anti-Plagiarism Strategies for Research Papers." (Chapter 15)
  <www.vanguard.edu/rharris/antiplag.htm>
Leland, Bruce H. "Plagiarism and the Web" (Chapter 13)
  <http://www.wiu.edu/users/mfbhl/wiu/plagiarism.htm>
Ryan, Julie J. C. H. "Student Plagiarism in an Online World." (Chapter 5)
  <http://www.asee.org/prism/december/html/student_plagiarism>
Ryan, Kevin. "The Six E's of Character Education: Practical Ways to Bring Moral Instruction to Life for Your Students." (Chapter 7)
  <http://education.bu.edu/CharacterEd/>

Web Addresses in Reprinted Articles

Ryan, Julie J. C. H. "Student Plagiarism In an Online World." (Chapter 5)
String Search Sites
<altavista.digital.com>
<www.lycos.com>
<www.netscape.com>
<www.metacrawler.com>
Search Help Sites
<www.searchinsider.com>
<www.cs.uwyo.edu/~drnelson/cs1100/TGSEARCH.html>
<www.zdnet.com/products/searchuser.html>
<www.albany.edu/library/internet/search.html>
Category Search Sites
<www.yahoo.com>
<www.infoseek.com>
<www.infospace.com>
<www.excite.com>
Online Bookstores
<www.amazon.com>
<www.barnesandnoble.com>
<www.borders.com>
People Search Sites
<www.bigfoot.com>
<www.bigyellow.com>
<www.whowhere.com>

Farmer: Cyber-Plagiarism Faculty Workshop (Chapter 12)
<http://www.chuckiii.com/cheats.shtml>
<http://www.collegepapers.com/>
<http://www.members.tripod.com/%7ETexasTwister/>
<http://www.researchpaper.com/>
<http://www.schoolsucks.com/>
<http://www.cheathouse.com/>
<http://www.cyberessays.com/5>
<http://www.nh.ultranet.com/~Imaccann/default_the_brain_trust.html>

Online Databases

(References Cited)
Bell & Howell Information and Learning-ProQuest
<http://proquest.umi.com>
InfoTrac
<http://web.infotrac.galegroup.com>
NewsBank
<http://infoweb.newsbank.com>
SIRS
<http://sks.sirs.com>

Index

Note: **w** = Web site; **c** = Copy-Me page

ABC Research.com **w**, 214

About Plagiarism, Pixels, and Platitudes **w**, 53

Academic integrity policies, 6–7, 92–114. *See also* Ethical school culture; Honor codes; Los Alamitos High School Academic Honesty Code
Development, 6–7, 93–98, 116, 134
Examples, 104–11
Implementation, 66, 97–101, 104, 113, 116, 132, 142
Publicity, 101, 104, 110
Student participation, 46, 98–99, 113

Academic Term Papers **w**, 22, 214

Academic Writing **w**, 214

Acceptable use policies, 50, 97, 99–100, 116. *See also* Internet

ACI Writing Assistance Center **w**, 215

Administrators. *See also* Parents–Working with school staff
Leadership role, 7, 93–98, 100–103, 135
Responses to cheating or plagiarism, 97, 131–33, 135
Setting an ethical example, 100–103, 131–33

Advanced Placement students. *See* Students–Advanced Placement

The Advertising Council, 4, 48

Anti-Plagiarism Strategies for Research Papers, 193–96

Antiplagiarism software and Web sites, 50–54, 57–58. *See also* Plagiarism–Prevention strategies

AP students. *See* Students–Advanced Placement

Are Any of These Cheating? **c**, 125

Are Any of These Plagiarizing? **c**, 126

Are These Valid Reasons to Cheat or Plagiarize? **c**, 88

Assignments. *See* Homework; Writing assignments

Attitudes. *See* Parents–Attitudes; Students–Attitudes; Teachers–Attitudes

Audiocassettes. *See* Headsets

"Avoiding a Plagiarized Report," 198–200

Avoiding Plagiarism **w**, 53

"Beyond Research Reports," 201–204

Bibliographies. *See* Research papers

Bignerds.com **w**, 22, 215

Binders. *See* Internet–Binders for Internet sites

Blocker Middle School (TX) **w**, 104–105

Blocking software. *See* Internet–Blocking software

Board members. *See* School board members

Book reports, 19, 201–204

Books That Build Character, 75–76

Brand, Alice G., 198

Brownlee, Bonnie J., 189

Bushweller, Kevin, viii–ix

But I Changed Three Words! Plagiarism in the ESL Classroom, 127–28

Calculators, 2, 11, 15–16, 48, 147–48. *See also* Texas Instruments TI-92 electronic calculator

A Case of High School Plagiarism **c**, 137

Censorware. *See* Internet–Blocking software

The Center for Academic Integrity **w**, 46, 76–77, 95

Center for Applied and Professional Ethics (CAPE) **w**, 83–84

The Center for the 4th and 5th Rs **w**, 77

Center for the Advancement of Ethics and Character **w**, 6, 74–75, 78

CHARACTER COUNTS! **w**, 6, 39–40, 79

Character education, 4, 72–91. *See also* Literature for character education

Character Education Manifesto **w**, 78

Character Education Pages **w**, 84

Character Education Partnership **w**, 74–75, 79

Chat rooms. *See* Web sites–Clandestine

Cheat sheets, 3, 14, 148–49

Cheat sites. *See* Internet–Cheat sites; Web sites–Clandestine

Cheater.com **w**, 23, 215

Cheaters Paradise **w**, 12

Cheathouse–The Evil House of Cheat **w**, 23, 215–216

Cheating, 2–4, 6–8, 10–16. *See also* Internet–Cheat sites; Statistical data; Tests and testing

  Career/life implications, 85–87, 130–131

  College and university students, 33, 44–46, 93

  Definition, 6, 109–110, 116–17, 125

  Elementary school students, 31–32

  High school students, 30–44

  Indicators of possible cheating, 15–16, 125, 132–33, 147–50

  Informing parents, 66–68, 132–34, 138–39, 150

  Middle school students, 7, 31–32, 39–41, 142

  Penalties, 7, 37, 111, 129, 134–36, 139

  Prevention strategies, 3–4, 8, 15–16, 130–31, 141–51

  Reasons/excuses, 1, 5, 32–35, 37, 41–44, 86, 88, 93

  Responding to incidents, 7, 63, 66–68, 110, 131–36, 138–39

Cheating Leads to Cheating, 1

Cheating and Succeeding: Record Number of Top High School Students Take Ethical Shortcuts **c**, 36–38

ChuckIII.com **w**, 216

Citing online sources. *See* Research papers–Citing online sources

Citizens' High School (FL) **w**, 105

Cobbs, Lewis, 112–14

Collaboration, 6, 118–19, 122–24, 151. *See also* Parents–Working with school staff; Students from other cultures; Teachers–Collaboration with librarians

College Term Papers.com **w**, 216

College and university research on cheating. *See* Statistical data–College and university students

Collegiate Care Research Assistance **w**, 216

Combating Cybercheating: Resources for Teachers **w**, 53

Computer networks
  Security, 12–13, 144
  Tests and Testing, 13, 49

Computers. *See* Hand-held computers

Confronting students about possible dishonesty. *See* Cheating–Responding to incidents; Plagiarism–Responding to incidents

The Construction of Children's Character, 73–74

"Controlled Research: Putting Text to the Test," 198

Copiers. *See* Photocopiers

"Coping with Plagiarism Requires Several Strategies," 189

Copyright Basics **w**, 122

Copyright issues, 6, 121–22. *See also* Internet–Copyright issues; Web sites–Copyright issues

The Copyright Primer for Librarians and Educators, 121

The Copyright Website **w**, 122

Cyber Classics **w**, 19

Cyber Essays **w**, 216

Cyber-Plagiarism Faculty Workshop **c**, 158–60

Cyberplagiarism, 18

Davis, Susan J., 9, 182–87

Dear Teacher, Johnny Copied, 170–73

Note: **w** = Web site; **c** = Copy-Me page

Davis, Susan J., 9, 182–87
Dear Teacher, Johnny Copied, 170–73
Decreasing Plagiarism Using Critical Thinking Skills, 190
Dick, David D., 198–200
Digital watches, 11, 48. *See also* Pager watches
Dinner with a Famous American Author, 206–208
Distance learning, 13, 49–50
Does Cheating Harm Your Career? **c**, 87
Downcrap **w**, 217
Downloadable Term Papers: What's a Prof to Do?, 25–28
Downloading and creating a paper. *See* Online sites for reports and research papers–Downloading and creating a paper
Drum, Alice, 189

Editing services. *See* Online sites for reports and research papers–Editing services
Educational Testing Service (ETS) **w**, 4, 48
Elementary school students. *See* Cheating–Elementary school students; Plagiarism–Elementary school students; Plagiarism–Unintentional; Statistical data–Elementary school students; Students
El Toro High School (CA) **w**, 105
Electronic calculators. *See* Calculators
Electronic encyclopedias, 2, 20–21
Electronic plagiarism. *See* Plagiarism
An Electronic Scavenger Hunt **c**, 168
Electronic School **w**, 48
Email, 2, 13
Encyclopedias. *See* Electronic encyclopedias
ESL students. *See* Students from other cultures
Essay Depot **w**, 217
Essaybank **w**, 217
Ethical school culture, 7, 90, 98–103, 135
Ethics, 36–44, 72–91. *See also* Integrity
Ethics Across the Curriculum, 83
ETS. *See* Educational Testing Service

ExamSoft Xmn8r Examination Security Software **w**, 50
Excuses for cheating. *See* Cheating–Reasons/excuses; Plagiarism–Reasons/excuses; Students–Attitudes
Exploring Ethics through Children's Literature–Book 1, 76

Faculty. *See* Teachers
Falcone, Stephen V., 102–03
Farmer, Lesley, 158–60, 201–204
Faxes, 2, 13
Filtering software. *See* Internet–Blocking software
4Research'99 **w**, 214
Frager, Alan, 170–73
Freitas, David, 75
From Library Skills to Information Literacy, 176
Fuchs, Gaynell M., 205

Geosits, Margaret S., 205
"Get Smart: The Crucial Link Between Media Specialists and A+ Students," 191–92
Glatt Plagiarism Services **w**, 52
Gordon, Mark, 174
GP Genius Papers **w**, 217
Grades and grading. *See* Tests and testing
Graphing calculators. *See* Calculators

Hackers, 13, 49, 143–44
H.E. Huntington Middle School (CA) **w**, 105
Hall, Ann W., 190
Hand-held computers, 2, 11, 15, 48. *See also* 3Com Corporation PalmPilot
Harris, Robert A., 9, 193–96
Headsets, 14
The Heartwood Institute **w**, 76, 80
Help, But Not Too Much **c**, 69
High school students. *See* Cheating–High school students; Plagiarism–High school students; Statistical data–High school students; Students
High-Tech Devices Used for Cheating **c**, 15–16

Note: **w** = Web site; **c** = Copy-Me page

Hiredpens **w**, 217
Homework, 2, 12–13, 49, 68–70, 125–26, 151. *See also* Parents–Assisting with homework; Tutors
Homework Helper **w**, 68
Homework's Done **w**, 218
Honesty. *See* Ethics; Integrity
Honor codes, 46, 93–98, 104–14. *See also* Academic integrity policies; Ethical school culture; Los Alamitos High School Academic Honesty Code
Honor Codes: Teaching Integrity and Interdependence, 112–14
Honoring Tomorrow's Leaders Today, 71
How to Develop a Strong Program for Academic Integrity **c**, 95

Information literacy, 153, 191
Information Power: Building Partnerships for Learning, 121, 153
Infrared transmitters, 11, 48
The Institute for Global Ethics **w**, 80–81
IntegriGuard **w**, 52
Integrity, 5–6, 40, 43–44, 72–91. *See also* Ethics
Intelligent Essay Assessor **w**, 52
International Center for Character Education (ICCE) **w**, 75, 81
Internet. *See also* Acceptable use policies; Online sites for reports and research papers; Plagiarism; Web sites
  Binders for Internet sites, 155
  Blocking software, 4, 50–51
  Bookmarks/Favorites, 49
  Cheat sites, 12, 18–19
  Copyright issues, 19, 121–22
  Translation software, 12, 20
Ivyessays Papers **w**, 218

Jackson, Louise A., 170–73
Josephson, Michael, 1, 39–41, 60, 63, 82
Josephson Institute of Ethics **w**, 1, 3, 6, 31, 39–41, 61, 79, 82. See also *1998 Report Card on the Ethics of American Youth*
Jungle Page **w**, 218

Kidder, Rushworth M., 80, 130–31
Killer Essays **w**, 218
Kirk, William R., 205
Knowledge Reports **w**, 218–219
Kreis, Kathleen A., 190
Krouse, Paul C., 5, 35–36, 71. See also *Who's Who Among American High School Students*

Lab reports, 2, 151
Langley High School (VA) **w**, 106
Lasarenko, Jane, 191
Laser printers, 13–14
Laws. *See* Plagiarism–Legislative action
LEAD Project (Leadership through Ethical Action and Development), 76, 83
Legislation. *See* Plagiarism–Legislative action
Leland, Bruce H., 169
Lessons and lesson plans, 8–9, 117, 156, 159–60, 163, 189–92, 198–204, 206–212. *See also* Online sites–Use in instruction; Writing assignments
Librarians/Library media teachers. *See also* Teachers–Collaboration with librarians
  Information dissemination, 154–58
  Leadership role, 121
  Librarian–teacher teams, 8, 152–58
  Teaching role, 104, 153–58
  Technological literacy, 48, 154–55
  Workshops, 154, 159–60
Literature for character education, 75–76, 80, 83
Locating original of a plagiarized paper. *See* Plagiarism–Locating original of a plagiarized paper
Los Alamitos High School Academic Honesty Code, 108–11
Los Angeles Times poll, 5. *See also* Statistical data
Lying, 7, 40, 44, 62

Mad Papers **w**, 219
Make-up tests. *See* Tests and testing–Make-up tests

Note: **w** = Web site; **c** = Copy-Me page